Journal of
Early
Childhood and
Infant
Psychology

Volume 3
2007

PACE UNIVERSITY PRESS   NEW YORK

ISSN 1554-6144
ISBN 0-944473-82-2

Address Subscription Inquiries to:

Pace University Press
41 Park Row, Room 1510
New York, NY 10038

www.pace.edu/press
(212) 346-1405

Journal of Early Childhood and Infant Psychology

Editor
Barbara A. Mowder
Pace University-New York City

Associate Editors
Florence Rubinson
Brooklyn College of the City University of New York
K. Mark Sossin
Pace University-New York City
Anastasia Yasik
Pace University-New York City

Editorial Review Board

Phyllis Ackman
Pace University-New York City

Vincent C. Alfonso
Fordham University

Stephen J. Bagnato
University of Pittsburgh

Anni Bergman
New York University

Zeynep Biringen
Colorado State University

Bruce Bracken
College of William & Mary

Susan Chinitz
Albert Einstein College of Medicine

Gerard Costa
Youth Consultation Service Institute
for Infant & Preschool Mental Health

Grace Elizalde-Utnick
Brooklyn College of the
City University of New York

Nancy Evangelista
Alfred University

Madeline Fernández
Pace University-New York City

Gilbert M. Foley
Yeshiva University

Paul C. McCabe
Brooklyn College of the
City University of New York

David McIntosh
Ball State University

Gail Ross
New York Presbyterian Hospital

Mark D. Terjesen
St. John's University

Susan Vig
Children's Evaluation and
Rehabilitation Center

Serena Wieder
Silver Spring, Md.

Editorial Assistant
Keara Conway

Editorial Policy: The Journal of Early Childhood and Infant Psychology (JECIP) is a publication of the Association of Early Childhood and Infant Psychologists (AECIP). One aspect of AECIP's mission is to provide a vehicle for networking within early childhood and infant psychology, including fostering research, scholarship, and professional interactions. This journal (JECIP) focuses on publishing original contributions from a broad range of psychological perspectives relevant to infants, young children, parents, and caregivers. Manuscripts incorporating research, theory and applications within clinical, community, development, neurological, and school psychology perspectives are considered. In addition to data-based research, the journal accepts test and book reviews, position statements, literature reviews, program descriptions and evaluations, clinical studies and other professional materials of interest to psychologists working with infants, young children, parents, families, and caregivers.

Format: Manuscripts should be original work not currently submitted for publication to other journals. Authors must follow the guidelines of the *Publication Manual* of the American Psychological Association (Fifth Edition), and not exceed 30 pages including charts, tables, and references.

Submission: Submit five (5) copies and one (1) floppy disk of the manuscript for editorial review. Avoid including any identifying author information in the text. Selection of manuscripts is based on blind peer review. Include a cover page with the following information: the title of article, author(s) full name(s), title(s), institution of professional affiliations, and mailing and email address of primary author. The cover page will not be sent to reviewers.

Selection Criteria:
• Importance of topic in early childhood and infant psychology
• Accuracy and validity of content
• Contribution to professional practice in early childhood and infant psychology
• Clear and concise writing

Submit manuscripts to the editor at the following address:
Professor Barbara A. Mowder
Editor, JECIP
Psychology Department, Pace University
41 Park Row
New York, New York 10038
Address inquiries to BMowder@pace.edu

Journal of Early Childhood and Infant Psychology

Volume 3, 2007

Mini-series: Examining the Role of Attachment in Child Development: Implications for Practice in the Schools

Tammy L. Hughes & Angeleque Akin-Little	1	Attachment Theory: Implications for Practice in the Schools: An Introduction to the Mini-Series
Janice H. Kennedy & Charles E. Kennedy	7	Applications of Attachment Theory in School Psychology
Benjamin J. Lovett, Tanya L. Eckert, Nicole M. Talge, & Angeleque Akin-Little	27	Attachment Intervention Programs: A Guide for School Psychologists
Thomas J. Kehle, Melissa A. Bray, & Sarah E. Grigerick	47	Infant and Child Attachment as it Relates to School-Based Outcomes
Clayton R. Cook, Steven G. Little, & Angeleque Akin-Little	61	Interventions Based on Attachment Theory: A Critical Analysis
Shane R. Jimerson, Brianna Coffino, & L. Alan Sroufe	79	Commentary: Building School-Based Interventions on Attachment Theory and Research

Chantal Cyr   **95**   Commentary: Attachment in the Schools:
Marinus H. van   Toward Attachment-Based Curricula
IJzendoorn

General Articles

Daniel S. Schecter, Annette   **119**   Child Mental Representations of
Zygmunt, Kimberly A..   Attachment When Mothers Are
Trabka, Mark Davies,   Traumatized: The Relationship of
Elizabeth Colon, Ann   Family-Drawings to Story-Stem
Kolodji, & James E. McCaw   Completion

Graciela Elizalde-   **141**   Young Selectively Mute English
Utnick   Language Learners: School-Based
                                      Intervention Strategies

Tammy Kaminer, Beatrice   **163**   Mothers' Dependent and Self-Critical
Beebe, Joseph Jaffe,   Depressive Experience is Related
Kristin Kelly, & Liza   to Speech Content with Infants
Marquette

Elizabeth H. Snyder,   **185**   Examining Attention Networks in
Deborah Winders Davis,   Preschool Children Born with Very
Barbara M. Burns, &   Low Birth Weights
Julia B. Robinson

Rebecca J. Morgan &   **205**   Structural Validity of the Early
James C. Di.Perna   Childhood Longitudinal Study
                                      Measure of Parental Beliefs About
                                      School Readiness

Reviews

Madeline Fernández &   **223**   Bayley III: A Preliminary Overview
Michele Zaccario

Nicole Pernod   **235**   *Strengthening Parent-Child*
                                      Relationships Through Play (2nd ed.)

Attachment Theory: Implications for Practice in Schools

Guest Editors:
Tammy L. Hughes, Duquesne University
Angeleque Akin-Little, Walden University

Bowlby's (1969, 1988) theory of attachment highlights the importance of the early parent-child relationship in facilitating appropriate emotional, social, and cognitive development in children (Ainsworth, 1989; Bowlby, 1988; Brazelton & Greenspan, 2000; Bretherton, 1992; Karen, 1998; Sroufe, Carlson, Levy, & Egeland, 1999). The benefits of adequate attachment are thought to be long lasting and provide a stable base from which subsequent growth experiences can flourish (Brazelton & Greenspan, 2000). For example, the relationship between attachment security in infancy and subsequent child behavior and later academic success (Bohlin, Hagekull, & Rydell, 2000; Main & Cassidy, 1988; Waters, Wippman, & Sroufe, 1979) has been documented. Additionally, secure attachment relationships have been shown to mediate the negative impacts of low social economic status and other social contextual risk factors (Pasco-Fearon & Belsky, 2004). Similarly, disrupted and insecure attachment has been associated with, for example, the development of psychopathology (e.g., Lyons-Ruth, 1996; Solomon & DeJong, 1995; Sroufe, 1979) such as oppositional defiant disorder and conduct disorder (Denham, Blair, Schmidt, & DeMulder, 2002; Thompson, 1994), anxiety and depression (Gerhardt, 2004), and underdeveloped social competence (Denham et al.; Thompson).

Highlighting the need to understand attachment over the course of development are the findings that attachment patterns, with intervention, may not remain stable over time (Goodman, 2007). Thus, understanding children's early attachment history and current attachment patterns is crucial for providing intervention services. Although the implications of attachment theory and research for practice are profound, much of the research has been concentrated within the field of developmental psychology, and has not been widely disseminated into the practice of school psychology where applied, school-based interventions could be implemented. The school is most children's first social system outside of the family where children may form strong attachment-like relationships with other

All correspondence should be addressed to Angeleque Akin-Little, Ph.D., 152 Shady Acres Rd., Tupelo, MS 38804. Phone: (662) 841-0008. Electronic mail may be sent to drsakinlittle@netzero.com.

adults, particularly teachers. However, how attachment may be generalized beyond the traditional parent-child relationship with important *others*, as described by both Bowlby (1969, 1988) and Ainsworth (1989), warrants examination.

This mini-series provides an opportunity to review the current status of attachment research in relation to child outcomes in school settings. In addition, much of the commentary provides a context for conceptualizing child attachment difficulties for applied psychologists. This series addresses the theoretical tenants of attachment, including the importance of early attachment relationships and how attachment patterns form internalized mental representations in addition to how attachment experiences relate to school-based (e.g., academic, behavioral) outcomes.

Attachment and the other dynamic developmental processes that may affect high-risk as well as typical children offer avenues for conceptualizing and implementing mental health and other interventions in educational contexts. For example, there are implications for consultation with parents and teachers, parent education programs, and comprehensive individualized intervention plans. The school psychologist is in a key position to provide leadership in applying attachment theory to school based programming promoting children's academic success and mental health.

The opening paper by Kennedy and Kennedy provides an overview of John Bowlby's theory of attachment describing risk factors for the development of insecure attachment. These authors highlight the importance of quality teacher-student relationships and children's positive adaptation to school, especially for high-risk students who may not have a supportive adult at home. The authors provide a unique discussion of the implications related to a lack of secure attachment in terms of the behavioral trajectories for children and adolescents. They conclude with valuable information on assessment and intervention from the perspective of school psychologists practicing in educational settings.

In the second paper, Lovett, Eckert, Talge, and Akin-Little begin with a brief overview/review of the research on relationships between attachment organization and psychopathology. The article also contains a description of three attachment interventions (i.e., "Circle of Security" Program, Biobehavioral Intervention Model, and Attachment Intervention within Head Start). The authors describe some support found in the results of studies with small sample sizes but also highlight problems with treatment integrity when considering group level data (e.g., Head Start). These authors conclude with an examination of three possible roles that school psychologists may play in relation to the development of positive attachment in the school setting.

In the third paper, Kehle, Bray, and Grigerick posit that children who develop insecure, ambivalent, or avoidant attachment with caregivers as infants face the very probable outcome of being unable to initiate and maintain friendships during their school career. They further suggest that these children are likely to have less than successful relationships with teachers. The implications of this lack of peer and teacher support include an inability for these individuals to attain success at friendships throughout their entire lives.

The last article by Cook, Little, and Akin-Little presents meta-analytic findings which assessed the efficacy and methodological adequacy of contemporary studies on attachment-based interventions. The data on treatment integrity, as reported by Lovett et al., along with any meaningful measures of consumer satisfaction, was found to be virtually non-existent in the current literature. The implications for any consequential interpretation of the true efficacy of the interventions analyzed or the ability to generalize the results is discussed. Further, the results of the analysis revealed that attachment interventions produce on average, weak to moderate effects across caregiver and child outcomes. The meta-analysis of the efficacy of attachment theory and treatment/interventions was based upon the Kratochwill and Stoiber (2002) guidelines for evaluating evidence-based interventions. The authors note that many attachment intervention studies were not considered because they did not meet the requirements for efficacious treatment as outlined by the current practice standards articulated by Kratochwill and Stoiber.

Finally, we present two excellent commentaries. The first is authored by Shane Jimerson, who holds a Ph.D. in both school and developmental psychology; Alan Sroufe, an international expert on developmental psychology; and Brianna Coffino, a graduate student with Alan Sroufe at the University of Minnesota. The second is written by Dutch psychologists Chantal Cyr and Marinus H. van Ijzendoorn. Notably, Dr. Van Ijzendoorn is an internationally known expert in this field and has published many meta-analytic findings in the past 15 years directly related to the effectiveness of attachment interventions. Both provide a framework for moving the field of attachment research into applied psychology. Indeed, they highlight the questions that warrant further consideration and promise to generate a meaningful dialogue for the purpose of understanding and helping children.

The literature on the application of attachment theory to the practice of school psychology is sparse. A PsychInfo search of the major journals in School Psychology (i.e., *Journal of School Psychology, Psychology in the Schools, School Psychology Quarterly,* and *School Psychology Review)* revealed limited studies on this topic. This mini-series seeks to provide information on this important subject tailored specifically for applied psychologists who work with children in schools. We also provide an analysis and critique of the literature in terms of the effectiveness of attachment interventions and the methodology of the published studies. It is our hope that bridging the theory-into-practice gap, this mini-series addresses how developmental and attachment theories can inform educational consultation and intervention practices for children. It is also our hope that the information provided therein will aid school psychologists in the selection of appropriate and efficacious interventions.

References

Ainsworth, M.D.S. (1989). Attachments beyond infancy. *American Psychologist, 44,* 709-716.

Bohlin, G., Hagekull, B., & Rydell, A. (2000). Attachment and social functioning: A longitudinal study from infancy to middle childhood. *Social Development, 9,* 24-39.

Bowlby, J. (1969). *Attachment* (2nd Ed.). New York: Basic Books.

Bowlby, J. (1988). *A secure base.* New York: Basic Books.

Brazelton, B. T., & Greenspan, S. I. (2000). *The irreducible needs of children: What every child must have to grow, learn and flourish.* Cambridge, MA: Perseus Publishing.

Bretherton, I. (1992). The origins of Attachment Theory: John Bowlby and Mary Ainsworth. *Developmental Psychology, 28,* 759-775.

Denham, S. A., Blair, K., Schmidt, M., & DeMulder, E. (2002). Compromised emotional competence: Seeds of violence sewn early? *American Journal of Orthopsychiatry, 72,* 70-82.

Gerhardt, S. (2004). *Why love matters: How affection shapes a baby's brain.* New York: Brunner-Routledge.

Goodman, G. (2007). Attachment-based intervention with prepubertal children: The impact of parent, child, and therapist mental representations on intervention points of entry. *Journal of the Humanities and Social Scientists,* 1. Retrieved November 16, 2006, from http://www.scientificjournals.org/articles/1065.html

Karen, R. (1998). *Becoming attached: First relationships and how they shape our capacity to love.* New York: Oxford University Press.

Kratochwill, T., & Stoiber, K. A. (2002). Evidence based interventions in school psychology: Conceptual foundations of the Procedural and Coding manual of Division 16 and the Society for the Study of School Psychology Task Force. *School Psychology Quarterly, 17,* 341-383.

Lyons-Ruth, K. (1996). Attachment relationships among children with aggressive behavior problems: The role of disorganized early attachment patterns. *Journal of Consulting and Clinical Psychology, 64,* 64-73.

Main, M., & Cassidy, J. (1988). Categories of response to reunion with the parent at age 6: Predictable from infant attachment classifications and stable over a 1-month period. *Developmental Psychology, 24,* 415-426.

Pasco-Fearon, R. M., & Belsky, J. (2004). Attachment and attention: Protection in relation to gender and cumulative social-contextual adversity. *Child Development, 75,* 1677-1693.

Solomon, J., & De John, A. (1995). Children classified as controlling at age six: Evidence of disorganized representational strategies and aggression at home and at school. *Development and Psychopathology, 7,* 447-463.

Sroufe, L. A. (1979). The coherence of individual development: Early care, attachment, and subsequent development issues. *American Psychologist, 34,* 834-841.

Sroufe, L. A., Carlson, E., Levy, A., & Egeland, B. (1999). Implications of attachment theory for developmental psychopathology. *Development and Psychopathology, 11,* 1-13.

Thompson, R. (1994). Emotional regulation: A theme in search of definition. *Monographs of the Society for Research in Child Development, 59,* 25-52.

Waters, E., Wippman, J., & Sroufe, L. A. (1979). Attachment, positive affect, and competence in the peer group: Two studies in construct validation. *Child Development, 50,* 821-829.

Applications of Attachment Theory in School Psychology

Janice H. Kennedy
Georgia Southern University

Charles E. Kennedy
Burke County Schools

School psychologists and educators concerned with facilitating children's adaptations and successes in school embrace a variety of theoretical perspectives. Attachment theory offers an innovative and critical perspective on issues such as the dynamics of students' and teachers' approaches to interpersonal relationships and the impact of qualitative differences in teacher-student relationships on students' success in social, behavioral and academic domains throughout school. In this paper an overview of Bowlby's ethological theory of attachment provides the foundation for consideration of these issues, along with the risk factors related to the development of insecure attachment in children, behavioral trajectories of children and adolescents according to attachment classification, and available methods of assessment and implications for intervention.

School psychologists have traditionally focused on prevention, assessment, and intervention strategies for a myriad of factors that influence school performance. Skills that enhance the performance of these tasks include a thorough knowledge of both adaptive and maladaptive developmental processes. Moreover, the effective practice of school psychology requires a strong theory and research-based perspective (Merrell, 2002). One such perspective is Bowlby's (1969/1982) ethological attachment theory, which provides an essential framework for understanding the impact of early social-emotional relationships

All correspondence should be addressed to Dr. Janice H. Kennedy, Department of Psychology, Georgia Southern University, P.O. Box 8041, Statesboro, GA 30460. Electronic mail may be sent to jkennedy@georgiasouthern.edu.

on cognitive-affective structures the child uses to construct views of the world, self, and others.

Attachment theory addresses social-emotional development from the perspective of both process and outcome and has identified a variety of markers predictive of later academic performance, social competence, and psychopathology. Subsequently, the theory offers school psychologists a theoretically and empirically based framework from which to approach hypothesis generation relevant to assessment and individualized intervention planning. Attachment theory provides an awareness of and new meanings derived from the child's history and the subtleties of observed child, parent and teacher behaviors in the current context.

In the current paper, we present an overview of John Bowlby's ethological theory of attachment and describe risk factors for the development of insecure attachment. Behavioral trajectories of children and adolescents according to attachment classification are discussed. Finally, student-teacher interactions within an attachment perspective and implications for assessment and intervention are presented.

Brief Overview of Bowlby's Ethological Theory of Attachment

Attachment is an affectional bond between child and primary caregiver that develops over the first 18 months of life (Ainsworth, 1989). Infants are born with a propensity to direct precursory attachment behaviors to human figures (e.g., crying, looking, clinging) to which caregivers are particularly likely to respond. These behaviors elicit caregiving and bring the caregiver into close proximity with the infant, ensuring protection from environmental dangers and a sense of security. Over time, infants begin to direct these responses primarily to one or a few caregivers. Around 7-8 months of age, infants show attachment to caregivers by protesting their leaving and grieving for them during their absence. During toddlerhood, children form a goal-corrected partnership in that they can begin to perceive events during interactions with mother from her perspective (Bowlby, 1969/1982). For example, toddlers may be less insistent than infants in demanding that their needs be met immediately if they have developed confidence in the caregiver's dependability in meeting their needs. During this time, infants are forming an internal working model (IWM)—a hypothetical construct of the attachment relationship which informs them about their own self-worth and the dependability of others to provide needed attention and care (Main, Kaplan, & Cassidy, 1985).

The IWM provides mental representations of self and others and appears to be the mechanism by which early experiences influence the quality of later attachment relationships. With development of language and cognitive abilities these representations become more elaborate, stable and symbolic (Bretherton & Munholland, 1999). They form the basis for expectations of dependability and responsiveness of others and affective tone within interpersonal relationships (Cicchetti, Toth, & Lynch, 1995; Main et al., 1985), both within and beyond the family. These representations are viewed as guiding and structuring cognition, language, affect and behavior through the development of both adaptive and maladaptive strategies for coping with stress and seeking social support (Cicchetti et al., 1995). For example, if a child expects people to be accepting and responsive based on prior experiences, the individual may project a friendly demeanor to new acquaintances' neutral behavior. The acquaintance may respond in kind (in a manner consistent with expectations), shaping the kinds of experiences a child has through development.

Ainsworth and her colleagues (e.g., Ainsworth & Bell, 1970) were first to provide empirical evidence for Bowlby's attachment theory. Using the Strange Situation Procedure, Ainsworth and Bell classified infants into one of three categories: (1) secure, in which infants use the mother as a secure base for exploration and seek contact with her after separation; (2) anxious-ambivalent (later called "resistant"), in which infants are unable to use the mother as a secure base and are often angry and push her away upon reunion; (3) anxious-avoidant, in which infants fail to use the mother as a secure base for exploration and avoid the mother upon reunion or approach her only indirectly. Later a fourth category was described—disorganized-disoriented—in which there is no predictable or effective pattern of eliciting caregiving behaviors by infants when stressed (Main & Solomon, 1990).

Each of these attachment classifications may be considered on a continuum of emotional regulation for managing affect, events and relationships (Dozier, Stovall, & Albus, 1999). This conceptualization places the anxious-avoidant style, with its overly organized strategies for controlling and minimizing affect at one end of the continuum, and the relatively uncontrolled, poorly managed affect of anxious-resistant styles at the opposite end. Secure attachment, falling along the midpoint of the emotional continuum, reflects a balance of the two extremes of emotional regulation. Those with disorganized-disoriented attachment classifications may present a range of behaviors involving under-controlled emotional reactions such as impulsive verbal and/or physical aggression or over-controlled responses in which emotions are difficult to express and behavior may reflect withdrawal and difficulty handling conflict (Jacobite & Hazen, 1999). Thus, their emotional reactions are unpredictable and typically maladaptive.

Precursors of Insecure and Disorganized Attachment Patterns

Early experiences with the caregiver are important in developing secure attachment relationships. Although under stress the drive to achieve proximity to caregivers is universal, the method used by infants to express their desire for proximity to the caregiver is dependent on caregivers' responses to them in the past. Certain parental factors are predictive of attachment security throughout development. Of particular importance are sensitivity and responsiveness (e.g., DeWolff & van IJzendoorn, 1997; Hane & Fox, 2006). Ainsworth and Bell (1970) reported that caregivers of anxious-resistant infants were unreliably responsive to infant needs, had poor timing in response to infant distress, and often obtrusively interrupted infant play. Caregivers of anxious-avoidant infants were unresponsive to infant needs and often rejected infant attempts to achieve proximity.

Caregivers of infants with a disorganized-disoriented attachment style are often psychiatrically distressed and/or are dealing with unresolved personal loss (Main & Solomon, 1990). These mothers appear to be either frightened and/or are seen as frightening by their infants. This pattern is typically associated with a high-risk home environment, including such factors as abuse, stress and poverty (Main & Solomon), resulting in compromised emotional availability to the infant (Lyons-Ruth, Easterbrooks, & Cibelli, 1997).

Attachment classifications remain relatively stable across time, especially if the environment remains stable (Waters, Merrick, Treboux, Crowell, & Abersheim, 2000). Attachment researchers generally agree that early experiences with the primary caregiver are particularly important in forming one's later attachment style (e.g., Ainsworth , 1989) as the primary caregiver is assumed to serve as the prototype for future relationships.

Children's Attachment Styles and Associated Behavioral Outcomes

Greenberg, Speltz and DeKlyen (1993) outline four interrelated sources of potential risk factors for poor developmental outcome: biological and/or neuro-logical vulnerabilities, family or community stressors, poor parental manage-ment, and insecurity of attachment. These factors are associated with higher risk for both internalizing and externalizing behavior problems, presumably at least partially via the IWM. Although insecure attachments are not necessarily patho-logical (Goldberg, 1997), current research does suggest a strong relation between one's early attachment classification and later social, emotional, behavioral and academic outcomes (Jacobsen & Hofmann, 1997; Moss & St-Laurent, 2001).

Children with secure attachment histories are more likely to develop internal representations of others as supportive, helpful and positive and to view them-selves as competent and worthy of respect (Jacobsen & Hofmann, 1997) than children with insecure attachment. Securely attached children relate more posi-tively to both peers and adults, demonstrate greater ego-resiliency, engage in more complex play, and receive higher sociometric ratings than children classi-fied as insecure (e.g., Howes, Matheson, & Hamilton, 1994). They also have been found to exhibit more flexible and socially appropriate emotional expression and control (Cassidy, 1994), show more focused attention and participation in class, and earn higher grades (Jacobsen & Hofmann) than insecurely attached children. Securely attached children also demonstrate better functioning goal-corrected partnerships, characterized by more mature perspective-taking, mutual communication of affect and joint planning (Crittenden, 1992) than insecure or disorganized-disoriented peers. In similar fashion secure adolescents report more satisfying interpersonal relationships and greater trust in others (Larose & Bernier, 2001), as well as less drug use (Schindler, Thomasius, Gemeinhardt, Kustner, & Eckert, 2005). They also exhibit a more positive, integrated view of self, are more prone to positive self-disclosure, and cope more adaptively with stressful situations (Mikulincer, 1995). Sroufe (2005), reporting results of a 30-year longitudinal study, found that security of infant attachment was related to adult self-reliance, capacity for emotional regulation, and social competence, emphasizing the organizational nature of the attachment construct throughout development.

The anxious-avoidant child uses less effective strategies in stressful situations (Kobak, Cole, Ferenz-Gillies, Fleming, & Gamble, 1993) to self-regulate negative affect than securely attached children. They may resist seeking help from others and demonstrate less dependence upon their social network (Larose & Bernier, 2001). In this process they limit access to their own feelings and view others as undependable or rejecting. Anxious-avoidant children thus fail to develop trusting relationships with others, seeing others as unable to provide emotional closeness and comfort, and thus feeling socially and emotionally isolated. These children may show more externalizing and aggressive, antisocial behavior (Renkin, Egeland, Marvinney, Mangelsdorf, & Sroufe, 1989), reflected by lying, bullying, and interpersonal insensitivity. Adolescents with an anxious-avoidant attachment style also demonstrate distancing strategies to minimize emotional stress (Dozier, Lomax, Tyrrell, & Lee, 2001). In clinical settings, their distrust of others, lack of comfort with interpersonal issues and tendencies toward nondisclosure contribute to their being less responsive to therapy (Dozier et al, 2001).

Children with an anxious-resistant attachment style typically exhibit hyperactivation of the attachment system when under stress (Kobak et al, 1993) as reflected in exaggerated emotional reactions and/or behaviors, when compared to children in other attachment classifications. Even under conditions of minimal distress, exploration of both social and learning environments is sacrificed for maintenance of proximity to and attention of the caregiver. These children may lack self-confidence, become reticent in unfamiliar settings and may become more socially isolated from peers (Jacobsen & Hofmann, 1997). Yet they tend to orient more frequently toward adults (Sroufe, Carlson, Levy, & Egeland, 1999) than securely attached children. Anxious-resistant children may be easily over-stimulated and present as reactive, impulsive, restless and easily frustrated

(Sroufe et al.). They show higher frequencies of internalizing problems (Warren, Houston, Egeland, & Sroufe, 1997) and are more likely to exhibit passive withdrawal behavior (Renkin et al., 1989). Adolescents with this classification demonstrate a greater frequency of anxiety disorders, dysthymic traits and borderline personality disorder than secure or other insecure categories (Cassidy, 1994).

The greatest risk for later psychopathology exists with disorganized attachment (Moss et al., 2006). Infants classified as disorganized-disoriented typically fail to develop an organized strategy for successfully coping with separation distress (Abrams, Rifkin, & Hesse, 2006). Studies have demonstrated a link, especially for high-risk samples, between disorganized-disoriented attachment and later behavior problems in preschool and school-aged children (Moss et al., 2006; Speltz, 1990). These problems orient primarily around aggressive and disruptive behaviors and social isolation (Campbell et al., 2004; Carlson, 1998). Jacobite and Hazen (1999) suggest that under stress the disorganized child sees others as potential threats and might shift between social withdrawal and defensively aggressive behavior, thus exhibiting difficulties in responding appropriately and contingently to others. Over time these individuals are at risk for borderline personality (Lyons-Ruth & Jacobvitz, 1999) and dissociative disorders (Carlson).

Retrospective studies of childhood psychopathologies and attachment history corroborate these findings and demonstrate the magnitude of the problem. Among students with externalizing, disruptive behavior problems, Lyons-Ruth et al. (1997) reported that 71-87% had histories of disorganized-disoriented attachment. In other samples (Greenberg, Speltz, DeKlyen, & Endivia, 1991), a large proportion (80-84%) of clinic-referred children between ages 3-6 years were classified as insecure, with 32-40% exhibiting the disorganized-disoriented attachment pattern. Estimates of disorganized-disoriented attachment among maltreated children may be as high as 77% (van IJzendoorn, Schuengel, & Bakermans-Kranenburg, 1999).

Both disruptive, externalizing disorders (e.g., oppositional defiant disorder, conduct disorder, attention deficit hyperactivity disorder), and internalizing disorders (e.g., depression) show higher incidence levels in those with disorganized status (Graham & Easterbrooks, 2000; Moss, Cyr, & Dubois-Comtois, 2004). Victims of physical and sexual abuse, as well as individuals with suicidal ideation, are also more likely to have a disorganized status whereas those experiencing neglect are more frequently associated with anxious-resistant status (Adam, Sheldon-Keller, & West, 1996). Anxious-resistant individuals also may demonstrate high levels of self-disclosure, disposing them to greater risk of rejection and social isolation (Mikulincer, 1995). An anxious-avoidant attachment history is related to greater levels of social isolation, limited self-disclosure and less social support seeking behavior (Jacobsen & Hofmann, 1997; Larose & Bernier, 2001).

As one enters the social world outside the family, other relationships that provide emotional support and protection may develop. Howes (1999) described characteristics of potential attachment figures beyond the primary caregiver as providing continuity, physical and emotional support, and an emotional investment in the child's life. Day care providers, teachers (Howes 1999), and psychotherapists (Dozier, Cue, & Barnett, 1994) in particular may serve these functions and develop relationships with children that are qualitatively similar to parent-child attachment relationships.

Student-Teacher Relationships

From an attachment theory perspective, the child's IWM of parental sensitivity, availability and responsiveness inform expectations of relationships with peers and adults outside the family. These internal representations, especially in the early grades, are predictive of the child's adjustment to school, social and academic competency, and level of expressed anger and/or aggression, as well as the quality of the teacher-student relationship (DeMulder, Denham, Schmidt, & Mitchell, 2000). Secure relationships with early child care providers and teachers, as the child's model of early teacher relationships, impact and predict qualitative aspects of future teacher-student relationships (Howes, 1999; Howes et al., 1994). The quality of these relationships influences the child's cognitive and social development as well as school engagement (Birch & Ladd, 1998; Howes et al., 1994).

Learning is facilitated within the context of exploration from a secure base (Bowlby, 1969/1982). A secure base depends on the child's IWM of caregivers as sensitive, available, and responsive, allowing anxiety-free cognitive and social learning. Secure parental attachment enhances the child's probability of effectively using the teacher as a secure base (Kobak, Little, Race, & Acosta, 2001). In a similar fashion, teacher sensitivity, responsiveness, and reciprocity promote and build on the parent-child secure attachments and appear to help compensate for insecure parent-child relationships (Meehan, Hughes, & Cavell, 2003), allowing students to explore academic and social environments from a secure base.

A number of studies have demonstrated that positive relationships with teachers facilitate learning and school success (e.g., Hamre & Pianta, 2001; Reddy, Rhodes, & Mulhall, 2003). Wentzel (2002) reported that warmth and support shown to students by middle school teachers was associated with positive academic performance and social behavior. Younger children with positive teacher relationships demonstrate more autonomy, positive peer relationships and greater achievement orientation and are characterized as closer to teachers, less dependent and less inclined to experience conflictual relationships (Howes et al., 1994; Jacobsen & Hofmann, 1997). Student-teacher relationships characterized by teachers as close were associated with students' positive attitudes toward school, self-direction, cooperation, and active participation, as well as improved academic performance (Birch & Ladd, 1998).

Children who show poor adjustment to the demands of school, both academic and peer-related, have been found to have less positive relationships with teachers. Some studies (e.g., Birch & Ladd, 1998; Kobak et al., 2001) have reported that both dependent and conflict-prone students tended to have poor self-direction, show less exploration of the learning environment and demand more of the teacher's time. They also have reported that children perceived by teachers as more dependent and/or conflict-prone seek greater proximity to and emotional involvement with teachers; these children are often reported to have a history of disorganized-controlling or insecure attachment. Kobak and colleagues (2001) note that the disorganized child's strategies for attainment of the teacher's attention are typically viewed by teachers as inappropriate and stressful, resulting in less productive relationships.

Interaction Between Teachers' and Students' IWMs

Both individuals in a stable dyadic relationship have attachment histories (IWMs) and associated perceptual, behavioral, and interpersonal strategies that influence the future direction of the relationship, as well as behavioral goals and strategies that are important within that relationship. For example, Dozier et al. (1994) found that a clinician's ability to attend and respond effectively to the needs of clients varied according to the clinician's attachment status, as well as to the match between therapist's and client's attachment status (Dozier et al., 2001). Preoccupied (resistant) clinicians are more effective with dismissing (avoidant) clients, while dismissing clinicians have more success with preoccupied clients. Insecure clinicians overall reacted to more surface-level, obvious issues and provided interventions which supported, rather than countered, the client's IWM and thus reinforced their existing maladaptive strategies. Within educational settings, Pianta (1999) reported similar observations of teachers in their interactions with students.

Secure, as compared to insecure, adults are typically more capable of objective evaluation of their own relationship histories, tend to have more constructive coping strategies (Kobak et al., 2001), have more positive and optimistic views of themselves and others (Mikulincer, 1995) and are more sensitive to the attachment needs of children (Crowell & Feldman, 1988). Individuals with a dismissing (avoidant) status distance themselves emotionally, appear less sensitive and responsive to the needs of others, may experience difficulty recognizing their own lack of warmth, and may be perceived as less accessible and supportive. Their expectations for students' maturity and self-direction may be unrealistic, based on their own lack of trust in interpersonal relationships and their needs for self-reliance. Preoccupied (resistant) individuals tend to be intermittently responsive to students' needs, fail to look beyond the surface-level implications of behavior, and may become emotionally reactive and perhaps inappropriately embroiled in relationships. Students may perceive the former as unconcerned, rejecting or threatening while the latter may be seen as socially and emotionally intrusive.

Generally, anxious-avoidant students are viewed by teachers as passively aggressive, angry, distant and uncooperative and the anxious-resistant students as overly dependent, demanding of attention and prone to be emotionally reactive and impulsive. Students with disorganized status may be viewed as having more conflict-laden relationships and as exhibiting more aggression, emotional reactivity, and unpredictable behavior (Jacobite & Hazan, 1999; Moss et al., 2006).

As quality and nature of relationships typically reflect the attachment needs and related interpersonal strategies of each participant, teachers may be more accepting of and effective with students of one versus another attachment style. Secure teachers should be more likely than teachers with insecure styles of attachment to recognize the anxious-avoidant students' aloofness and anger, the anxious-resistant students' dependency, and the disorganized students' acting out behavior, as expressions of past experiences and current needs. Approaches to problem resolution by teachers secure in attachment style are expected to be more sensitive to students' needs and to foster positive, supportive, and trusting relationships, as compared to approaches of problem resolution by insecure teachers. Problem resolutions that take into account students' needs and perspectives are expected to facilitate students' development of positive IWMs and an appreciation for reciprocity in relationships.

Interventions with Insecurely Attached Children

Insecure attachment status reflects individuals' adaptive strategies and are not, in themselves, pathological, yet may signal risk for future pathology (Goldberg, 1997). Traditional clinically derived diagnoses, such as oppositional defiant disorder, typically result in treatment plans that do not consider students' attachment status. However, each attachment style reflects different needs and mechanisms for emotional regulation (Dozier et al., 1994). Barber and Muenz (1996) note the importance of these distinctions for differential treatment. The avoidant student's oppositional behavior may reflect anger related to perceived rejection, and acting out behavior associated with resistant status may be directed toward gaining teacher attention. Expressions of childhood depression as predominately externalizing with interpersonal hostility has been related to avoidant status while ambivalent status has been associated with internalizing self-blame.

The literature provides numerous examples prior to school age of effective attachment-based interventions within research and clinical domains (e.g., Lieberman, 1992; Speltz, 1990); yet there have been relatively few such applications reported in educational settings. Effective intervention often involves implementation of multiple strategies. Researchers consistently stress the need for early identification of home- and school-based risk factors, parent and teacher education and individualized student-oriented intervention. It is also important to consider that the child's IWM, as well as associated behavioral strategies, appears to become increasingly rigid and resistant to modification with age (Thompson, 1999).

Traditionally, early identification of children at risk and intervention are facilitated through addressing such issues as: (a) reduction and/or management of home and school-based contextual risks; (b) development of both parent and teacher support systems including linkages with available agency resources; (c) strategies to reduce home- and school-based conflict while promoting parent/teacher sensitivity, clarity of communication, cooperation, appropriate behavioral monitoring and disciplinary practices; and (d) improving parent and child attitudes toward and connectedness to the school. Other papers in this issue address some of these challenges. The above processes are enhanced by the consideration of attachment-related dynamics (IWM) of parent-child and teacher-student relationships.

The unique position of school psychologists allows direct teacher contact in dealing with common goals in addressing the needs of referred students. Assessment-oriented interviews and observations naturally extend into a consultative relationship with teachers, offering potential learning experiences and insights relevant to current and future aspects of classroom dynamics and management strategies. Helping teachers recognize student behavior as interactions between current contexts and prior relationship histories facilitates recognition of underlying student motivations and needs. Moreover, an awareness of the potential interactive impact of their own and the student's interpersonal strategies, expectations, and goals can modify the tenor of classroom environments and student-teacher relationships. Such insights can improve teacher-student relationships, student academic commitment and peer relationships, as well as reduce behavior problems and school dropout (Greenberg & Hickman, 1991; Marcus & Sanders-Reio, 2001). A brief example of an intervention strategy is given below.

Student-oriented interventions may be facilitated through attachment-informed application of traditional strategies. A goal of cognitive-behavioral approaches has been to facilitate changes in perceptions of self and others (IWMs), thus enhancing adaptive behavior. Speltz (1990) used behavior management techniques to control high frequency disruptive behavior in the classroom while simultaneously addressing parent-child attachment issues. Approaches of particular relevance include the reduction of teacher-student conflict (Pianta, Steinberg, & Rollins, 1995), a shift from punitive disciplinary strategies to positive management techniques and the maintenance of stable predictable classroom environments. Kobak and colleagues (2001) suggest the use of therapists (or counselors/teachers) in special education classes for high-risk students to assist in behavior management and help interpret disruptive behaviors as expressions of unmet attachment needs. Goals for students involve skill building in areas such as accurate perception, interpretation and communication of internal feeling states, clear communication, development of cooperative, trusting relationships, and the establishment of balanced emotional regulation through modulation of hyperactivation or deactivation-oriented emotional responses to events and individuals. Attachment-oriented interventions emphasize the development of secure, adaptive working models of self, others and relationships. Involvement of school counselors can be instrumental on an on-going basis in developing these skills by students.

A Note on Assessment of Attachment

Methodologies applicable to assessment of attachment style have evolved within research contexts and typically are impractical for use in school settings due to time constraints and lack of comprehensive clinical norms. However, decades of attachment research have identified patterns of behavioral strategies, vulnerabilities, and personality traits uniquely associated with each attachment classification (Rosenstein & Horowitz, 1996; Sroufe et al., 1999).

Within school settings the attachment paradigm may best contribute to the assessment process by providing a new perspective, allowing more comprehensive acquisition of clinically significant information that may help guide both evaluation and intervention planning and contribute to the total assessment outcome (Kennedy & Kennedy, 2004). From an attachment perspective, key assessment issues should at least include identification of: (a) significant disruptions in the attachment process resulting from child separations or losses by divorce, death, multiple caregivers, or foster placements; (b) past and current family-based risks such as marital discord, parental psychiatric, and/or substance abuse issues; (c) the IWMs and associated interpersonal/behavioral strategies of the child, parent and teacher with attention to their interactional dynamics; and (d) contributing contextual issues.

The school psychologist may address these and related issues utilizing comprehensive family, developmental, medical and school histories; parent, student, and teacher interviews; and multi-contextual observations of the child's interactions with the parent, teacher, and peers. Teacher interviews may explore both the student's presenting problem(s) and the teacher's expectations, style of relating, and attitudes toward the student. Observations of the child's interactions with the parent and teacher reflect each individual's attachment needs, IWMs, capacity for emotional regulation, levels of conflict, perspective taking, and clarity of communication. Functional behavior analysis may expand definitions of antecedents of target behaviors to include unmet attachment needs. The use of standardized instruments such as parent/teacher behavior rating scales and student self-report scales, while providing significant insight into relational and behavioral patterns, also have potential to differentiate attachment-specific patterns (Moss et al., 2006). The Student-Teacher Relationship Scale (Pianta et al., 1995) has been useful in both research and school settings, assessing teacher-student relationship dimensions paralleling child-parent attachment relationships. Some investigators (e.g., Fury, Carlson, & Sroufe, 1997; Jacobsen & Hofmann, 1997; Solomon, George, & de Jong, 1995) have employed family drawings and picture/story-stem completion strategies to assess the child's IWMs. While findings effectively differentiate response patterns by attachment status and may provide school psychologists with added insight when using traditional projective techniques, these procedures lack sufficient replication and clinical norms for general application.

A Case Study

Upon entering kindergarten, Allison exhibited hypervigilance, with daily episodes of crying, prolonged tantrum behavior, and occasional physical aggression. At other times she was described as passive aggressive and resistant, often doing the opposite of whatever she was asked to do, while looking at the teacher for a reaction. When seemingly happy, she constantly sought teacher contact, attention and approval. Yet any perception of disapproval immediately resulted in negative behavior. The teacher reported daily multiple disciplinary problems and citations because of Allison's inappropriate behavior.

An interview by the school psychologist with the mother and child indicated an interactional pattern in which the mother was relatively passive and only intermittently and insensitively responsive to the child. Allison's mother, a single parent with several other children, noted her own diagnosis of clinical depression and problems coping with life's demands.

In developing an intervention strategy, the school psychologist explored expectations and feelings by the teacher for Allison, as well as defining problematic behavior and desired changes. Together with the teacher, Allison's classroom behavior was then considered within the framework of her history and working model of relationships (attachment style), and the teacher was guided through a process of linking the child's past experiences to emotional needs reflected by her classroom behavior. Teacher awareness and sensitivity to the child's dynamics and needs facilitated receptivity to and development of management and disciplinary strategies focusing on positive, supportive interactions designed to build trust and positive working models of teacher-student relationships such that a sense of autonomy could be strengthened and dependency on the teacher's constant attention could be reduced. Allison's records, over a 30-day period, reflected a shift from multiple daily disciplinary citations to approximately two weeks without notable problems.

Summary and Conclusions

One may reasonably ask why ethological attachment theory is so important to understanding child development. After all, causative statements about attachment cannot be made with confidence, since ethically only quasi-experimental studies can assess the relationship between attachment classification and outcome. Others have criticized attachment research findings as being an artifact of temperament (e.g., Kagan, Snidman, Zentner, & Peterson, 1999), a particular experimental procedure (e.g., Bronfenbrenner, 1979), or American culture (Jackson, 1993; Takahashi, 1990). Sroufe and Waters (1977), in a classic paper suggest that secure attachment is such an important development because it is a marker for optimal functioning (particularly in young children), like other milestones we look for at certain ages as indicators of healthy functioning such as reflex activity, object permanence, and school readiness skills such as motor, social, and cognition levels. The development of these abilities informs us about prior experiences in the child's life and predicts to future successes or problems. Specifically, security of attachment predicts present and future well-being, both in terms of social and intellectual competence. Children who have a realistic and positive sense of their own self-worth and the dependability of others they may encounter in the world are more able to take advantage of learning opportunities they may have in the schools and elsewhere.

In formulating attachment theory, Bowlby (1969/1982) conceptualized the mother-infant relationship as a prototype for all subsequent social and emotional relationships across the lifespan. The quality of the attachment relationship is influenced by the infant's perception of caregiver sensitivity, availability, and responsiveness and may further be molded by various contextual issues (NICHD Early Child Care Research Network, 2006). Secure attachment fosters in the child the capacity for open communication, balanced emotional regulation, trust, and reciprocal goal-corrected partnerships. One's IWM is dynamic and constantly evolving in that adaptations within each new context are informed by, and influence, the individual's IWM (Shaw & Dallos, 2005; Sroufe et al., 1999). Longitudinal studies (e.g., Sroufe, 2005) verify the lifespan continuity and influence of IWMs and interpersonal/behavioral strategies associated with each attachment style.

Attachment theory stresses the meaning of behavior rather than the form it may take (Bowlby, 1969/1982; Crittenden, 1992). It is important to recognize that the child's, parent's, teacher's and the school psychologist's behavior reflect their ongoing adjustments to relational/situational stressors via their IWMs. Professionals working with children, regardless of their attachment status, may benefit from an awareness and understanding of their own relational representations and their impact on student and classroom dynamics. Parent-child attachment status predicts qualitative aspects of the teacher-student relationship and both relate to present and future student cognitive, social/emotional competence and potential risk for maladjustment.

An attachment-oriented perspective allows professionals the opportunity to consider the whole child within the evaluation process and the development of a comprehensive service plan. These two processes may be enhanced by further research leading to development of age-appropriate assessment strategies for use by practitioners working directly with children in a range of settings. As behavioral correlates of attachment status at different ages continue to be identified and refined, the need for further research articulating effective intervention strategies and informing application of attachment-oriented practice with school-age children is critical. Of equal importance is the need to dispel the often-held perception that identified problems reside solely within the student and that interventions should be designed accordingly. Acknowledgment of interdependent influences within dyadic relationships reflecting individual histories, adaptive strategies and needs can enhance assessment, intervention planning, and the potential for positive change.

References

Abrams, K. Y., Rifkin, A., & Hesse, E. (2006). Examining the role of parental frightened/frightening subtypes in predicting disorganized attachment within a brief observational procedure. *Development and Psychopathology, 18*, 345-362.

Adam, K. S., Sheldon-Keller, A. E., & West, M. (1996). Attachment organization and history of suicidal behavior in clinical adolescents. *Journal of Consulting and Clinical Psychology, 64*, 264-272.

Ainsworth, M. D. S. (1989). Attachments beyond infancy. *American Psychologist, 44*, 709-716.

Ainsworth, M. D. S., & Bell, S. (1970). Attachment, exploration, and separation: Illustrated by the behavior of one-year-olds in a Strange Situation. *Child Development, 41*, 49-67.

Barber, J. P., & Muenz, L. R. (1996). The role of avoidance and obsessiveness in matching patients to cognitive and interpersonal therapy: Empirical findings from the Treatment for Depression Collaborative Research Program. *Journal of Counseling and Clinical Psychology, 64*, 951-958.

Birch, S. H., & Ladd, G. W. (1998). Children's interpersonal behaviors and teacher-child relationships. *Developmental Psychology, 34*, 934-946.

Bowlby, J. (1969/1982). *Attachment and loss. Vol. 1. Loss.* New York: Basic Books.

Bretherton, I., & Munholland, K. (1999). IWMs in attachment relationships. In J. Cassidy & P. Shaver (Eds.), *Handbook of attachment* (pp. 89-114). New York: Milford Press.

Bronfenbrenner, U. (1979). *The ecology of human development: Experiments by nature and design.* Cambridge: Harvard University Press.

Campbell, S. B., Brownell, C. A., Hungerford, A., Spieker, S. J., Mohan, R., & Blessing, J. S. (2004). The course of maternal depressive symptoms and maternal sensitivity as predictors of attachment security at 36 months. *Development and Psychopathology, 16,* 231-252.

Carlson, E. (1998). A prospective longitudinal study of attachment disorganization/disorientation. *Child Development, 69,* 1107-1128

Cassidy, J. (1994). Emotional regulation: Influence of attachment relationships. In N. A. Fox (Ed.), The development of emotional regulation: Biological and behavioral considerations. *Monographs of the Society for Research in Child Development, 59(2-3),* 228-249.

Cicchetti, D., Toth, S. L., & Lynch, M. (1995). Bowlby's dream come full circle: The application of attachment theory to risk and psychopathology. In T. H. Ollendick & R. J. Prinze (Eds.), *Advances in clinical and child psychology* (pp. 1-75). New York: Plenum Press.

Crittenden, P. M. (1992). Treatment of anxious attachment in infancy and early-childhood. *Development and Psychopathology, 4,* 575-602.

Crowell, J. A., & Feldman, S. S. (1988). Mothers' internal models of relationships and children's behavioral and developmental status: A study of mother-child interaction. *Child Development, 59,* 1273-1285.

DeMulder, E. K., Denham, S., Schmidt, M., & Mitchell, J. (2000). Q-sort assessment of attachment security during the preschool years: Links from home to school. *Developmental Psychology, 36,* 274-282.

DeWolff, M. S., & van IJzendoorn, M. H. (1997). Sensitivity and attachment: A meta-analysis on parental antecedents of infant attachment. *Child Development, 68,* 571-591.

Dozier, M., Cue, K., & Barnett, L. (1994). Clinicians as caregivers: The role of attachment organization in treatment. *Journal of Consulting and Clinical Psychology, 62,* 793-800.

Dozier, M., Lomax, L., Tyrrell, C. L., & Lee, S. W. (2001). The challenge of treatment with clients with dismissing states of mind. *Attachment & Human Development, 3,* 62-76.

Dozier, M., Stovall, K. C., & Albus, K. E. (1999). Attachment and psychopathology in adulthood. In J. Cassidy & P. R. Shaver (Eds.), *Handbook of attachment* (pp. 497-519). New York: Milford Press.

Fury, G., Carlson, E. A., & Sroufe, L. A. (1997). Children's representations of attachment relationships in family drawings. *Child Development, 68,* 1154-1164.

Goldberg, S. (1997). Attachment and childhood behavior problems in normal, at-risk and clinical samples. In L. Atkinson & K. J. Pucker (Eds.), *Attachment and psychopathology* (pp. 171-195). New York: Milford Press.

Graham, C. A., & Easterbrooks, M. A. (2000). School-aged children's vulnerability to depressive symptomatology: The role of attachment security, maternal depressive symptomatology, and economic risk. *Development and Psychopathology, 12,* 201-213.

Greenberg, G. E., & Hickman, C. W. (1991). Research and practice in parent involvement: Implications for teacher education. *Elementary School Journal, 91,* 279-288.

Greenberg, M. T., Speltz, M. L., & DeKlyen, M. (1993). The role of attachment in the early development of disruptive behavior problems. *Development and Psychopathology, 5,* 191-213.

Greenberg, M. T., Speltz, M. L., DeKlyen, M., & Endivia, M. C. (1991). Attachment security in preschoolers with and without externalizing behavior problems: A replication. *Development and Psychopathology, 3,* 413-430.

Hamre, B. K., & Pianta, R. C. (2001). Early teacher-child relationships and the trajectory of children's school outcomes through eighth grade. *Child Development, 72,* 625-638.

Hane, A. A., & Fox, N. A. (2006). Ordinary variations in maternal caregiving influence human infants' stress reactivity. *Psychological Science, 17,* 550-556.

Howes, C. (1999). Attachment relationships in the context of multiple caregivers. In J. Cassidy & P. R. Shaver (Eds.), *Handbook of attachment* (pp. 671-687). New York: Milford Press.

Howes, C., Matheson, C. C., & Hamilton, C. E. (1994). Maternal, teacher, and child care history correlates of children's relationships with peers. *Child Development, 65,* 264-273.

Jackson, J. F. (1993). Multiple caregiving among African Americans and infant attachment: The need for an emic approach. *Human Development, 36,* 87-102.

Jacobite, D., & Hazen, N. (1999). Developmental pathways from infant disorganization to childhood peer relationships. In J. Cassidy & P. R. Shaver (Eds.), *Handbook of attachment* (pp. 671-687). New York: Milford Press.

Jacobsen, T., & Hofmann, V. (1997). Children's attachment representations: Longitudinal relations to school behavior and academic competency in middle childhood and adolescence. *Developmental Psychology, 33*, 703-710.

Kagan, J., Snidman, N., Zentner, M., & Peterson, E. (1999). Infant temperament and anxious symptoms in school age children. *Development and Psychopathology, 11*, 209-224.

Kennedy, J. H., & Kennedy, C. E. (2004). Attachment theory: Implications for school psychology. *Psychology in the Schools, 41*, 247-259.

Kobak, R. R., Cole, H. E., Ferenz-Gillies, R., Fleming, W. S., & Gamble, W. (1993). Attachment and emotional regulation during mother-teen problem-solving: A control theory analysis. *Child Development, 64*, 231-245.

Kobak, R., Little, M., Race, E., & Acosta, M. C. (2001). Attachment disruptions in seriously emotionally disturbed children: Implications for treatment. *Attachment & Human Development, 3*, 243-258.

Larose, S., & Bernier, A. (2001). Social support processes: Mediators of attachment state of mind and adjustment in late adolescence. *Attachment & Human Development, 3*, 96-120.

Lieberman, A. F. (1992). Infant-parent psychotherapy with toddlers. *Development and Psychopathology, 4*, 559-574.

Lyons-Ruth, K., Easterbrooks, M. A., & Cibelli, C. D. (1997). Infant attachment strategies, infant mental lag, and maternal depressive symptoms: Predictors of internalizing and externalizing problems at age 7. *Developmental Psychology, 33*, 681-692.

Lyons-Ruth, K., & Jacobvitz, D. (1999). Attachment disorganization: Unresolved loss, relational violence, and lapses in behavioral and attentional strategies. In J. Cassidy & P. R. Shaver (Eds.), *Handbook of attachment* (pp. 520-554). New York: Milford Press.

Main, M., Kaplan, N., & Cassidy, J. (1985). Security in infancy, childhood, and adulthood: A move to the level of representation. In I. Bretherton & E. Waters (Eds.), Growing points in attachment theory and research. *Monographs of the Society for Research in Child Development, 50* (1-2, Serial No. 209), 66-106.

Main, M., & Solomon, J. (1990). Procedures for identifying infants as disorganized/disoriented during the Ainsworth Strange Situation. In M. Greenberg, D. Cicchetti, & E. M. Cummings (Eds.), *Attachment in the preschool years: Theory, research and intervention* (pp. 121-160). Chicago: University of Chicago Press.

Marcus, R. F., & Sanders-Reio, J. (2001). The influence of attachment on school-completion. *School Psychology Quarterly, 16*, 427-444.

Meehan, B. T., Hughes, J. N., & Cavell, T. A. (2003). Teacher-student relationships as compensatory resources for aggressive children. *Child Development, 74*, 1145-1157.

Merrell, K. W. (2002). Social-emotional interventions in schools: Current status, progress, and promise. *School Psychology Review, 31*, 143-147.

Mikulincer, M. (1995). Attachment style and mental representations of the self. *Journal of Personality and Social Psychology, 69*, 1203-1215.

Moss, E., Cyr, C., & Dubois-Comtois, K. (2004). Attachment at early school age and developmental risk: Examining family contexts and behavior problems of controlling-caregiving, controlling-punitive, and behaviorally disorganized children. *Developmental Psychology, 40*, 519-532.

Moss, E., Smolla, N., Cyr, C., Dubois-Comtois, K., Mazzarello, T., & Berthiaume, C. (2006). Attachment and behavior problems in middle childhood as reported by adult and child informants. *Development and Psychopathology, 18*, 425-444.

Moss, E., & St-Laurent, D. (2001). Attachment at school age and academic performance. *Developmental Psychology, 37*, 863-874.

NICHD Early Child Care Research Network. (2006). Infant-mother attachment classification: Risk and protection in relation to changing maternal caregiving quality. *Developmental Psychology, 42*, 38-58.

Pianta, R. C. (1999). *Enhancing relationships between children and teachers.* Washington, DC: American Psychological Association.

Pianta, R. C., Steinberg, M. S., & Rollins, K. B. (1995). The first two years of school: Teacher-child relationships and deflections in children's classroom adjustment. *Development and Psychopathology, 7*, 295-312.

Reddy, R., Rhodes, J. E., & Mulhall, P. (2003). The influence of teacher support on student adjustment in the middle school years: A latent growth curve study. *Development and Psychopathology, 15*, 119-138.

Renkin, B., Egeland, B., Marvinney, D., Mangelsdorf, S., & Sroufe, L. A. (1989). Early childhood antecedents of aggression and passive-withdrawal in early elementary school. *Journal of Personality, 57*, 257-281.

Rosenstein, D. S., & Horowitz, H. A. (1996). Adolescent attachment and psychopathology. *Journal of Counseling and Clinical Psychology, 64*, 244-253.

Schindler, A., Thomasius, P. S., Gemeinhardt, B., Kustner, U., & Eckert, J. (2005). Attachment and substance use disorders: A review of the literature and a study in drug dependent adolescents. *Attachment & Human Development, 7*, 207-228.

Shaw, S. K., & Dallos, R. (2005). Attachment and adolescent depression: The impact of early attachment experiences. *Attachment & Human Development, 7*, 409-424.

Solomon, J., George, C., & de Jong, A. (1995). Children classified as controlling at age six: Evidence of disorganized representational strategies and aggression at home and at school. *Development and Psychopathology, 7*, 447-463.

Speltz, M. L. (1990). The treatment of preschool conduct problems: An integration of behavioral and attachment concepts. In M. T. Greenberg & E. M. Cummings (Eds.), *Attachment in the preschool years* (pp. 399-426). Chicago: University of Chicago Press.

Sroufe, L. A. (2005). Attachment and development: A prospective, longitudinal study from birth to adulthood. *Attachment & Human Development, 7,* 349-367.

Sroufe, L. A., Carlson, E. A., Levy, A. K., & Egeland, B. (1999). Implications of attachment theory for developmental psychopathology. *Development and Psychopathology, 11,* 1-13.

Sroufe, L. A., & Waters, E. (1977). Attachment as an organizational construct. *Child Development, 48,* 1184-1199.

Takahashi, K. (1990). Are the key assumptions of the "Strange Situation" procedure universal? A view from Japanese research. *Human Development, 33,* 23-30.

Thompson, R. A. (1999). Early attachment and later development. In J. Cassidy & P. R. Shaver (Eds.), *Handbook of attachment* (pp. 265-286). New York: Milford Press.

van IJzendoorn, M. H., Schuengel C., & Bakermans-Kranenburg, M. J. (1999). Disorganized attachment in early childhood: Meta-analysis of precursors, concomitants, and sequelae. *Development and Psychopathology, 11,* 225-249.

Warren, S. L., Houston, L., Egeland, B., & Sroufe, L. A. (1997). Child and adolescent anxiety disorders and early attachment. *Journal of the American Academy of Child and Adolescent Psychiatry, 36,* 637-644.

Waters, E., Merrick, S., Treboux, D., Crowell, J., & Abersheim, L. (2000). Attachment security in infancy and early adulthood: A 20-year longitudinal study. *Child Development, 71,* 684-689.

Wentzel, K. R. (2002). Are effective teachers like good parents? Teaching styles and student adjustment in early adolescence. *Child Development, 73,* 287-301.

Attachment Intervention Programs: A Guide for School Psychologists

Benjamin J. Lovett & Tanya L. Eckert
Syracuse University

Nicole M. Talge
University of Minnesota

Angeleque Akin-Little
Walden University

Children's early emotional attachments with caregivers constitute an important developmental task, with individual differences in attachment style predicting later psychopathology. A
wide variety of intervention programs are available to promote
secure attachments, in an effort to reduce risk for negative
mental health outcomes. This article briefly reviews the
research on relationships between attachment organization and
psychopathology before discussing general issues in attachment interventions, describing the details of three such interventions, and concluding with recommendations for school
psychologists' involvement with these intervention programs.

School psychologists hold increasingly expanding roles in American school
systems (Fagan, 2002). Once limited to intelligence testing and certifying children for special education classes, today they consult with teachers regarding
behavior problems, monitor the academic skill development of low achieving students, and serve as a mental health resource for school staff and children alike.
One recent area of role expansion is services for preschool children. School psychologists are often called upon to conduct readiness evaluations, design preventive interventions, and train preschool teachers and parents in behavior
management strategies. In addition, school psychologists have started to focus on
improving the social and emotional adjustment of young children (ages 0-5) by

---

All correspondence should be addressed Benjamin J. Lovett, Department of
Psychology, Syracuse University, 430 Huntington Hall, Syracuse, NY, 13244.
Electronic mail may be sent to bjlovett@syr.edu.

using a conceptual framework that is *child-centered, partnership-based,* and *population-focused* (Fantuzzo, McWayne, & Bulotsky, 2003). As Schakel (1988) noted, given the importance of the developmental changes that occur during the early childhood years, school psychologists have good reason to be interested in including young children in their scope of practice.

School psychologists are often involved with young children suspected of having disabilities and their families. For these young children, federal policy (P.L. 99-457, amended by P.L. 102-119) mandates assessment and early intervention services (Sandall, Hemmeter, Smith, & McLean, 2004). As a result, school psychologists determine eligibility services, link children and families to appropriate early intervention programs, and verify whether intervention programs are meeting the needs of young children and their families (Greenwood, Luze, & Carta, 2002). Furthermore, a focus on young children was identified as an important theme for future work in the 2002 Conference on the Future of School Psychology (Dawson et al., 2003/2004).

A major issue in young children's development involves the formation of foundational emotional relationships, attachments, with parents and other important adults (Thompson, 1998). In the present paper, we review the nature and diversity of interventions that have been designed to help parents to improve their children's attachment security. Our purpose is not to train school psychologists to deliver attachment interventions, but to give personnel who provide psychological services to preschoolers enough information to speak knowledgably to primary caregivers about some of the kinds of intervention programs available, and to support children who have participated in these programs. We begin by briefly reviewing attachment theory and associated research, focusing on the relationships between attachment insecurity and disorganization and psychopathology in children and adults. We then describe general issues in attachment interventions and give details concerning three intervention programs. We conclude with a discussion of the school psychologist's role in enhancing attachment security.

The Origins and Consequences of Individual Differences in Attachment Security

Basic Concepts in Attachment Theory

Modern theories of attachment have their roots in psychodynamic and ethological traditions. John Bowlby, widely recognized as the founder of modern attachment theory, combined Freud's view on the potential of early experiences to exert long-lasting effects on behavior with ethological insights on the fundamental utility and survival value of relationships (Sroufe, 1986). Bowlby noted that human infants are dependent upon caregivers for relatively protracted periods of time relative to other species, and argued that enduring emotional relationships with caregivers evolved to promote survival in this context. His conceptualization of attachment also recognized the active contribution of children to relationships with their caregivers (Sroufe, 1986), and as such, viewed attachment as fundamentally dyadic in nature.

Variations in attachment organization have been examined in a variety of contexts, but Mary Ainsworth's Strange Situation remains the most well-known and influential in the field. This paradigm, typically employed with children between 12 and 18 months of age, involves observing children's responses to a scripted series of separations and reunions with their primary caregiver as well as an unfamiliar adult (Ainsworth, Blehar, Waters, & Wall, 1978). Initially, three patterns of attachment behaviors (secure, insecure-avoidant, and insecure-resistant) were identified based on these observations and, more recently, a fourth pattern (disorganized) was also identified. Securely attached children may display distress upon separation from their caregiver but then seek proximity and happily welcome the caregiver back upon return.

Children classified as showing any of the remaining attachment patterns do not display such confidence in the caregiver. Insecure-avoidant children separate easily from their caregivers, appear indifferent upon reunion, and may respond in an affiliative manner towards an unfamiliar adult (even in the absence of the caregiver). This attachment pattern has been associated with overly intrusive parenting or the rebuffing of bids for attention and interaction. The second insecure attachment pattern, resistant, is characterized by difficulty in separating from their caregiver, and also fussing or crying upon reunion. These behaviors are thought to follow, in part, from unresponsive or inconsistent parenting. Finally, disorganized attachments, which have been observed among maltreated children, are typified by a lack of behavioral cohesion or goal-directedness. Children may display contradictory behavior as well as stereotypies or freezing, and may even display apprehension towards the caregiver (Kennedy & Kennedy, 2004).

Although several independent, longitudinal samples have associated the quality of caregiving during the first year with the aforementioned attachment patterns (Thompson, 1998), attachment relationships have multiple determinants. What constitutes sensitive parenting, for example, depends upon characteristics of the caregiver and child alike. Children with difficult, irritable temperaments may not only elicit certain behaviors from parents, but also require more consistent support or guidance than children otherwise described as agreeable or "easy." Furthermore, the effect and significance of sensitive parenting may differ depending upon the surrounding context in which the care is provided (e.g., play time vs. providing comfort when distressed; Thompson, 1998). Prospective studies with high risk samples also suggest that attachment patterns are not always static. For example, increases in life stress have been associated with insecure attachment styles, particularly when parents' coping strategies are poor (Egeland & Farber, 1984). Generally speaking, however, secure attachments display greater stability across time than insecure attachments (Thompson, 1998), a finding with particular relevance for the viability of interventions.

Attachment and Psychopathology

Our interest in attachment is due in part to concerns that insecure attachments lead to the development of maladaptive behavior patterns. These relationships are complex and moderated by many factors, but they are also robust and therefore worth considering in some detail. In their comprehensive review of relationships between attachment and psychopathology, Kobak, Cassidy, Lyons-Ruth, and Ziv (2006) argued, following Bowlby, that these relationships exist at three levels of analysis. First, an individual child's attachment organization (i.e., style of attachment) may put him or her at risk for the development of various kinds of psychopathology, and most research focuses on these relationships. Second, the quality of care provided for the child may directly affect the child's behavior in pathological ways. Finally, a nonoptimal social and environmental context of caregiving (e.g., physically abusive parenting) may lead to psychopathology.

Much of the research on attachment and psychopathology uses attachment organization assessed during the period of infancy to predict later psychopathology. Generally, the predictive value is lowest in low-risk samples, suggesting that insecure attachment alone is insufficient to induce psychopathology (Greenberg, 1999). However, when children from higher risk samples (e.g., single parent families, those receiving welfare assistance) are examined, a substantial relationship between attachment insecurity and higher risk for a variety of types of psychopathology is reliably found (Kobak et al., 2006). Relationships between specific types of attachment insecurity and corresponding varieties of psychopathology are less robust, but generally, an avoidant attachment style is more predictive of externalizing behavior disorders than internalizing problems, whereas the resistant attachment style shows the opposite pattern (Kennedy & Kennedy, 2004). Finally, the disorganized attachment style is predictive of the worst outcomes, including fearful behavior symptomatic of anxiety disorders as well as reactive aggression stemming from misperceptions of others as threatening (Jacobvitz & Hazen, 1999).

A second line of attachment research has examined concurrent relationships between attachment and psychopathology in preschool children. This research relies on experimental paradigms similar to the Strange Situation, in that the child is separated from and then reunited with a caregiver and the child's response is observed. Several studies by Greenberg and his colleagues (e.g., Speltz, Greenberg, & DeKlyen, 1990) have found that preschool-age boys diagnosed with oppositional defiant disorder (ODD) have higher rates of insecure attachment than boys from a nonclinical comparison group. Other research examining preschoolers' attachment organization has found that, just as with infant studies, disorganized attachment is most strongly and consistently related to problem behavior (Kobak et al., 2006).

The associations between insecure attachment styles and higher rates of psychopathology are robust enough to motivate attachment-focused interventions. However, before describing these interventions, we should note two caveats regarding these associations from a developmental psychopathology perspective. First, as Thompson (2000) points out, some children are more affected by nonsecure attachment styles than others. Even if the relationship between insecure attachment and psychopathology is causal, the mediating mechanisms do not operate in a vacuum, and they interact with many other risk and protective factors to influence mental health. Second, children's cognitive representations (i.e., their "internal working models") of their relationships with caregivers are known to be an important mediator between early attachment organization and outcomes in the domain of interpersonal functioning (Pietromonaco & Barrett, 2000), and this representation is susceptible to change by subsequent experiences. Despite these caveats, the probabilistic risk of increased psychopathology associated with insecure and disorganized attachments is high enough to interest school psychologists and other professionals in proactively intervening to promote secure attachments. Moreover, many scholars consider secure attachment to be predictive of positive outcomes that extend beyond a lack of psychopathology to such qualities as social competence and self-esteem (Thompson, 1998).

Intervening to Improve Attachment: General Strategies and Issues

Attachment research and attachment-based clinical interventions have not generally been as integrated as one might expect. Ziv (2005) argued that this was in part due to disputes between Bowlby and his fellow psychoanalysts. Whatever the cause, today there are a large number of therapeutic programs for individuals of any age, all of these purporting to be based on the principles of attachment theory. Mercer (2006) described several of the more controversial interventions that have scant empirical support, some involving physical restraint, emotional withholding, and other authoritarian tactics. As Robinson (2002) notes, research on the parental behaviors associated with secure attachment immediately suggests a general approach quite different from these controversial therapies:specifically, the provision of "a caregiving relationship context that is available, sensitive, and responsive, in which attachment can develop" (p. 15).

Given this general approach, several conceptual and practical issues immediately arise. First, how individualized will the intervention be? Clearly, individual differences in the enduring traits of parents and children influence parent-child interaction and the continually developing relationship between them. However, highly individualized treatments make dissemination, training, and efficacy evaluation more difficult since, in a sense, they become a different intervention each time they are administered. On the other hand, manualized interventions can be too rigid and may be obviously inappropriate for parents or children with certain characteristics, making their participation in these interventions ethically questionable.

A second question is raised by Kobak and colleagues' (2006) taxonomy of developmental pathways linking attachment and psychopathology: At which level should attachment interventions intervene? The most direct method of intervention might seem to be working with the child, assessing and (if necessary) modifying his or her internal working model of the attachment relationship. However, such a method would unnecessarily exclude the parent, possibly a crucial weakness for an intervention designed to affect parent-child relationships. Alternatively, clinicians might intervene at the level of parent behavior by training the parent to be more sensitive and responsive to the child's needs. Challenges for interventions that operate at this level would include ensuring that parental skills are retained and generalized across situations. Finally, although some scholars would hesitate to call these "attachment interventions," programs could be implemented at the level of contextual factors, aimed at modifying the social and environmental conditions (e.g., poverty, parental psychological disorder) that may be substantial (albeit indirect) contributors to insecure and disorganized attachments. Unfortunately, the causal nature of the relationship between these conditions and attachment style is poorly understood, making for an uncertain foundation for intervention. Also, intervening at this level would be quite costly to implement.

A final question is logistical: For whom should the interventions be designed? The three-fold model of prevention found in the public health literature is helpful here. In a primary prevention program our aim would be to prevent insecure attachments from forming, and our audience would theoretically include all parents. An intensive one-on-one or small-group intervention would not be feasible at this level, but a less intensive intervention (such as brochures or information sheets on attachment for pediatricians to give to parents) might be possible. Secondary prevention programs focus on members of "at-risk" populations, so we might invite new parents from these populations to attend small-group seminars on parenting skills. Finally, in a tertiary prevention program, we would seek out children already demonstrating insecure attachment styles and aim to keep these styles from leading to psychopathology, either by enhancing attachment security or by assessing and treating any early mental health consequences. Since a tertiary prevention program would have the smallest audience, it could afford to be more intensive and might involve more one-on-one contact time with intervention agents.

Degree of individualization, level of focus, and scope of audience are only a few of the many dimensions on which available attachment intervention programs vary. We have selected three such programs that illustrate the diversity of attachment interventions. Unlike many other programs, these three each have at least one published evaluation study associated with them, and each provides enough concrete information about the actual implementation of the intervention to give outsiders the experience of participating in the program. However, although these three programs are "public" in that they have published evaluation studies and intervention manuals, the programs are still in the stage of being tested and refined. The field of attachment interventions is young, and not all of the promising programs reviewed here may withstand continued empirical evaluation.

Intervening to Improve Attachment: Three Sample Programs

The "Circle of Security" Program

In an attempt to shift patterns of attachments among high-risk caregiver-child dyads, Cooper, Hoffman, Powell, and Marvin (2005) developed a group-based intervention that incorporates parent education and psychotherapy to promote appropriate interactions among Head Start and Early Head Start parents and their young children. The intervention program, the Circle of Security project, aims to teach caregivers about their children's attachment needs, strengthen their ability to observe and improve their own caregiving skills, and address any residual parental obstacles that interfere with caregiver-child relationships. A classification of caregivers' defensive sensitivities (into separation-sensitive, esteem-sensitive, and safety-sensitive) is used to individualize the program for each participant. The program relies heavily on edited videotapes of caregiver-child interactions, incorporates parent-friendly teaching tools, and has been field-tested among Head Start and Early Head Start recipients (Cooper, Hoffman, Marvin, & Powell, 2000).

Four specific principles influenced the development of this training program (Cooper et al., 2005). First, the quality of child-caregiver attachment plays an influential role in children's developmental trajectories. Second, permanent changes in child-caregiver attachment can be achieved by caregivers changing their behaviors, including understanding their children's relationship needs, developing observational and inferential skills, engaging in reflective functioning, regulating emotions, and developing empathy. Third, improved child-caregiver relationships can be achieved when caregivers learn to interact within a secure-base relationship. Fourth, targeting both the strengths and weaknesses of individual caregivers can result in better long-term changes in caregivers' behavior. As a result, the goals of the Circle of Security intervention protocol include: (a) establishing the therapist and the group as a secure base for the caregivers, (b) increasing the caregivers' sensitivity and responsiveness, (c) increasing the caregivers' competence in identifying their child's cues, (d) increasing the caregivers' empathy, and (e) increasing the caregivers' understanding of their own developmental history and how it affects their current behavior (Hoffman, Marvin, Cooper, & Powell, 2006).

Intervention sessions are implemented on a weekly basis for 75 minutes. Throughout the program, trained clinicians work with small groups of caregivers of young children (1 to 4 years of age). Using videotapes of attachment-caregiving interactions obtained prior to the onset of the program, caregivers are encouraged to increase their sensitivity and appropriate responsiveness to their children's signals, reflect on their perceptions regarding caregiving interactions, and identify experiences that affect their caregiving capabilities. During the first phase of the program, clinicians review the videotaped child-caregiver dyad interactions obtained during the Strange Situation procedure, facilitate a discussion of the caregiver's observed parenting skills, and require the group of caregivers to identify "over-used strengths" and "under-used capacities" that were exhibited by the caregiver. During the second phase of the program, underdeveloped parenting skills are further targeted and caregivers are asked to examine defensive processes that inhibit their ability to use these underdeveloped skills. The final phase of the program focuses on reinforcing positive caregiver changes and identifying directions for future improvement. More detailed descriptions of the procedures have been provided by Hoffman and colleagues (2005, 2006).

Child behavior problems, parent internalizing problems (e.g., depression, anxiety), environmental factors (e.g., stress), and caregiver-child attachment patterns are assessed at pretreatment, posttreatment, and one year following treatment. The caregiver-child attachment patterns are derived from the interactions observed during the Strange Situation procedure. These interactions are coded using a combination of attachment classification systems (Ainsworth et al., 1978; Britner, Marvin, & Pianta, 2005; Cassidy & Marvin, with the MacArthur Working Group on Attachment, 1992) by clinical psychologists and graduate students certified in the attachment coding procedures. In addition, caregivers' strengths and weaknesses are identified using the Caregiver Behavior Classification System (Britner et al., 2005), and their core attachment sensitivities are analyzed using the Circle of Security Interview (Cooper, Hoffman, Marvin, & Powell, 1999).

Although the program has been implemented with more than 75 caregivers and preliminary results suggest that the program resulted in significant changes for caregivers' behaviors and their children's attachment patterns, outcome data have been largely restricted to case studies (Marvin, Cooper, Hoffman, & Powell, 2002; Powell, Cooper, Hoffman, & Marvin, in press). Recently, a large-scale evaluation of the Circle of Security intervention was conducted with 65 toddler- or preschooler-caregiver dyads from Head Start or Early Head Start programs (Hoffman et al., 2006). In this study, most of the caregivers were female (86%)

and White/Caucasian (86%), with an average age of 24 years. The gender of the children was relatively equal, and their average age was 32 months.

Prior to the commencement of the program, all child-caregiver dyads were assessed during a laboratory session (i.e., pre-assessment). The Circle of Security intervention was implemented approximately 8 weeks following the pre-assessment and continued over a 20-week period. Following completion of the intervention, all child-caregiver dyads were reassessed (i.e., post-assessment). The results of this study indicated a statistically significant difference in the number of children classified with disorganized attachment following the intervention. From pre- to post-assessment, 69% of the children classified with disorganized attachment ($n = 27$) shifted to a classification of organized attachment, whereas 15% of the children classified with organized attachment ($n = 4$) shifted to a classification of disorganized attachment. Similarly, a statistically significant difference in the number of children with insecure attachment classifications was observed following the intervention. From pre- to post-assessment, 44% of the children classified with insecure attachment ($n = 23$) shifted to a classification of secure attachment, whereas 8% of the children classified with secure attachment ($n = 1$) shifted to a classification of insecure attachment. A total of 31% of the participants classified with disorganized attachment ($n = 12$) and 56% of the participants classified with insecure attachment ($n = 29$) were unresponsive to the intervention and did not change their attachment classifications. These findings are promising and suggest that the Circle of Security program may be effective for addressing attachment-related problems for at-risk toddlers and young children.

A Biobehavioral Intervention Model

In an attempt to promote the foster care of young children and their surrogate caregivers, Dozier, Lindhiem, and Ackerman (2005) developed the Attachment and Biobehavioral Catch-Up training program. Given the physiological, behavioral, and emotional dysregulation observed in many foster care children (Dozier et al., 2006) combined with the disproportionately higher number of foster children with disorganized attachments or less coherent attachment patterns (Dozier, Stovall, Albus, & Bates, 2001; Stovall-McClough & Dozier, 2004), the authors developed their program to address the unique needs of foster care infants and their caregivers. Their program is principally influenced by analyses of the evidence-based literature, suggesting that if stable, responsive, and nurturing foster care is provided during sensitive periods in children's development of neuroendocrine regulation and attachment, early difficulties can be remediated (Dozier, Albus, Fisher, & Sepulveda, 2002).

The theoretical and empirical rationale for their biobehavioral intervention model is based on three phenomena that Dozier and colleagues (2002) have observed occurring among infants and young children in foster care placements. First, foster children are inclined to omit behavioral signals that result in foster caregivers engaging in non-nurturing behaviors (Stovall & Dozier, 2000; Tyrell & Dozier, 1999). Second, some foster caregivers are reluctant to provide nurturance, even when their foster children provide clear behavioral signals for nurturance (Stovall & Dozier, 2000). Third, foster care children are at greater risk for experiencing regulatory difficulties (Fisher, Gunnar, Chamberlain, & Reid, 2000). To address these critical needs, four core training components are embedded in the program, including: (a) helping caregivers provide nurturance to their infants, (b) teaching caregivers to provide nurturance in the absence of infant cues, (c) supporting caregivers to provide predictable interpersonal routines, and (d) creating safe, non-threatening environments. These training components are intended to promote infant organized attachment, regulate infant behavior and biobehavioral systems, and improve caregiver behaviors (e.g., gentle, comforting interactions).

Ten intervention sessions are implemented for 60 minutes in the caregivers' homes by a professional trained in the procedures. To promote caregiver nurturance (components one and two), four sessions review the importance of foster children receiving nurturing care, discuss infant behaviors that elicit and inhibit care, encourage caregivers to provide nurturing care (even in the absence of infant cues), and recognize caregivers' experiences that may affect responding. Five sessions address the third component, in which caregivers are taught to provide predictable interpersonal routines. During these sessions, caregivers are instructed to read their children's behavioral signals (e.g., engagement, disengagement), identify appropriate situations for childhood autonomy, and provide opportunities for their children to direct parent-child interactions. Finally, one session addresses the importance of caregivers providing a safe, non-threatening environment. In this session, caregivers are trained to promote children's expression of negative emotions and respond in a supportive manner.

Although the procedures for each session are standardized, some sessions are individualized to meet the unique needs of the caregivers (e.g., caregiver state of mind; Dozier & Sepulveda, 2004). Homework activities are also assigned throughout the training program. In addition, videotaped sessions of caregiver-infant interactions are reviewed with caregivers to provide additional instruction, feedback, and reinforcement related to the core training components. At annual intervals, caregivers' behaviors (e.g., sensitivity, nurturance, commitment) and infants' behaviors (e.g., attachment, problem behaviors, regulatory behaviors, neuroendocrine functioning) are assessed. Detailed descriptions of the procedures used in this program have been published (Dozier et al., 2002) as well as manualized (Dozier et al., 2006).

Preliminary case studies suggest that the training program promotes caregivers' commitment to their foster care infants and results in favorable caregiver-infant attachment (Dozier et al., 2005; Fisher, 2001). In addition, a recent randomized clinical trial of the Attachment and Biobehavioral Catch-Up training program was conducted with 60 foster care children (Dozier et al., 2006). Typically-developing children ($n = 104$) who had not been placed in foster care were also included in secondary outcome analyses. Most of the foster care children were African American (63%), with an average age of 17 months. An equal number of male and female foster care children participated. The foster care children were randomly assigned to one of two conditions: Attachment and Biobehavioral Catch-Up ($n = 30$) or Developmental Education for Families ($n = 30$). The Developmental Education for Families intervention emphasized children's cognitive and linguistic development, was based on work by Ramey and colleagues (Ramey, McGinness, Cross, Collier, & Barrie-Blackley, 1982; Ramey, Yeates, & Short, 1984), and has been shown to improve children's cognitive functioning (Brooks-Gunn, Klebanov, Liaw, & Spiker, 1993). Both interventions were conducted over 10 hour-long sessions. Post-intervention outcome measures, that included assays of children's diurnal cortisol production and caregivers' reports of their children's problem behaviors, were collected.

The results of this study indicated that children assigned to the Attachment and Biobehavioral Catch-Up intervention showed significantly lower cortisol values than children participating in the Developmental Education for Families intervention. In addition, the cortisol levels for the children assigned to the Attachment and Biobehavioral Catch-Up condition were not different from those levels obtained from the typically-developing participants, whereas statistically significant differences were observed between the foster care children assigned to the Developmental Education for Families condition and the typically-developing participants. Results of the parent-reported behavior problems indicated that there was no statistically significant difference between the behavior problems reported by the parents assigned to the two interventions. However, observed differences were in the predicted direction of the caregivers receiving the Attachment and Biobehavioral Catch-Up intervention reporting fewer behavior problems for their toddlers, relative to younger infants, and relative to caregivers receiving the Developmental Education for Families intervention. It should also be noted that a statistically significant interaction (i.e., condition by age) was found, wherein caregivers of foster care children assigned to the Attachment and Biobehavioral Catch-Up intervention reported fewer behavior problems for toddlers than infants. No age differences were observed for caregivers of foster care children assigned to the Developmental Education for Families intervention.

The findings from this randomized clinical trial provide empirical support for the Attachment and Biobehavioral Catch-Up intervention in regularizing the biological system of foster care children to the point that their functioning is comparative to typically-developing children. The outcomes were less robust with respect to caregivers' reports of their foster care children's behavior problems.

Attachment Intervention within Early Head Start

In an attempt to improve caregiver-infant interactions within the context of an Early Head Start partnership program (i.e., a community site working with a local university research team), Spieker, Nelson, DeKlyen, and Staerkel (2005) developed a comprehensive attachment intervention that was embedded within the federally-mandated program. The partnership program was part of a national evaluation of parent and child outcomes associated with family participation in Early Head Start programs (Office of Research and Evaluation, Head Start Bureau, 2001, 2002).

By embedding their attachment intervention within the context of the Early Head Start Program, Spieker and colleagues (2005) were able to examine three objectives. First, they examined whether caregivers' participation in the attachment intervention enhanced parent-child interactions and parent-child attachment to a greater extent than caregivers who were assigned to a control condition. Second, they investigated whether caregivers' early attachment relationships or internalizing symptoms moderated the effectiveness of the attachment intervention. Third, they explored whether demographic variables and caregivers' early attachment relationships influenced participation in the intervention.

In an attempt to enhance early attachments, this intervention commenced while the caregivers were pregnant. Home visits were divided into three 30 minute segments: (a) assessment and activities linked with the Individual Learning Plan, required for Early Head Start participation, (b) support and training regarding home environment issues, including parent-child interactions, and (c) the attachment intervention (i.e., Parent-Child Communication Coaching Program). The intervention aimed to improve caregiver-infant interactions, promote secure caregiver-infant attachment relationships, and maintain a positive relationship between the home visitor and family. As part of the intervention, 10 protocols were developed that focused on topics relevant to prenatal and infant development: (a) recognizing the fetus, (b) gaining family acceptance, (c) creating attachment moments, (d) creating a close physical proximal environment, (e) understanding infant states and behavioral cues, (f) learning contingent imitation, (g) recognizing infant emotional and verbal expressions, (h) facilitating parent-child communication before language, (i) engaging in preverbal activities, and (j) encouraging book reading with the child. These intervention protocols were implemented over the course of five developmental phases: pregnancy, newborn to 3 months, 4-8 months, 9-24 months, and 24-36 months (Speiker et al., 2005).

As each intervention protocol was introduced to the caregivers, the protocol and corresponding steps were reviewed by the home visitors. A home-based activity, informational handout, and homework assignment were provided for each intervention step contained in the protocol. In addition, video-feedback techniques were used in conjunction with some intervention steps. At key developmental periods (i.e., feeding, imitation, eliciting emotions, nonverbal gestures), home visitors videotaped the interactions between caregivers and infants. Following an analysis of the videotape and consultation with the university research team, the home visitors reviewed the interactions with the caregivers and provided feedback. The caregivers' psychosocial functioning and representations of early attachment relationships were assessed in addition to infant attachment security. An overview and description of the procedures have been published (Spieker et al., 2005).

To date, the only empirical data examining the effectiveness of the Parent-Child Communication Coaching Program was included in the original work describing the intervention procedures (Spieker et al., 2005). In this study, a total of 135 caregivers of infants less than 6 months of age were recruited to participate in the project. To be eligible to participate in the project, caregivers needed to be living at or below the poverty level. Caregivers were randomly assigned to either the Early Head Start program ($n = 65$) or the control condition ($n = 70$), with the caregivers participating in the Early Head Start program receiving intensive family support that started during pregnancy and continued through the child's third year. Consistent with Early Head Start program guidelines, the program addressed child, family, staff, and community development (Administration for Children and Families, 2003). Parent training and support through home visits was provided on a weekly basis, and mental health services, stress management classes, and vocational counseling were also offered to the caregivers.

Overall, very low rates of program participation and treatment integrity were reported. Caregivers participated in less than 25% of the scheduled home visits and only 36% of the intervention protocols were completed. Furthermore, there was no caregiver who completed all of the interventions steps with the home visitor. Intervention protocols that had the highest completion rates included gaining family acceptance during pregnancy (51%) and facilitating parent-child communication before language, 9 to 24 months (45%). Conversely, 4 of the 10 intervention protocols had completion rates less than 20%, including engaging in preverbal activities with infant, 9 to 24 months (1%); understanding infant states and behavioral cues, newborn to 3 months (4%); recognizing the fetus during pregnancy (18%); and creating attachment moments during pregnancy (18%). These exceptionally low levels of treatment integrity, within the context of poor program participation rates, may account for the lack of intervention effects observed. The authors found that neither parent-child interactions nor infant attachment patterns were affected by caregivers' participation in the attachment intervention. Furthermore, at the end of the intervention, a higher proportion of children in the control group had secure attachments.

Additional analyses examined whether caregiver characteristics, such as maternal depression or early attachment relationships, moderated the effect of the attachment intervention. Results of these analyses indicated that the intervention had a significantly greater effect on depressed caregivers than non-depressed caregivers. Depressed caregivers receiving the attachment intervention tended to engage in more caregiver warmth/sensitivity than depressed caregivers assigned to the control condition. No significant findings were attributed to any other caregiver characteristic.

Attachment Interventions and the School Psychologist

We have discussed general issues common to all attachment interventions and have given detailed descriptions of three interventions that illustrate the diversity of available programs. What should school psychologists be expected to do with this knowledge? What is their role in promoting secure attachments? In this concluding section we outline three possible roles for school psychologists, representing a range of levels of involvement.

A first role is that of an information or referral source. Psychologists who are knowledgeable about the dimensions on which attachment interventions vary can direct families to intervention programs with characteristics from which each particular family can benefit the most. Admittedly, knowledge of the demonstrated efficacy of each program is important information when making referral decisions, and school psychologists trained as data-based problem solvers will be best able to understand and interpret evaluation research on attachment programs when making such decisions. However, even a basic knowledge of attachment theory can be helpful in knowing which questions to ask parents to determine whether risk factors for attachment insecurity are present and whether an insecure or disorganized attachment style is already developing.

A second possible role for school psychologists involves supporting attachment interventions using skills in such areas as behavior analysis. Parenting practices may be an important determinant of attachment organization, but the importance of "child effects" on parenting are also well known (e.g., Bell & Chapman, 1986). As such, it may be much easier for parents to provide the type of receptivity and sensitivity associated with the secure attachment style if certain child behaviors (e.g., noncompliance, oppositionality) can be reduced. Although direct intervention with toddlers may not always be feasible or appropriate, school psychologists can advise parents on general behavior management techniques (e.g., differential reinforcement, ignoring attention-maintained problem behavior) that might allow parent-child dyads to benefit from attachment intervention programs.

Finally, many school psychologists may take on a more direct role by aiding in the maintenance of gains made during attachment interventions by monitoring and supporting preschool and school-age students who have benefited from these interventions. School psychologists who work with preschool populations should be aware of children who have participated in attachment interventions and should become knowledgeable about the specific programs in the local area that families tend to utilize. Open communication with parents and teachers, and making oneself available for consultation with these individuals, can help to ensure that the benefits from the interventions are not lost.

Concern for healthy development of children's emotional relationships may seem less central as an area of focus for school psychologists today, at a time when academic skills get more media coverage and government attention. However, the maladaptive behavior that is associated with insecure and disorganized attachment styles can itself be a risk factor for academic problems (Nelson, Benner, Lane, & Smith, 2004). Even if this were not the case, school psychologists cannot overlook early interpersonal patterns that can lead to psychopathology when these patterns may be amenable to change and so many programs are available to try to change them. An understanding of attachment and attachment interventions, then, confers a responsibility on school psychologists, but with that responsibility comes an opportunity to affect children's social development in positive ways.

References

Administration for Children and Families. (2003). *Serving infants and toddlers: A resource guide for measuring services and outcomes.* Washington, DC: U.S. Department of Health and Human Services.

Ainsworth, M. D. S., Blehar, M. C., Waters, E., & Wall, S. (1978). *Patterns of attachment: Psychological study of the Strange Situation.* Hillsdale, NJ: Erlbaum.

Bell, R. Q., & Chapman, M. (1986). Child effects in studies using experimental or brief longitudinal approaches to socialization. *Developmental Psychology, 22,* 595-603.

Britner, P. A., Marvin, R. S., & Pianta, R. C. (2005). Maternal caregiving and child attachment patterns in the preschool Strange Situation. *Attachment and Human Development, 7,* 83-102.

Brooks-Gunn, J., Klebanov, P. K., Liaw, F., & Spiker, D. (1993). Enhancing the development of low birth weight, premature infants: Changes in cognition and behavior over the first three years. *Child Development, 64,* 736-753.

Cassidy, J., & Marvin, R. S., with the MacArthur Working Group on Attachment. (1992). *A system for classifying individual differences in the attachment-*

behavior of 2 ½ to 4 ½ year old children. Unpublished coding manual, University of Virginia.

Cooper, G., Hoffman, K., Marvin, R., & Powell, B. (1999, June/July). *The Circle of Security Interview.* Unpublished materials, Marycliff Institute, Spokane, WA.

Cooper, G., Hoffman, K., Marvin, R., & Powell, B. (2000). *Attachment-based intervention with at-risk Head Start child-parent dyads.* Paper presented at the National Head Start Research Meetings, Washington, DC.

Cooper, G., Hoffman, K., Powell, B., & Marvin, R. (2005). The Circle of Security intervention: Differential diagnosis and differential treatment. In L. J. Berlin, Y. Ziv, L. Amaya-Jackson, & M. T. Greenberg (Eds.), *Enhancing early attachments: Theory, research, intervention, and policy* (pp. 127-151). New York: Guilford.

Dawson, M., Cummings, J. A., Harrison, P. L., Short, R. J., Gorin, S., & Palomares, R. (2003/2004). The 2002 multisite conference on the future of school psychology: Next steps. *School Psychology Quarterly, 18,* 497-509. *School Psychology Review, 33,* 115-125.

Dozier, M., Albus, K., Fisher, P. A., & Sepulveda, S. (2002). Interventions for foster parents: Implications for developmental theory. *Development and Psychopathology, 14,* 843-860.

Dozier, M., Lindhiem, O., & Ackerman, J. P. (2005). Attachment and biobehavioral catch-up: An intervention targeting empirically identified needs of foster infants. In L. J. Berlin, Y. Ziv, L. Amaya-Jackson, & M. T. Greenberg (Eds.), *Enhancing early attachments: Theory, research, intervention, and policy* (pp. 178-194). New York: Guilford.

Dozier, M., Manni, M., Gordon, M. K., Peloso, E., Gunnar, M. R., Stovall-McClough, K. C., et al. (2006). Foster children's diurnal production of cortisol: An exploratory study. *Child Maltreatment: Journal of the American Professional Society on the Abuse of Children, 11,* 189-197.

Dozier, M., Peloso, E., Lindheim, O., Gordon, M. K., Manni, M., Sepulveda, S., et al. (2006). Developing evidence-based interventions for foster children: An example of a randomized clinical trial with infants and toddlers. *Journal of Social Issues, 62,* 767-785.

Dozier, M., & Sepulveda, S. (2004). Foster mother state of mind and treatment use: Different challenges for different people. *Infant Mental Health Journal, 25,* 368-378.

Dozier, M., Stovall, C., Albus, K., & Bates, B. (2001). Attachment for infants in foster care: The role of caregiver state of mind. *Child Development, 72,* 1467-1477.

Egeland, B., & Farber, E. A. (1984). Infant-mother attachment: Factors related to its development and changes over time. *Child Development, 55,* 753-771.

Fagan, T. K. (2002). School psychology: Recent descriptions, continued expansion, and an ongoing paradox. *School Psychology Review, 31,* 5-10.

Fantuzzo, J., McWayne, C., & Bulotsky, R. (2003). Forging strategic partnerships to advance mental health science and practice for vulnerable children. *School Psychology Review, 32,* 17-37.

Fisher, P. A. (2001). *Physical growth, cortisol, and neuropsychological functioning among maltreated preschoolers in the foster care system.* Paper presented at the biennial meeting of the Society for Research in Child Development, Minneapolis, MN.

Fisher, P. A., Gunnar, M. R., Chamberlain, P., & Reid, J. B. (2000). Preventive intervention for maltreated preschoolers: Impact on children's behavior, neuroendocrine activity, and foster parent functioning. *Journal of the American Academy of Child and Adolescent Psychiatry, 39,* 1356-1364.

Greenberg, M. T. (1999). Attachment and psychopathology in childhood. In J. Cassidy & P. R. Shaver (Eds.), *Handbook of attachment: Theory, research, and clinical applications* (pp. 469-496). New York: Guilford.

Greenwood, C. R., Luze, G. J., & Carta, J. J. (2002). Best practices in assessment of intervention results with infants and toddlers. In A. Thomas & J. Grimes (Eds.), *Best practices in school psychology – IV* (pp. 1219-1230). Bethesda, MD: The National Association of School Psychologists.

Hoffman, K. T., Marvin, R. S., Cooper, G., & Powell, B. (2006). Changing toddlers' and preschoolers' attachment classifications: The Circle of Security intervention. *Journal of Consulting and Clinical Psychology, 74,* 1017-1026.

Jacobvitz, D., & Hazen, N. (1999). Developmental pathways from infant disorganization to childhood peer relationships. In J. Solomon & C. G. George (Eds.), *Attachment disorganization* (pp. 127-159). New York: Guilford.

Kennedy, J. H., & Kennedy, C. E. (2004). Attachment theory: Implications for school psychology. *Psychology in the Schools, 41,* 247-259.

Kobak, R., Cassidy, J., Lyons-Ruth, K., & Ziv, Y. (2006). Attachment, stress, and psychopathology: A developmental pathways model. In D. Cicchetti & D. J. Cohen (Eds.), *Developmental psychopathology* (2nd ed., Vol. 1, pp. 333-369). New York: Wiley.

Marvin, R., Cooper, G., Hoffman, K., & Powell, B. (2002). The Circle of Security project: Attachment-based intervention with caregiver-pre-school child dyads. *Attachment and Human Development, 4,* 107-124.

Mercer, J. (2006). *Understanding attachment: Parenting, child care, and emotional development.* Westport, CT: Praeger.

Nelson, J. R., Benner, G. J., Lane, K., & Smith, B. (2004). Academic achievement of K-12 students with emotional and behavioral disorders. *Exceptional Children, 71*, 59-73.

Office of Research and Evaluation, Head Start Bureau. (2001). *Building their futures: How Early Head Start programs are enhancing the lives of infants and toddlers in low-income families (Summary report)*. Washington, DC: Administration on Children, Youth and Families, U.S. Department of Health and Human Services.

Office of Research and Evaluation, Head Start Bureau. (2002). *Making a difference in the lives of infants and toddlers and their families: The impacts of Early Head Start (Executive summary)*. Washington, DC: Administration on Children, Youth and Families, U.S. Department of Health and Human Services.

Pietromonaco, P. R., & Barrett, L. F. (2000). The internal working models concept: What do we really know about the self in relation to others? *Review of General Psychology, 4*, 155-175.

Powell, B., Cooper, G., Hoffman, K., & Marvin, R. (in press). The Circle of Security project: A case study. In D. Oppenheim & D. Goldsmith (Eds.), *Clinical application of attachment theory: Bridging the gap between theory, research, and practice*. New York: Guilford.

Ramey, C. T., McGinness, G. D., Cross, L., Collier, A. M., & Barrie-Blackley, S. (1982). The Abecedarian approach to social competence: Cognitive and linguistic intervention for disadvantaged preschoolers. In K. Borman (Ed.), *The social life of children in a changing society* (pp. 14-174). Hillsdale, NJ: Erlbaum.

Ramey, C. T., Yeates, K. O., & Short, E. J. (1984). The plasticity of intellectual development: Insights from preventative intervention. *Child Development, 55,* 1913-1925.

Robinson, J. R. (2002). Attachment problems and disorders in infants and young children: Identification, assessment, and intervention. *Infants and Young Children, 14*, 6-18.

Sandall, S., Hemmeter, M. L., Smith, B. J., & McLean, M. E. (2004). *DEC recommended practices: A comprehensive guide for practical application*. Longmont, CO: Sopris West.

Schakel, J. A. (1988). Providing services to preschool-aged children: A role for school psychologists. *School Psychology International, 9*, 163-173.

Speltz, M. L., Greenberg, M. T., & DeKlyen, M. (1990). Attachment in preschoolers with disruptive behavior: A comparison of clinic-referred and nonproblem children. *Development and Psychopathology, 2*, 31-46.

Spieker, S. J., Nelson, D. C., DeKlyen, M., & Staerkel, S. (2005). Enhancing early attachments in the context of early head start. In L. J. Berlin, Y. Ziv, L. Amaya-Jackson, & M. T. Greenberg (Eds.), *Enhancing early* attachments: Theory, research, intervention, and policy (pp. 61-78). New York: Guilford.

Sroufe, L. A. (1986). Appraisal: Bowlby's contribution to psychoanalytic theory and developmental psychology: Attachment, separation, loss. *Journal of Child Psychology and Psychiatry, 27,* 841-849.

Stovall, K. C., & Dozier, M. (2000). The development of attachment in new relationships: Single subject analyses for ten foster infants. *Development and Psychopathology, 12,* 133-156.

Stovall-McClough, K. C., & Dozier, M. (2004). Forming attachments in foster care: Infant attachment behaviors during the first 2 months of placement. *Development and Psychopathology, 16,* 253-271.

Thompson, R. A. (1998). Early sociopersonality development. In W. Damon (Ed.), *Handbook of child psychology* (5th ed., Vol. 3, pp. 25-104). New York: Wiley.

Thompson, R. A. (2000). The legacy of early attachments. *Child Development, 71,* 145-152.

Tyrell, C., & Dozier, M. (1999). Foster parents' understanding of children's problematic attachment strategies: The need for therapeutic responsiveness. *Adoption Quarterly, 2,* 49-64.

Ziv, Y. (2005). Attachment-based intervention programs: Implications for attachment theory and research. In L. J. Berlin, Y. Ziv, L. Amaya-Jackson, & M. T. Greenberg (Eds.), *Enhancing early attachments: Theory, research, intervention, and policy* (pp. 61-78). New York: Guilford.

Infant and Child Attachment as it Relates to School-Based Outcomes

Thomas J. Kehle, Melissa A. Bray, & Sarah E. Grigerick
University of Connecticut

A ubiquitous finding is that children without friendships are at-risk for psychological and social dysfunction throughout the lifespan. The assumption is that a child's lack of social support and failure to develop friendships in the primary grades may be partially the result of insecure attachment during infancy. The quality of parent-infant attachment is most likely influenced by both environmental and biological factors as articulated in social pain theory. The child who forms an insecure (e.g., avoidant, ambivalent) attachment may face difficulties in the school setting when trying to form successful peer relationships. Further, those children who lack peer support often lack teacher support as well. The classroom environment becomes psychologically oppressive and consequently not only does the motivation to excel academically become seriously attenuated, but the physical health of these children is also threatened. In summary, children who lack peer acceptance probably also lack adult acceptance beginning with their caretakers in infancy. This article will explore the life course that persists following insecure attachments.

For children, school is an environment in which social expectations for behavior must be learned, and the repercussions of success or failure can be enduring. Two theories of human development, Bowlby's (1987) model of attachment and MacDonald and Leary's (2005) theory of social pain, provide some insight into the explanation and prediction of social dysfunction in children.

First, Bowlby's (1987) ethological theory of attachment has provided a framework for understanding how children view themselves in relation to the social world. Children's adaptive behaviors may function to elicit caring, support, and nourishment from a primary caregiver, typically their mother. According to

All correspondence should be addressed to Thomas Kehle, Ph.D., University of Connecticut, 249 Glenbrook Road, Unit 2064, Storrs, CT 06269-2064. Phone: (860) 486-4031. Electronic mail may be sent to thomas.kehle@uconn.edu.

Bowlby, it is this attachment relationship that teaches the child that other people can be depended upon for social support and results in a psychologically secure child capable of demonstrating appropriate levels of independent exploration and social contact seeking. Conversely, a poor attachment relationship may affect attempts at friendship formation and the development of social competence in the child (Elicker, Englund, & Sroufe, 1992).

Using the Strange Situation method, Ainsworth and Bell (1970) were the first researchers to empirically document the different attachment styles theorized by Bowlby. Under direct observation of mother and child interactions during and following a separation, the subjects were classified into one of three attachment categories: (a) secure, (b) anxious-ambivalent, and (c) anxious-avoidant. A fourth category of insecure attachment, disorganized-disoriented, was later identified by Main and Solomon (1990). For insecurely attached children, their social world can be perceived as dangerous and confusing with low expectations of empathy or gratification in response to social need. Possible consequences of these experiences are a negative self-concept and a low sense of self-worth (Verschueren, Marcoen, & Schoefs, 1996).

A second theory, social pain theory (MacDonald & Leary, 2005), has its roots in the biological premise of species evolution and adaptive survival. Because early humans were reliant on acceptance into the social group for physical survival, MacDonald and Leary theorized that the neurologically-based pain sensors that guide a person's response to physical danger evolved into a system that warned of emotional danger or social exclusion through the aversive experience of "pain affect." These feelings of pain are supposedly influenced by social rejection that through negative reinforcement result in the individual moving away from the rejection toward a more accepting social group.

Children are particularly sensitive to these pain cues; their early survival requires that signs of physical distress are responded to with needed food, water, or safety, all accompanied by a mother's calming touch. For securely attached children, social pain provides easy to understand cues to human behavior that, if attended to, lead to expected results. With an internal working model of the self as deserving of social contact and others as reliably providing support when necessary, social pain – much like the burn of a hot stove – is a brief, soon abated signal to steer the securely attached child away from social danger and toward social inclusion. In contrast, the insecurely attached child is at increased risk of not having fundamental needs met. If the child is lacking in adult attention or contact, these seemingly small experiences, which are typically abated in the securely attached child, may manifest themselves through physical symptoms or behavioral outcomes.

With respect to both Bowlby's (1987) attachment and MacDonald and Leary's (2005) social pain theories, investigators have found that insecure attachment is correlated with specific outcomes at each stage of a child's life, with a specific emphasis on early childhood. The subsequent sections will not only detail the results of this research, but will attempt to show how these outcomes are mediated by the child's attachments and experience of social pain, resulting in a more thorough understanding of these children and a firmer foundation for intervention study.

Preschool, Kindergarten, and Primary Grades

The classroom environment is a complex social system requiring interaction with both teachers and peers that influence academic and behavioral outcomes throughout the child's schooling. The extent to which children are able to establish and maintain reciprocal positive relationships influences a diverse array of protective factors, including school adjustment and academic achievement (Birch & Ladd, 1997; Ladd & Price, 1987). Knowing this, researchers are challenged to understand how children develop the social competence that will affect the quality of these peer and teacher relationships in the preschool and early elementary years.

Attachment theory (Bowlby, 1987) has long provided a foundation for this kind of inquiry. Children engaged in secure attachment relationships with their primary caregivers have been shown to be relatively successful at engaging peers in play, and to have developed positive friendships by age 5 (Kerns & Barth, 1995; Youngblade & Belsky, 1992). These same children are also apt to be judged as socially competent and task oriented by their teachers (Pianta, Longmaid, & Ferguson, 1999; Wentzel, 1991). A recent study conducted by Szewczyk-Sokolwski, Bost, and Wainwright (2005) found attachment security to account for approximately 50% of the total variance in children's peer acceptance, based on preschool peer nomination measures. The researchers concluded that security of attachment was as important in predicting a child's level of social competence as the internal characteristics, such as temperament, that had traditionally been weighted the heaviest. These results suggest that attachment security affects more than just the child's internal view of the world — there is something inherently unique in the interaction style and behavior between an insecurely attached child and the individual and social groups they encounter in a school setting.

The correspondence between a child's level of attachment security and expression of externalizing and internalizing behaviors may account for some of these findings, as investigators have shown that insecure and disorganized attachment styles in the first two years of life predict behavioral difficulties in the pre-elementary years (Sroufe, 2005). The National Institute of Child Health and Human Development - Early Child Care Research Network (NICHD-ECCRN, 2006) recently reported that children who were classified in infancy as avoidant were rated higher on behaviors such as aggression, anxiety, and withdrawal than those children with other attachment classifications. This finding replicated an earlier study correlating less secure attachment with poor social competence and preschool aggression (Schmidt, DeMulder, & Denham, 2002).

Aggression and anxiety have implications for the development of social support networks that can be partially explained by the mediating effect of social pain theory. A 3-year longitudinal study by Persson (2005) found that children who engaged in aggressive acts during preschool were less likely to be the recipients of peer-initiated prosocial behavior. Similar results were found when relational aggression was the focus of research (Crick et al., 2006). A study conducted by Howes, Hamilton, and Matheson (1994) noted an inverse relationship between children's physical aggression and their secure relationships with preschool teachers.

This lack of a secure teacher-child relationship also influences peer rejection rates (Chang, 2003). Chang found the largest variance in peer support levels to be a function of the teacher response to a child's aggressive behavior. Increased levels of peer rejection were related to aggressive behavior throughout the school years, especially when social support was withdrawn early in childhood (Ialongo, Vaden-Kiernan, & Kellam, 1998).

Further, the behavioral consequences of insecure attachment are not exclusive to externalizing disorders; reports of conditions such as social anxiety have been found to be higher among insecurely attached children as well (Bohlin, Hagekull, & Rydell, 2000). In a study of preschoolers, McIntyre, Lounsbury, Hamilton and Mantooth (1980) found that children with high levels of anxiety engaged in play less and watched others play more than less anxious children. Once these children enter kindergarten, anxiety and peer exclusion begin to co-exist and stabilize over time, predicting depressive symptoms by the fourth grade (Gazelle & Ladd, 2003). Many of these results can be interpreted through the mediating link of social pain theory, which maintains that anxiety is often the mind's response to the body's anticipation of pain, whether physical or social (MacDonald & Leary, 2005). Insecurely attached children have a high sensitivity to the pain of rejection, which, when combined with a constant vigilance against and anticipation of that social exclusion, may make them less likely to join in play groups or approach peers.

Given that social exclusion was historically as much a threat to human survival as physical danger, social pain theory suggests that people react to social threats in much the same way as they react to fear for their physical well-being, with a fight-or-flight "panic" response. This aggressive reaction is not cognitively mediated, but rather an instantaneous, defensive response to a real or perceived threat, which, while highly functional in relation to physical threats of danger, is counterproductive when dealing with the pain of social rejection (MacDonald & Leary, 2005). Being armed with this knowledge and a deeper understanding of the interactions between insecure attachment, social rejection, aggression, and

social pain can help school psychologists be more effective in both the prevention of and intervention with behavioral disorders in at-risk children.

Early Childhood Experiences and Implications for Future School Outcomes

The behavioral problems that are manifested by insecurely attached children
in the early school years endure as they enter adolescence. An insecure attachment style has been negatively linked to school-based outcomes such as student
attention level, classroom participation, and grade point average, as well as psychologically-based outcomes such as insecurity about self and school adjustment
(Granot & Mayseless, 2001; Jacobsen & Hofmann, 1997). In addition, the implications of the poor student-teacher relationships routinely developed by insecure
children in the preschool and kindergarten years are predictive of relatively poor
school and social adjustment in adolescence (Blankemeyer, Flannery, &
Vazsonyi, 2002; Hamre & Pianta, 2001). Poor peer relations are also predictive
of relatively lower academic achievement as well as lower peer preference
scores, lower high school graduation rates, and increased criminal activities
(Parker & Asher, 1987; Risi, Gerhardstein, & Kistner, 2003).

Zsolnai (2002) found that certain factors intrinsic to social competence, such
as friendliness and openness, were inversely related to intrinsic motivation and
academic self-concept, both of which are prerequisites for successful school and
life outcomes. These personality factors are associated with the low self-worth,
depression, and anxiety often experienced by insecurely attached students, especially around times of school transition (Papini & Roggman, 1992). Again, social
pain theory can help to interpret psychologically-based outcomes of insecure
attachment including depression and anxiety (Abela et al., 2005; Margolese,
Markiewicz & Doyle, 2005). Both depression and anxiety are thought to function as a buffer between the self and social pain — the body's defensive stance
against extraversion and social risk taking (MacDonald & Leary, 2005).

Of special concern to school psychologists is the convergence of outcomes
such as poor school adjustment, aggression, depression, peer exclusion, and anxiety into a high risk factor for the commission of school violence (Shafii & Shafii,
2003). Malecki and DeMaray (2003) found that children who brought weapons
to middle school reported receiving less social support than did their unarmed
peers. Case studies of 15 school shootings revealed that having experienced
social rejection and feelings of depression were characteristic of the majority of
perpetrators (Leary, Kowalski, Smith, & Phillips, 2003). Aggressive behavior is
a risk factor for both perpetrators and victims of school violence, as students with
aggressive attitudes who were both victims of aggression and perpetrators of
aggression reported having lower levels of adult support and lower academic
grades than their non aggressive peers (Brockenbrough, Cornell, & Loper, 2002).

Aggressive students who had been the target of school violence reported that they brought weapons to school and participated in school fights more often than did their non-victim, non-aggressive peers (Brockenbrough et al, 2002). The paradox here is striking: committing an act of school violence is unlikely to gain the rejected student more friends, or the depressed student less isolation. Yet, social pain theory again mediates this link. When the experience of social pain is indistinguishable from the experience of physical pain, an aggressive "kill or be killed" response may make evolutionary, if not conventional, sense (MacDonald & Leary, 2005).

Insecure Attachment and the Experience of Physical Pain

There is the belief, both in social pain theory and somatization research, that the experience of social pain often leads to feelings of physical pain, especially if internalizing behaviors, such as anxiety and depression, are present (MacDonald & Leary, 2005). The child psychology and medical literature, though not extensive, has examined areas relating physical pain to children's levels of aggression, anxiety, and attachment security. In a sizeable study of children ages 2 through 6, Ramchandani et al. (2005) found that recurrent abdominal pain was associated with feelings of anxiety in both children and their mothers. Further, anxious children experienced headaches and limb pain in conjunction with stomach aches more frequently than their less anxious peers. These studies find that a child's pain experience is often mediated by the anxiety symptoms of the mother, which, in addition to providing modeling and reinforcement, may in fact interfere with the attachment bond itself. Research into the relationship between separation anxiety and vulnerability to pain experiences in preschoolers and kindergarteners found that children who scored higher on measures of insecure attachment also responded to pictorial depictions of children in pain with less self-confidence and more helplessness than securely attached children (Walsh, Symons, & McGrath, 2004).

As for the link between aggression and pain, a study by Pakalnis, Gibson, and Colvin (2005) found significant comorbidity between the experience of migraine headaches in children and adolescents and a clinical diagnosis of oppositional defiant disorder. As both attachment issues and the externalizing and internalizing disorders that stem from them affect the body's pain experience in ways that are physical as well as psychological, social pain theory provides a platform from which to explore these results. One explanation may be that for children who anticipate and experience rejection more frequently, the body's pain management systems have become overburdened, leaving the socially excluded child susceptible to intensified feelings of physical pain (MacDonald, Kingsbury, & Shaw, 2005).

The above literature is entirely based on correlational data. There is a dearth of empirically based literature that clearly establishes the efficacy of interventions designed to promote healthy, or attenuate insecure, attachments. It will be subsequently argued that healthy attachments are a consequence of characteristics that are nurtured from infancy throughout life and that these characteristics can be enhanced. Consequently, even given an early childhood history of insecure attachments, interventions are available that can mitigate the predicted negative outcomes.

R.I.C.H. Theory and the Development of Appropriate Attachments

The relationship between physical health and social functioning has been discussed by Kehle and Bray (2004) within the context of their more encompassing R.I.C.H. theory, which defines happiness as being synonymous with psychological health. With respect to their theory, Kehle and Bray define happiness as belonging to those individuals who: make use of their resources (R) in the achievement of age-appropriate independence, possess an ability to initiate and maintain intimacy (I), have achieved competence relative to peers (C), and possess good physical health (H). These four characteristics are all interrelated to the extent that they are each incorporated into the others' definitions; they encompass all possible reinforcers; they are relatively obtainable by all individuals; and the improvement in any one results in the improvement of the remaining three. In sum, the R.I.C.H. theory posits that a psychologically healthy, and therefore happy, individual is one who possesses resources, intimacy, competence, and heath.

The R.I.C.H. theory was derived from the analysis of responses that resulted from questioning mothers' concerns with their children's development. Specifically, a single question was asked, "What do you want your child to be like when they grow up?" Irrespective of culture, situation, or the child's age, mothers essentially want the same four things for their children. A faithful interpretation of the mothers' responses was that they wanted their children to grow up to have resources, intimacy, competence, and physical health (Kehle, 1989, 1999; Kehle & Barclay, 1979; Kehle & Bray, 2004; Kehle, Bray, Chafouleas, & McLoughlin, 2002; Kehle, Clark, & Jenson, 1993). The appropriate allocation of *resources* results in a feeling of independence or professionalism that is defined as being synonymous with a sense of individual freedom, or a sense of control over one's time and daily life. *Intimacy* is defined as friendship, and involves empathy, appreciation, and enjoyment of a friend's company. An individual has feelings of *competence* relative to some societal or personal standard. Competence is attributed to one's own abilities and is situation specific. Consequently, one may feel competent in some aspects of life but not in others.

In addition to being physically healthy, the individual needs to be aware of and maintain allegiance to the practices that are conducive to physical *health*.

The R.I.C.H. theory assumes that the enhancement of one of these characteristics will result in the enhancement of the others, while the attenuation of one results in the lessening of all three. Relative to education, allowing a student greater independence in assuming responsibility for his or her own learning decisions (resources) would also serve to promote the remaining R.I.C.H. characteristics (competence, intimacy, and health). The use of external rewards, either symbolic or material, as a means of motivating students is often interpreted by the children themselves as a manipulation, which is inversely related to the students' sense of independence. Though widely advocated and employed, external rewards likely function to insidiously erode a student's intrinsic motivation to learn (Deci, Koestner, & Ryan, 2001). However, when rewards promote a student's sense of independence, his or her intrinsic motivation to pursue learning is enhanced.

The results of Deci et al.'s (2001) meta-analytic study on the motivational effects of extrinsic and intrinsic rewards indicate that it is important for educators to provide choice, which in turn fosters a sense of independence that facilitates intrinsic motivation. Ultimately, the student should have a sense of "not working" in that he or she intrinsically enjoys their selection of school environments and has choices as to what they learn. For example, a student assigned homework that is perceived as nothing other than "busy" work would definitely have a sense of working. It is perceived as an unnecessary and an educationally illegitimate intrusion on his or her time. External contingencies that are perceived as manipulative are inversely related to the individual student's sense of developing professionalism. In accordance with R.I.C.H. theory, the student learns best that which he or she is intrinsically interested in.

According to the R.I.C.H. theory, all individuals can acquire the four characteristics. In a relative sense, all children are capable of promoting their independence, establishing intimacy, experiencing the satisfaction of competence, and enjoying physical health. In addition, the four characteristics allow for the evaluation of processes. Interventions can be evaluated relative to their worth in promoting movement toward the attainment of the four R.I.C.H. characteristics. For example, if the educational system requires the preschooler to become skilled at walking a balance beam, its worth, or lack thereof, can be judged relative to its influence in promoting the R.I.C.H. characteristics.

Implications for School Psychology and Directions for Future Research

Two main implications can be drawn from the research linking attachment and social pain theories. First, developing successful peer relationships early in life is even more important for insecurely attached children than previously thought, given that social exclusion is likely to result in feelings of painful affect that will provide an ever-increasing deterrent to friendship initiations as the child ages. Second, these children may be more likely to experience physical symptoms of pain that can interfere not only with the building of social support networks, but with the achievement of academic success as well (Breuner, Smith, & Womack, 2004). According to the proposed R.I.C.H. theory, enhancing the resources, intimacy, competence, and health characteristics of children, especially those with insecure attachments, may contribute to improving social, behavioral, and academic difficulties, as well as enhancing psychological health and functioning.

Interventions for children, including those children with insecure attachments, may promote movement toward attaining each of the R.I.C.H. characteristics. For example, school personnel may wish to concentrate their efforts on instituting interventions that have demonstrated success in raising the friendship profile of low-status children, especially those identified as being insecurely attached to their primary caregivers, in order to enhance intimacy. While much of the recent attention in the social support literature has focused on child-deficit based social skills interventions, given both the lack of generalization demonstrated by most programs and the disappointing effect sizes they produce as recorded by meta-analytic studies, peer based treatments may prove more promising in remediating these difficulties (Forness & Kavale, 1996; Magee-Quinn, Kavale, Mathur, Rutherford, & Forness, 1999). One such intervention worthy of future study with insecurely attached student populations is Fantuzzo et al.'s (1996) Resilient Peer Treatment (RPT), which pairs withdrawn and resilient children to stimulate habitual, positive play experiences within the regular classroom environment.

As children grow older they may begin to suffer the physical effects of peer exclusion, and research should be undertaken to link common pain disorders, such as stomach- and head-aches, to attachment security. Once the connection has been made, identifying and intervening with these students through proven school-based techniques, such as relaxation training, can be undertaken (Larsson, Carlsson, Fichtel, & Melin, 2005). The hope is that once the problems of peer exclusion and an overtaxed pain management system have been addressed, the comorbid behavioral disorders of the insecurely attached child – aggression, anxiety, and depression, among others – will cease to exist and the overall health characteristics will be improved. Finally, to address the resource and competence characteristics, school personnel should provide students with independence in task choice and the assignment of tasks and goals that are challenging yet attainable.

Summary

The classroom environment is essential to children's development of appropriate peer relationships and social competencies. Children with insecure attachment often fall rapidly behind their securely attached counterparts, viewing the classroom as psychologically oppressive and failing to gain both the academic and emotional education that would facilitate future success in school and relationships. R.I.C.H. theory suggests that students lacking in intimate relationships, whether with parents, teachers or peers, are at risk for deficiencies in all other aspects of life (resources, competency and health). Of particular importance is the recognition that students experiencing social pain may be at risk for more than poor school outcomes; they may also endure physical pain, and be more likely to exhibit behavioral problems. In order to eliminate the negative effects of social pain, the environments in which children learn and live must be capable of promoting success in all four aspects of the R.I.C.H. theory. By building on teacher and caregiver acceptance, as well as on peer friendship in the earliest school settings, the child with insecure attachment will have increased opportunities for successful academic, psychological, and behavioral outcomes.

References

Abela, J. R. Z., Hankin, B. L., Haigh, E. A. P., Adams, P., Vinokuroff, T., & Trayhern, L. (2005). Interpersonal vulnerability to depression in high-risk children: The role of insecure attachment and reassurance seeking. *Journal of Clinical Psychology and Adolescent Psychology, 34(1),* 182-192.

Ainsworth, M. D. S., & Bell, S. (1970). Attachment, exploration, and separation: Illustrated by the behavior of one-year-olds in a strange situation. *Child Development, 41,* 49-67.

Birch, S. H., & Ladd, G. W. (1997). The teacher-child relationship and children's early school adjustment. *Journal of School Psychology, 35,* 67-79.

Blankemeyer, M., Flannery, D. J., & Vazsonyi, A. T. (2002). The role of aggression and social competence in children's perceptions of the child-teacher relationship. *Psychology in the Schools, 39(3),* 293-304.

Bohlin, G., Hagekull, B., & Rydell, A. (2000). Attachment and social functioning: A longitudinal study from infancy to middle childhood. *Social Development, 9,* 24-39.

Bowlby, J. (1987). *Attachment and loss: Vol. 1. Attachment* (2nd ed.). New York: Basic Books.

Breuner, C. C., Smith, M. S., & Womack, W. M. (2004). Factors related to school absenteeism in adolescents with recurrent headache. *Headache: The Journal of Head and Face Pain, 44(3)*, 217-222.

Brockenbrough, K. K., Cornell, D. G., & Loper, A. B. (2002). Aggressive attitudes among victims of violence at school. *Education and Treatment of Children, 25(3)*, 273-287.

Chang, L. (2003). Variable effects of children's aggression, social withdrawal, and prosocial leadership as functions of teacher beliefs and behaviors, *Child Development, 74(2)*, 535-548.

Crick, N. R., Ostrov, J. M., Burr, J. E., Cullerton-Sen, C., Jansen-Yeh, E., & Ralston, P. (2006). A longitudinal study of relational and physical aggression in preschool. *Journal of Applied Developmental Psychology, 27(3)*, 254-268.

Deci, E. L., Koestner, R., & Ryan, R. M. (2001). Extrinsic rewards and intrinsic motivation in education: Reconsidered once again. *Review of Educational Research, 71*, 1-27.

Elicker, J., Englund, M., & Sroufe, L. A. (1992). Predicting peer competence and peer relationships in childhood from early parent-child relationships. In R. Parke & G. W. Ladd (Eds.), *Family and peer relationships: Modes of Linkage* (pp. 77-106). Hillsdale, NJ: Lawrence Erlbaum.

Fantuzzo, J., Sutton-Smith, B., Atkins, M., Stevenson, H., Coolahan, K., Weiss, A., & Manz, P. (1996). Peer-mediated treatment of socially withdrawn maltreated preschool children: Cultivating natural community resources. *Journal of Consulting and Clinical Psychology, 64(6)*, 1377-1386.

Forness, S. R., & Kavale, K. A. (1996). Treating social skill deficits in children with learning disabilities: A meta-analysis of the research. *Learning Disability Quarterly, 19(1)*, 2-13.

Gazelle, H., & Ladd, G. W. (2003). Anxious solitude and peer exclusion: A diathesis-stress model of internalizing trajectories in childhood. *Child Development, 74(1)*, 257-278.

Granot, D., & Mayseless, O. (2001). Attachment security and adjustment to school in middle childhood. *International Journal of Behavioral Development, 25(6)*, 530-541.

Hamre, B. K., & Pianta, R. C. (2001). Early teacher-child relationships and the trajectory of children's school outcomes through the eighth grade. *Child Development, 72(2)*, 625-638.

Howes, C., Hamilton, C. E., & Matheson, C. C. (1994). Children's relationship with peers: Differential associations with aspects of the teacher-child relationship. *Child Development, 65(1)*, 253-263.

Ialongo, N. S., Vaden-Kiernan, N., & Kellam, S. (1998). Early peer rejection and aggression: Longitudinal relations with adolescent behavior. *Journal of Developmental and Physical Disabilities, 10(2)*, 199-213.

Jacobsen, T., & Hofmann, V. (1997). Children's attachment representations: Longitudinal relations to school behavior and academic competency in middle childhood and adolescence. *Developmental Psychology, 33(4),* 703-710.

Kehle, T. J. (1989, March). *Maximizing the effectiveness of interventions: The RICH model.* Paper presented at the annual meeting of the National Association of School Psychologists, Boston.

Kehle, T. J. (1999, August). *RICH-based interventions.* Invited address at the annual meeting of the American Psychological Association, Boston.

Kehle, T. J., & Barclay, J. R. (1979). Social and behavioral characteristics of mentally handicapped students. *Journal of Research and Development in Education, 12(4),* 46-56.

Kehle, T. J., & Bray, M. A. (2004). R.I.C.H. Theory: The promotion of happiness. *Psychology in the Schools, 41,* 43-49.

Kehle, T. J., Bray, M. A, Chafouleas, S. M., & McLoughlin, C. S. (2002). Promoting intellectual growth in adulthood. *School Psychology International, 23(2),* 233-240.

Kehle, T. J., Clark, E., & Jenson, W. R. (1993). The development of testing as applied to school psychology. *Journal of School Psychology, 31(1),* 143-161.

Kerns, K. A., & Barth, J. M. (1995). Attachment and play: Convergence across components of parent-child relationships and their relations to peer competence. *Journal of Social and Personal Relationships, 12(2),* 243-260.

Ladd, G. W., & Price, J. M. (1987). Predicting children's social and school adjustment following the transition from preschool to kindergarten. *Child Development, 58(5),* 1168-1189.

Larsson, B., Carlsson, J., Fichtel, A., & Melin, L. (2005). Relaxation treatment of adolescent headache sufferers: Results from a school-based replication series. *Headache: The Journal of Head and Face Pain, 45(6),* 692-704.

Leary, M. R., Kowalski, R. M., Smith, L., & Phillips, S. (2003). Teasing, rejection, and violence: Case studies of the school shootings. *Aggressive Behavior, 29,* 202-214.

MacDonald, G., Kingsbury, R., & Shaw, S. (2005). Adding insult to injury: Social pain theory and response to social exclusion. In K. D. Williams, J. P. Forgas, & W. von Hippel (Eds.), *The social outcast: Ostracism, social exclusion, rejection, & bullying* (pp. 77-90). New York: Psychology Press.

MacDonald, G., & Leary, M. R. (2005). Why does social exclusion hurt? The relationship between social and physical pain. *Psychological Bulletin, 131*(2), 202-223.

Main, M., & Solomon, J. (1990). Procedures for identifying infants as disorganized-disoriented during the Ainsworth Stange Situation. In M.

Greenberg, D. Cicchetti, & E. M. Cummings (Eds.), *Attachment in the preschool years: Theory, research and intervention* (pp. 121-160). Chicago: University of Chicago Press.

Magee-Quinn, M., Kavale, K. A., Mathur, S. R., Rutherford, R. B., Jr., & Forness, S. R. (1999). A meta-analysis of social skill interventions for students with emotional or behavioral disorders. *Journal of Emotional and Behavioral Disorders, 7(1),* 54-64.

McIntyre, A., Lounsbury, K., Hamilton, M. L., & Mantooth, J. M. (1980). Individual differences in preschool object play: The influences of anxiety proneness and peer affiliation. *Journal of Applied Developmental Psychology, 1,* 149-161.

Malecki, C. K., & DeMaray, M. K. (2003). Carrying a weapon to school and perceptions of social support in an urban middle school. *Journal of Emotional and Behavioral Disorders, 11(3),* 169-178.

Margolese, S. K., Markiewicz, D., & Doyle, A. B. (2005). Attachment to parents, best friend, and romantic partner: Predicting different pathways to depression in adolescence. *Journal of Youth and Adolescence, 34(6),* 637-650.

NICHD Early Child Care Research Network (2006). Infant-mother attachment classification: Risk and protection in relation to changing maternal caregiving quality. *Developmental Psychology, 41(1),* 38-58.

Pakalnis, A., Gibson, J., & Colvin, A. (2005). Comorbidity of psychiatric and behavioral disorders in pediatric migraine. *Headache: The Journal of Head and Face Pain, 45(5),* 590-596.

Papini, D. R., & Roggman, L. A. (1992). Adolescent perceived attachment to parents in relation to competence, depression, and anxiety: A longitudinal study. *Journal of Early Adolescence, 12(4),* 420-440.

Parker, J. G., & Asher, S. R. (1987). Peer relations and later personal adjustment: Are low-accepted children at risk? *Psychological Bulletin, 102(3),* 357-389.

Persson, G. E. B. (2005). Young children's prosocial and aggressive behaviors and their experiences of being targeted for similar behavior by peers. *Social Development, 14(2),* 206-228.

Pianta, R. C., Longmaid, K., & Ferguson, J. E. (1999). Attachment-based classifications of children's family drawings: Psychometric properties and relations with children's adjustment in kindergarten. *Journal of Clinical Child Psychology, 28(2),* 244-255.

Ramchandani, P. G., Hotopf, M., Sandhu, B., Stein, A., & ALSPAC Study Team (2005). The epidemiology of recurrent abdominal pain from 2 to 6 years of age: Results of a large population-based study. *Pediatrics, 116(1),* 46-50.

Risi, S., Gerhardstein, R., & Kistner, J. (2003). Children's classroom peer relationships and subsequent educational outcomes. *Journal of Clinical Child and Adolescent Psychology, 32(3),* 351-361.

Schmidt, M. E., DeMulder, E. K., & Denham, S. A. (2002). Kindergarten social-emotional competence: Developmental predictors and psychosocial implications. *Early Child Development and Care, 172,* 451-462.

Shafii, M., & Shafii, S. L. (2003). School violence, depression, and suicide. *Journal of Applied Psychoanalytic Studies, 5(2),* 155-169.

Sroufe, L. A. (2005). Attachment and development: A prospective, longitudinal study from birth to adulthood. *Attachment & Human Development, 7(4),* 349-367.

Szewczyk-Sokolowski, M., Bost, K. K., & Wainwright, A. B. (2005). Attachment, temperament, and preschool children's peer acceptance. *Social Development, 14(3),* 379-397.

Verschueren, K., Marcoen, A., & Schoefs, V. (1996). The internal working model of the self, attachment, and competence in five-year-olds. *Child Development, 67(5),* 2493-2511.

Walsh, T. M., Symons, D. K., & McGrath, P. J. (2004). Relations between young children's responses to the depiction of separation and pain experiences. *Attachment & Human Development, 6(1),* 53-71.

Wentzel, K. R. (1991). Social competence at school: Relation between social responsibility and academic achievement. *Review of Educational Research, 61(1),* 1-24.

Youngblade, L. M., & Belsky, J. (1992). Parent-child antecedents of 5-year-olds' close friendships: A longitudinal analysis. *Developmental Psychology, 28(4),* 700-713.

Zsolnai, A. (2002). Relationship between children's social competence, learning motivation, and school achievement. *Educational Psychology, 22(3),* 317-329.

Interventions Based on Attachment Theory: A Critical Analysis

Clayton R. Cook
University of California, Riverside

Steven G. Little & Angeleque Akin-Little
Walden University

Attachment-based interventions represent a class of intervention strategies that focus on enhancing caregiver-child interaction patterns. The present study assesses the efficacy and methodological adequacy of contemporary studies on attachment-based interventions. The results of our analysis revealed that attachment interventions produce on average weak to moderate effects across caregiver and child outcomes. Also, it was found that data on treatment integrity or consumer satisfaction are essentially nonexistent in the literature, hindering the interpretation and generalizability of study findings. Evaluation of individual study effect sizes around the overall weighted mean effect size indicated considerable variability in the magnitude of effect produced by attachment interventions across studies. The discussion focuses on the evidence-based status of interventions based on attachment theory and promising directions for attachment researchers to take in the research.

Over the past decade, several researchers have evaluated the efficacy of interventions predicated on elements of attachment theory. The common denominator of these interventions is their focus on improving the quality of the caregiver-child relationship. According to attachment theory, the quality of early caregiver-child interaction patterns set the stage for later (a)typical development (Ainsworth, Blehar, Waters, & Wall, 1978). That is, infants and young children direct a large portion of their behaviors (e.g., crying, looking, babbling) to caregivers, which is intended to secure help for negotiating the demands of their environments (Bowlby, 1982). The extent to which caregivers fail to respond to these cues, the greater the likelihood that the child will manifest some type of attach-

All correspondence should be addressed to Steven G. Little, Ph.D., 152 Shady Acres Rd., Tupelo, MS 38804. Phone: (662) 841-0008. Electronic mail may be sent to slittle2@waldenu.edu.

ment disorder and experience the range of possible negative outcomes that accompany such disorders, including poor self-regulation and rejection from peers (Carlson & Sroufe, 1995). Research has also shown that in homes where caregiver-child attachment is characterized as warm and loving, children are likely to develop competence even in the face of adverse conditions (Masten & Coatsworth, 1998).

Given the implications that early attachment bonds have for the development of children, from a preventive standpoint, interventions designed to improve the attachment between caregivers and young ones is a palpable approach to preventing serious social, emotional, or behavioral problems. Many researchers have, in fact, adopted this perspective and implemented attachment-related interventions with caregivers and preschool-aged children as the targets of their interventions. Although there is considerable intuitive appeal to the notion of interventions based on attachment theory, it is important that practitioners are aware of the empirical support for such interventions before they blindly implement them. This logic is consistent with the evidence-based movement that has pervaded many professional disciplines (APA, 2005; Kratochwill, 2003; Kratochwill & Stoiber, 2000, 2002; Sackett, Straus, Richardson, Rosenberg, & Haynes, 2000; Weisz & Hawley, 2002).

Evidence-Based Practice

In August of 2005 the American Psychological Association adopted a policy with regard to evidence-based practice in psychology (EBPP). The purpose of this policy is to promote effective psychological practice by using evidence derived from clinically relevant research (APA, 2005). Specific statements have also been developed by APA's Divisions 16 (Kratochwill, 2003) and 12 (Weisz & Hawley, 2002). The Division 16 procedures, which will be adhered to in the current study, review only research that has been peer-reviewed. Interventions are rated across nine dimensions: (a) measurement, (b) comparison group, (c) primary/secondary outcomes significant, (d) educational/clinical significance, (e) durability of effects, (f) identifiable intervention components, (g) implementation fidelity, (h) replication, and (i) school- or field-based site (see Kratochwill, 2003). The inclusion of comparison groups in a study is given specific importance as without a relevant comparison group it is difficult to fully evaluate the merits of the results. Implementation fidelity is another of the essential characteristics. Also called treatment integrity, it refers to the extent to which an intervention is implemented as designed (Gresham, 1989, 2004). Without adequate implementation fidelity it is impossible to know if any reported results are a function of the intervention.

Meta-Analyses on Attachment Interventions

To date, two meta-analyses have been performed to evaluate the effects of attachment interventions (Bakersmans-Kranenburg, van Ijzendoorn, & Juffer, 2003, 2005), both providing modest support for the efficacy of attachment interventions. The Bakersmans-Kranenburg and colleagues (2003) meta-analysis included 70 studies ($N = 842$) detailing 88 intervention effects published between 1978 and 2001 on both sensitivity and/or attachment. To be included, intervention had to start before the child's age of 54 months. With regard to enhancing maternal sensitivity, results indicated a moderate effect size ($d = 0.33$). Infant attachment security was the focus of 29 intervention studies ($n = 1,503$) included in a separate analysis. Results indicated a "small but significant" (Bakersmans-Kranenburg et al., 2003, p. 206) effect size ($d = 0.19$). The authors conclude that infant attachment insecurity is more resistant to improvement than maternal sensitivity but there does appear to be a relationship between the two. In other words, as maternal sensitivity improves, so does infant attachment security. Bakersmans-Kranenburg et al. (2005) examined the effectiveness of early childhood interventions in preventing disorganized attachment. Fifteen prevention studies published between 1988 and 2005 were combined in the meta-analysis. Overall, the results failed to support the efficacy of interventions to prevent or change disorganized attachment in infants ($d = 0.05$; *range* = -0.49 to 0.53).

These meta-analyses notwithstanding, to date no systematic evaluation of the methodological adequacy of these studies (e.g., treatment integrity and acceptability, psychometric properties, and adequacy of comparison group) to reveal deeper insight into the quality of the evidentiary support for attachment-related interventions has been conducted. Therefore, the goal of this paper is to perform an evidence-based analysis of the literature evaluating the effects of interventions predicated on attachment theory. Using the criteria developed by the Task Force on Evidence-Based Interventions in School Psychology (Kratochwill, 2003), particular attention will be paid to a host of methodological aspects of the primary studies.

Method

Rather than perform an analysis of all the extant empirical literature on attachment-based interventions, we chose to collect and evaluate only those studies within a decade period of time from 1997-2006. We used several search methods to identify our final list of studies. Our first step was to search two electronic databases (PsychInfo and ERIC) using combinations of the following search terms: *attachment, intervention, therapy, treatment, children, child, infant,* and *toddler.* Next, we conducted ancestral searches on important review studies to locate additional studies for possible inclusion into our study. This resulted in a list of 878 studies. We then performed a title and abstract analysis on these studies to identify those that were actual treatment studies. Out of the 878 studies, only 22 met final inclusion criteria. However, one study contained two studies in one article (Wagner & Clayton, 1999); therefore, the total number of studies analyzed was 23. Of the excluded studies, the majority were excluded on the basis of failing to implement an actual intervention based on attachment theory. The remaining studies were excluded because they included samples of older students (> 5 years old) or they did not provide sufficient evidence for computing effect sizes.

Coding Scheme

Based on recommendations from the Task Force on Evidence-Based Interventions in School Psychology (Kratochwill, 2003), we chose to code seven variables that would help us evaluate the evidence-based status of attachment-related interventions. In addition, we generated both a quantitative, in the form of effect size estimates, and qualitative, in the form of a narrative review, depiction of the efficacy of each of the primary studies. The following is a variable-by-variable description of the seven variables.

Sample size. The number of caregiver-child dyads included in each study was recorded in order to depict the total number of dyads across studies and to calculate an overall weighted mean effect size.

Age of children. Age of the infants, toddlers, or children in each sample was recorded to discern whether age of the child potentially moderates the effectiveness of attachment interventions. We first looked to record the mean age in months of the sample at onset of the intervention for each study, but in many instances studies reported only the range of ages across children. In these cases, we simply recorded the age range.

Age of parents. The mean age or age range of the parents included in each study was recorded. Also, if provided, the standard deviation around the mean value was recorded to provide readers with an understanding of the variability of parent ages in a given sample.

Treatment focus. This variable was created to denote who was the focal point of the treatment. That is, was the focus of the treatment solely on parents (mother, father, or both), the children, or both parents and children.

Psychometric properties of dependent measures. Adequate psychometric properties of the dependent measures used in each study to evaluate the impact of the intervention is an important element of determining the overall effects of an intervention. Thus, three levels of classification were created to reflect the quality: (a) Yes (psychometric properties reported for all variables), (b) Partial (psychometric properties reported for some but not all of the dependent measures), and (c) No (psychometric properties not reported for any of the dependent measures).

Treatment integrity. Treatment integrity refers to the degree to which an intervention is implemented as planned (Gresham, 1989). Treatment integrity has become a critical variable to assess when evaluating the evidence-based status of particular interventions. As such, we recorded Yes or No as to whether treatment integrity data were collected in each of the primary studies.

Social validity. From a practical standpoint, interventions that are deemed more acceptable by key consumers of the intervention (i.e., parents, children, intervention agents, etc.) are more likely to be adopted in actual practice (Riley-Tillman, Chafouleas, Eckert, & Kelleher, 2005). Therefore, treatment acceptability has important implications for the external validity or generalizability of interventions for producing positive outcomes in real-world contexts. Hence, we recorded whether or not each study assessed aspects of social validity either directly (e.g., participants) or indirectly (e.g., other family members not involved in treatment).

Data Analytic Strategy

To provide a quantitative index of the magnitude of the effect produced by each attachment intervention, we converted all individual study statistics into effect size estimates. Specifically, we converted all quantitative results into two effect size metrics: (a) Cohen's d and (b) Pearson Product Moment Correlation Coefficient (r). These individual effect sizes were then combined to produce both a weighted and unweighted mean effect size to depict the overall effect of attachment-related interventions across studies. One study had a much larger sample than the other studies ($N = 4410$) and would have too much influence on the weighted mean effect size. As a result, the sample was winsorized to equal 611, which was the value of the next largest sample size (O'Brien-Caughy, Huang, Miller, & Genevro, 2004).

Labeling effect sizes as small, medium, or large as recommended by Cohen (1977) may be misleading in interpreting effect sizes. As such, effect sizes were further transformed into the binomial effect size display (BESD), which is a readily interpretable heuristic that highlights the practical importance of an effect size (Rosenthal, Rosnow, & Rubin, 2000). The BESD shows the effect of group membership (i.e., treatment versus control) on the improvement/success rate of a given outcome. The BESD is a 2 X 2 contingency table with the columns representing group status (treatment versus control) and the rows representing improvement and nonimprovement rates, respectively. To calculate the values corresponding to each cell within the 2 X 2 contingency table, one puts the obtained r into the following equation:

$$IR/NIR = .50 \pm r/2$$

In this equation, IR represents the value of improvement rate for the treatment group $(.50 + r/2)$ and NIR represents the value of the nonimprovement rate for the treatment group $(.50 - r/2)$. The improvement and nonimprovement rates for the control group are simply the inverse of the improvement and nonimprovement rates of the treatment group. We did not conduct our own statistical analyses of potential moderators of treatment outcomes, but we did make inferences about potential moderators of intervention effectiveness that should represent the focus of future research.

Results

Results of the 23 studies are depicted in Table 1 (see pp 74-78). As one can see, across the studies, a total of 7,585 caregiver-child dyads were either both or singly exposed to an attachment-related intervention. Most of the studies described interventions that focused on both parents and children ($N = 16$; 70%) as the target of the intervention. The remaining studies isolated parents as the sole target of the attachment intervention. Of these studies, fathers were involved in only 1 (1 out of 7; 14%) study. In terms of the psychometric properties of the outcome measures, eight (35%) of the studies failed to provide information about the reliability and validity of the measures used to evaluate the efficacy of the attachment interventions. With regard to the age of the children, most of the studies involved children roughly 6-months of age or less (15 out of 23; 65%).

Effect Size Results

Examination of the individual study effect sizes revealed that there was considerable variability across the studies (d [*range*: min. = -.60 and max. = +1.22, $SD = .40$] and r [*range*: min. = -.28 and max. = .52, $SD = .17$]). The unweighted and weighted mean standardized effect sizes across the studies were .29 and .13, respectively. Cast in terms of a correlation coefficient, the unweighted and weighted mean effect sizes were .14 and .06, respectively. It is important to note the large difference between the weighted and unweighted mean effect sizes. The difference between the weighed and unweighted effect sizes is due to the fact that the two studies reporting the largest overall effects for attachment interventions also had the smallest sample sizes. Therefore, when weighting each individual study effect size by its sample size and calculating the mean effect size, the two studies with the largest effects had significantly less influence on the overall mean relative to the amount of influence they had on the unweighted mean.

To help understand the practical importance of the mean effect size found for attachment interventions we relied on the BESD. Applying the BESD to unweighted mean effect size, an r of .14 suggests that, on average, roughly 57%

of parent-child dyads exposed to the attachment intervention will improve compared to only 43% of controls. Although this may seem like a practically important effect, when interpreting the weighted mean effect size r, the results are less compelling. The weighted mean effect size of $r = .06$ indicates that, on average, 53% parent-child dyads will improve compared to 47% of the controls. An improvement rate of 50% indicates a null effect; the same proportion of individuals in both the control group and intervention group are likely to experience improvement. Therefore, the weighted mean effect size provides only modest support for the efficacy of attachment-based interventions.

Treatment Integrity

To our surprise, none of the studies reported data on the integrity of intervention implementation. Not only did none of the studies report actual treatment integrity data, but, from what we could discern, none of the studies even mentioned it. This raises serious concerns about the internal validity of the primary studies. That is, it is difficult to determine whether the null effects associated with some interventions are the result of a "bad" intervention or the result of inadequate implementation of an otherwise effective intervention. Without treatment integrity data, it is difficult to make decisions about the evidence-based status of attachment interventions.

Social Validity

Only one study reported assessing caregivers' acceptability of attachment interventions (Fraser, Armstrong, Morris, & Dadds, 2000). This is particularly troubling considering that to some extent the large research-to-practice gap in most areas of psychological study can be attributed to scientifically validated interventions that are not accepted by individuals in the "real-world" (Kazdin, 2000; Lewis, Hudson, Richter, & Johnson, 2004). What is needed, then, is a focus from researchers on those elements of attachment-based interventions that are liked most by clients and are also associated with the best outcomes. This will undoubtedly facilitate the adoption and implementation of empirically supported components of attachment interventions.

Discussion

The primary aim of this study was to conduct an evidence-based analysis of the literature on the efficacy of interventions based on attachment theory. The results of our analysis indicate that overall attachment related interventions appear to produce modest positive results in both child and parent outcome measures. However, depending on whether one chooses to interpret the unweighted or weighted mean effect size, one will likely arrive at different conclusions regarding the practical import of attachment interventions. Notably though, these results reflect primarily a main effect interpretation of the data, and there was considerable variability in the effectiveness of the interventions across individual studies. A look at the studies that produced the highest mean effect sizes suggests that attachment interventions involving both parents and children in the program are likely to produce the greatest psychotherapeutic benefit. There are several other findings that are worth mentioning.

First, the fact that none of the studies reported data on treatment integrity is problematic for a determination of the evidence-based status of attachment interventions. As Gresham (1989) has noted, there appears to be a "curious double standard" in published research. The curious double standard is the bias by journal editors to frequently request reliability data on the dependent measures used in a study, but almost never on the reliability of the independent variable or the intervention. Without treatment integrity data, it is difficult to make judgements regarding the internal validity of the intervention. That is, one cannot unambiguously determine that the attachment intervention was responsible for the changes in the dependent variable(s). It is quite possible that in the few studies that reported negative effects for the attachment interventions that the interventions were not implemented with integrity. If this were the case, then the lackluster findings should not be interpreted as supporting the notion that attachment interventions do not work, but rather the findings are the result of a poorly implemented intervention. A strong commitment to collect treatment integrity data in future research on attachment-related interventions will undoubtedly help provide a better picture of the evidentiary support of such interventions.

Also, given the lack of attention paid by researchers to consumers' satisfaction with, or acceptability of, attachment-related interventions, it is difficult to ascertain whether these interventions have sufficient effectiveness for application in real-world contexts. In the evidence-based literature, effectiveness is a term reserved for studies that assess the impact of interventions under real-world conditions, as opposed to efficacy studies that assess intervention under tightly controlled conditions. From the current literature base, it is difficult to determine whether attachment interventions are directly or indirectly accepted by important consumers. Future research will want to pay particular attention to the acceptability of attachment interventions to evaluate whether they hold promise for practitioners in the medical and psychological communities.

The primary limitation of our review was the failure to assess the differential impact of attachment interventions based on the baseline risk status of the parents (e.g., postpartum depression, low SES) and/or children (e.g., low birth weight, premature). It is quite possible that families experiencing greater risk at the onset of the study may benefit more or less from the attachment intervention than families with fewer risk factors. However, findings from Bakermans-Krazenburg et al. (2003) suggest that this may not necessarily be the case, as they found that sample characteristics did *not* moderate the effectiveness of attachment interventions. Although risk factors may not affect the immediate intervention outcomes, the authors hypothesize that risk factors would have implications for the generalization and maintenance of intervention effects. Nevertheless, researchers should explore whether risk factors impact the short- and/or long-term effectiveness of attachment-based interventions.

To conclude, while the results of this analysis may be interpreted as providing modest support for the efficacy of attachment-based interventions, it may be premature to derive such a conclusion. First, the weighted mean effect size d of .13 was quite a bit less than the unweighted mean effect size d of .29. This, along with the large variability in reported effect sizes suggests caution in interpretation. Second, when effect sizes were transformed into the binomial effect size display (BESD), the weighted mean effect size of $r = .06$ indicates that, on average, 53% parent-child dyads improved compared to 47% of the controls, suggesting a weak effect at best. Finally, the lack of treatment integrity and social validity data makes any of the results difficult to interpret. That being said, there are still some promising results presented in the literature; research in this area that conforms to the accepted standards for evidence-based practice is needed.

References

Ainsworth, M. S., Blehar, M. C., Waters, E., & Wall, S. (1978). *Patterns of attachment: A psychological study of the strange situation.* Hillsdale, NJ: Erlbaum Publishing.

American Psychological Association. (2005). *American Psychological Association Policy Statement on Evidence-Based Practice in Psychology.* Retrieved September 6, 2006 from http://www2.apa.org/practice/ebpstatement.pdf.

*Ammaniti, M., Speranza, A. M., Tambelli, R., Muscetta, S., Lucarelli, L., Vismara, L., Odorisio, F., & Cimino, S. (2006). A prevention and promotion intervention program in the field of mother-infant relationship. *Infant Mental Health Journal, 27,* 70-90.

*Bakermans-Krazenburg, M. J., Juffer, F., & van Ijzendoorn, M. H. (1998). Interventions with video feedback and attachment discussions: Does type of maternal insecurity make a difference? *Infant Mental Health Journal, 19,* 202-219.

Bakersmans-Kranenburg, M. J., van Ijzendoorn, M. H., & Juffer, F. (2003). Less is more: Meta-analysis of sensitivity and attachment interventions in early childhood. *Psychological Bulletin, 129*, 195-215.

Bakersmans-Kranenburg, M. J., van Ijzendoorn, M. H., & Juffer, F. (2005). Disorganized infant attachment and preventive interventions: A review and meta-analysis. *Infant Mental Health Journal, 26*, 191-216.

*Benoit, D., Madigan, S., Lecce, S., Shea, B., & Goldberg, S. (2001). Atypical maternal behavior toward feeding-disordered infants before and after intervention. *Infant Mental Health Journal, 22*, 611-626.

Bowlby, J. (1982). *Attachment and loss: Vol. 1.* New York: Basic Books.

*Brisch, K. H., Bechinger, D., Betzler, S., & Heinemann, H. (2003). Early preventive attachment-oriented psychotherapeutic intervention program with parents of a very low birthweight premature infant: Results of attachment and neurological development. *Attachment & Human Development, 5*, 120-135.

Carlson, E. A., & Sroufe, L. A. (1995). Contributions of attachment theory to developmental psychopathology. In D. Cicchetti & D. J. Cohen (Eds.), *Developmental psychopathology: Vol. 1, Theory and methods* (pp. 581-617). New York: Wiley.

*Cicchetti, D., Toth, S. L., & Rogosch, F. A. (1999). The efficacy of toddler-parent psychotherapy to increase attachment security in off-spring of depressed mothers. *Attachment & Human Development, 1*, 36-66.

Cohen, J. (1977). *Statistical power analysis for the behavioral sciences* (Rev. ed.). New York: Academic Press.

*Cohen, N. J., Muir, E., Lojkasek, M., Muir, R., Parker, C. J., Barwick, M., & Brown, M. (1999). Watch, wait, and wonder: Testing the effectiveness of a new approach to mother-infant psychotherapy. *Infant Mental Health Journal, 20*, 429-451.

*Constantino, J. N., Hashemi, N., Solis, E., Alon, T., Haley, S., McClure, S., Nordlicht, N., Constantino, M. A., Elmen, J., & Carlson, V. K. (2001). Supplementation of urban home visitation with a series of group meetings for parents and infants: Results of a "real-world" randomized, controlled trial. *Child Abuse & Neglect, 25*, 1571-1581.

*Field, T. M., Scafidi, F., Pickens, J., Promronidis, M., Palaez-Nogueras, M., Torquanti, J., Wilcox, H., Malphurs, J., Schanberg, S., & Kuhn, C. (1998). Polydrug-using adolescent mothers and their infants receiving early intervention. *Adolescence, 33*, 117-143.

*Fraser, J. A., Armstrong, K. L., Morris, J. P., & Dadds, M. R. (2000). Home visiting intervention for vulnerable families with newborns: Follow-up results of a randomized controlled trial. *Child Abuse & Neglect, 24*, 1399-1429.

*Goodson, B. D., Layzer, J. I., St. Pierre, R. G., Bernstein, L. S., & Lopez, M. (2000). Effectiveness of a comprehensive, five-year family support program for low-income children and their families: Findings from the Comprehensive Child Development Program. *Early Childhood Research Quarterly, 15,* 5-39.

Gresham, F. M. (1989). Assessment of treatment integrity in school consultation and prereferral intervention. *School Psychology Review, 18,* 37-50.

Gresham, F. M. (2004). Current status and future directions of school-based behavioral interventions. *School Psychology Review, 33,* 326-343.

*Heinicke, C. M., Fineman, N. R., Ponce, V. A., & Guthrie, D. (2001). Relation-based intervention with at-risk mothers: Outcomes in the second year of life. *Infant Mental Health Journal, 22,* 431-462.

*Juffer, F., Bakersmans-Kranenburg, M. J., & van IJzendoorn, M. H. (2005). The importance of parenting in the development of disorganized attachment: Evidence from a preventive intervention study in adoptive families. *Journal of Child Psychology and Psychiatry, 46,* 263-274.

*Juffer, F., Hoksbergen, R. A. C., Riksen-Walvern, J. M., & Kohnstamm, G. A. (1997). Early intervention in adoptive families: Supporting maternal sensitive responsiveness, infant-mother attachment, and infant competence. *Journal of Child Psychology and Psychiatry, 38,* 1039-1050.

Kazdin, A. E. (2000). Perceived barriers to treatment participation and treatment acceptability among antisocial children and their families. *Journal of Child and Family Studies, 9,* 157-174.

Kratochwill, T. R. (2003). *Procedural and coding manual for review of evidence-based interventions.* Madison, WI: Task Force on Evidence-Based Interventions in School Psychology.

Kratochwill, T. R., & Stoiber, K. C. (2000). Empirically supported interventions and School Psychology: Conceptual and practical issues: Part II. *School Psychology Quarterly, 15,* 233-253.

Kratochwill, T. R., & Stoiber, K. C. (2002). Evidence-based interventions in school psychology: Conceptual foundations of the Procedural and Coding Manual of Division 16 and the Society for the Study of School Psychology Task Force. *School Psychology Quarterly, 17,* 341-389.

*Lafreniere, P. J., & Capuano, F. (1997). Preventive intervention as means of clarifying direction of effects in socialization: Anxious-withdrawn preschoolers case. *Development and Psychopathology, 9,* 551-564.

Lewis, T. J., Hudson, S., Richter, M., & Johnson, N. (2004). Scientifically supported practices in emotional and behavioral disorders: A proposed approach and brief review of current practices. *Behavioral Disorders, 29,* 247-259.

Masten, A. S., & Coatsworth, J. D. (1998). The development of competence in favorable and unfavorable environments. *American Psychologist, 53,* 205-220.

*Moran, G., Pederson, D. R., & Krupka, A. (2005). Maternal unresolved attachment status impedes the effectiveness of interventions with adolescent mothers. *Infant Mental Health Journal, 26,* 231-249.

*O'Brien-Caughy, M., Huang, K. Y., Miller, T., & Genevro, J. L. (2004) The effects of the Healthy Steps for Young Children Program: Results from observations of parenting and child development. *Early Childhood Research Quarterly, 19,* 611-630.

*Onozawa, K., Glover, V., Adams, D., Modi, N., & Kumar, C. (2001). Infant massage improves mother-infant interaction for mothers with postnatal depression. *Journal of Affective Disorders, 63,* 201-207.

*Oppenheim, D., Goldsmith, D., & Koren-Karie, N. (2004). Maternal insightfulness and preschoolers' emotion and behavior problems: Reciprocal influences in a therapeutic preschool program. *Infant Mental Health Journal, 25,* 352-367.

Riley-Tillman, C. T., Chafouleas, S. M., Eckert, T. L., & Kelleher, C. (2005). Bridging the gap between research and practice: A framework for building research agendas in school psychology. *Psychology in the Schools, 42,* 459-473.

Rosenthal, R., Rosnow, R. L., & Rubin, D. B. (2000). *Contrasts and effect sizes in behavioral research: A correlational approach.* New York: Cambridge University Press.

Sackett, D. L., Straus, S. E., Richardson, W. S., Rosenberg, W., & Haynes, R. B. (2000). *Evidence based medicine: How to practice and teach EBM* (2nd ed.). London: Churchill Livingstone.

*Sajaniemi, N., Makela, J., Salokorpi, T., von Wendt, L., Hamalainen, T., & Hakamies-Blomqvist, L. (2001). Cognitive performance and attachment patterns at four years of age in extremely low birth weight infants after early intervention. *European Child & Adolescent Psychiatry, 10,* 122-129.

*Schuler, M. E., Nair, P., & Black, M. M. (2002). Ongoing maternal drug use, parenting attitudes, and a home intervention: Effects on mother-child interaction at 18 months. *Developmental Behavioral Pediatrics, 2,* 87-94.

Wagner, M. M., & Clayton, S. L. (1999). The Parents as Teachers Program: Results from two demonstrations. *The Future of Children, 9,* 91-115.

Weisz, J. R., & Hawley, K. M. (2002). *Procedural and coding manual for identification of beneficial treatments.* Washington, DC: American Psychological Association, Society for Clinical Psychology Division 12 Committee on Science and Practice.

*Zahr, L. K. (2000). Home-based intervention after discharge for Latino families of low-birth-weight infants. *Infant Mental Health Journal, 21*, 448-463.

* = studies included in the analysis

Table 1

Study Characteristics and Evidence-Based Analysis of Studies on Attachment-Related Interventions from 1997-2006

Study	Sample Size	Age of Children	Age of Parents	Treatment Focus	Psych. Properties	Treatment Integrity	Social Validity	Average ES	Findings
Ammaniti et al. (2006)	91	Birth	M = 32.5 SD = 4.19	Mother	Yes	No	No	d = .64 r = .31	The findings from this study revealed that a home visiting program focusing on attachment patterns significantly improved mothers' sensitive behaviors toward their children.
Benoit, Madigan, Lecce, Shea, & Goldberg (2001)	28	M = 18 months	M = 32.3 SD = 6.7	Both	Yes	No	No	d = 1.22 r = .52	The target intervention significantly reduced the number of atypical behaviors that caregivers exhibit during the course of play interactions with infants. Also found that increased parental sensitivity is likely to lead to reduction in problem behaviors of the infant.
Brisch, Bechinger, Betzler, & Heinemann (2003)	87	Range = 3-4 months	M = 30.9 SD = 4.9	Parents	No	No	No	d = -.60 r = -.28	Following intervention, the authors found a significantly higher proportion of infants with secure attachment patterns in the control compared to the attachment intervention condition. The authors attempted to explain the unexpected findings.
Cicchetti, Toth, & Rogosch (1999)	104	M =20 months	M = 31.7 SD = 4.36	Both	Partial	No	No	d = .24 r = .12	The attachment intervention for depressed mothers was able to produce modest changes in secure attachment when compared to a no treatment control condition.
Cohen et al. (1999)	67	Range = 10-30 months	M = 32.4 SD = 4.5	Both	No	No	No	d = .11 r = .06	The authors reported that the findings from this study provided partial, modest support for the efficacy of the intervention. The failure to find an increase in maternal sensitivity was a particularly notable finding.

Study	Sample Size	Age of Children	Age of Parents	Treatment Focus	Psych. Properties	Treatment Integrity	Social Validity	Average ES	Findings
Constantino et al. (2001)	148	M = 8.8 months	M = 26.1 SD = 7.2	Both	Yes	No	No	d = .00 r = .00	Although the intervention produced a trend in increasing mothers' sensitivity to emotional cues, it was unable to produce positive results across all outcomes.
Field et al. (1998)	126	birth	M = 18.1 SD = NP	Mother	No	No	No	d = .35 r = .17	The attachment focused intervention was able to move drug-mothers behaviors into the range of nondrug-mothers behavior.
Fraser, Armstrong, Morris, & Dadds (2000)	181	birth	M = 26 SD = 6	Both	Yes	No	Yes	d = .08 r = .04	The authors reported an inconsistent pattern of results across outcome measures. One notable positive finding was the significant reduction in potential for child abuse produced by the intervention.
Goodson, Layzer, St. Pierre, Bernstein, & Lopez (2000)	4410	NP	NP	Both	Yes	No	No	d = .06 r = .03	The findings from this study indicate that large scale intervention produced relatively no significant effects on children's cognitive or social-emotional development.
Heinicke, Fineman, Ponce, & Guthrie (2001)	64	birth	M = 24	Both	No	No	No	d = .35 r = .17	The home visiting mother/infant program made a significant impact on both mother's and child's functioning from birth to 2 years of life. Intervention mothers were more responsive, provided greater encouragement, to their children, and were able to better encourage their children to engage in tasks than control mothers.

Study	Sample Size	Age of Children	Age of Parents	Treatment Focus	Psych. Properties	Treatment Integrity	Social Validity	Average ES	Findings
Juffer, Bakersmans-Kranenburg, & van IJzendoorn (2005)	130	< 6 months	N/P	Mothers	Yes	No	No	$d = .44$ $r = .22$	Two interventions based on attachment therapy were implemented. When compared to the control condition, the video with feedback intervention produced much stronger effects than the book-only condition, which produced weak results. Overall, both interventions produced positive outcomes.
Juffer, Hoksbergen, Riksen-Walvern, & Kohnstamm (1997)	90	< 5 months	M = 35.5 SD = 3.4	Mothers	Yes	No	No	$d = .31$ $r = .15$	Two interventions based on attachment therapy were implemented. The less intense of the two was unable to produce consistent significant results across the dependent measures when compared to the control. The more intense intervention group, however, showed significantly better results than the control across most of the dependent variables.
Lafreniere & Capuano (1997)	43	Range = 31-70 months	M = 34.1 SD = NP	Mothers	Partial	No	No	$d = .91$ $r = .41$	Authors found that the six-month intervention program that focused on improving maternal competency through making them more aware of their child's developmental needs significantly improved interaction patterns as measured by an objective observation system.
Moran, Pederson, & Krupka (2005)	90	M = ~ 6 months	M = 18.4 SD = NP	Both	Yes	No	No	$d = .15$ $r = .08$	The brief intervention produced modest results on maternal sensitivity. However, there appeared to be an interaction between state of mind of mothers at baseline (secure vs. unresolved) and the effectiveness of the intervention. In fact, secure mothers were more likely to benefit from the intervention than unresolved mothers.

Study	Sample Size	Age of Children	Age of Parents	Treatment Focus	Psych. Properties	Treatment Integrity	Social Validity	Average ES	Findings
O'Brien-Caughy, Huang, Miller, & Genevro (2004)	611	Range = 16-18 months	20-29 years	Both	Yes	No	No	$d = .09$ $r = .05$	Authors reported that the intervention lead to improvements in mothers' interactions with their children. Close inspection revealed that there were no significant differences on many of the parent and child outcome measures.
Onozawa, Glover, Adams, Modi, & Kumar (2001)	25	Range = 9-11 months	15-45 years	Both	No	No	No	$d = 1.19$ $r = .51$	This study found clear benefits for the massage group over the control group on both parent and child outcome measures.
Oppenheim, Goldsmith, & Koren-Karie (2004)	42	< 3 months	$M = 32.6$ $SD = NP$	Both	Partial	No	No	$d = .37$ $r = .18$	Authors found that gains in mothers' insightfulness produced by the intervention corresponded to concomitant decreases in child behavior problems.
Sajaniemi et al. (2001)	115	6 months	NP	Both	No	No	No	$d = .28$ $r = .14$	Slight improvements in cognitive functioning were noted for children involved in the intervention group. The authors note that this is particularly encouraging considering the cumulative negative effects cognitive deficits can have on development.
Schuler, Nair, & Black (2002)	131	< 6 months	$M = 27.1$ $SD = 5.3$	Both	Yes	No	No	$d = .11$ $r = .06$	The intervention was found to have no measured effect on mother-child interaction at 18-months postpartum.
Wagner & Clayton (1999)	497	> 6 months	$M = 25.3$ $SD = NP$	Both	No	No	No	$d = -.02$ $r = -.01$	Results across multiple dependent measures were inconsistent. In all, results indicate that the PAT intervention was not successful.

Study	Sample Size	Age of Children	Age of Parents	Treatment Focus	Psych. Properties	Treatment Integrity	Social Validity	Average ES	Findings
Wagner & Clayton (1999)	355	< 6 months	M = 16.6 SD = NP	Both	No	No	No	d = .04 r = .02	Results of the PAT intervention for teenage mothers was unable to produce consistent positive results supporting its efficacy. Dosage up to 3 years; attrition high (over 40%)
Zahra (2000)	120	birth	M = 26.4 SD = 6.1	Mother	Partial	No	No	d = -.05 r = -.02	The attachment-based intervention failed to produce measurable improvements. In fact, the non-intervention group did significantly better than the intervention groups on two measures.

NP = Not Provided in Article

NOTE: One study (Wagner & Clayton, 1999) contained two separate studies and is listed twice in this table.

Building School-Based Interventions on Attachment Theory and Research

Shane R. Jimerson
University of California, Santa Barbara

Brianna Coffino & L. Alan Sroufe
University of Minnesota, Institute of Child Development

The central tenets of the attachment theory proposed by John Bowlby and Mary Ainsworth have now been supported by extensive empirical evidence. Attachment is recognized as a technical term in psychology, as it has an established meaning built from a body of research and theory. Thus, there is an opportunity to utilize the concepts and methods of the theory as a foundation for school-based interventions to promote student adjustment. In doing so, a certain degree of care will be required. Not every intervention, even those focusing on social relationships, and not every assessment procedure, would derive in a clear way from attachment theory. This article begins by briefly describing Bowlby's conception of attachment and the criteria for validating any concept or measure of attachment. The second section presents a synthesis of relevant findings from the Minnesota Study of Parents and Children, which provides evidence affirming that attachment history provides a foundation for individual development and later social relationships. The final section presents implications of attachment research and theory to the school setting, at times drawing from the preceding papers of this mini-series.

The attachment theory proposed by John Bowlby and Mary Ainsworth has been one of the most successful paradigms introduced to psychology in the last half century. Because of its salience and precision, the theory led to an outpouring of research and application, and the core hypotheses have now been amply supported (e.g., Cassidy & Shaver, in press; Grossmann, Grossmann, & Waters, 2005; Sroufe, Egeland, Carlson, & Collins, 2005a). Considering the stunning suc-

All correspondence should be addressed to Shane R. Jimerson; University of California at Santa Barbara; Department of Counseling, Clinical, and School Psychology; Phelps Hall; Santa Barbara, California 93106. Electronic mail may be sent to: jimerson@education.ucsb.edu.

cess of this theory, it is logical that there are many efforts to utilize and extend the theory in various ways. Extending attachment theory into educational domains, for example, is appropriate for it may indeed have much to offer, as is reflected in important past work (e.g., Pianta, 1999) and in papers in this special section. Previous and contemporary efforts are laudable. Both basic and applied work, including intervention studies, is timely, as is each topic raised in this mini-series.

In extending attachment theory, a certain degree of caution is warranted. When a paradigm is extended, especially when its success has been rapid, there is a risk of over-extension and inappropriate extension. Concepts may become blurred and may lose their distinctiveness from other related concepts. When altered definitions and new measures are introduced, if they differ from past work sufficiently, then one cannot rest the new work on previous validation studies. And there are risks in losing the gains in precision that have been made.

Attachment is now a technical term in psychology, in the same sense that negative reinforcement and habituation are technical scientific terms. Thus, attachment has an established meaning built upon a body of research and theory. Because of the substantial validation of Bowlby's attachment concept, adhering to his definition is important. Likewise, moving from established measures of attachment to alternative measures can be necessary, but such moves do carry the obligation to validate the measures according to criteria established by Bowlby and Ainsworth, or to create a new body of research, before concluding that attachment is being measured. In educational psychology, when one introduces a new measure, the custom is to validate it against established measures or against behavior meeting a definitive criterion. Hence, the following provides a brief description of what Bowlby meant by attachment and the criteria for validating any concept or measure of attachment, and also reviews data from a prospective, longitudinal study that support these concepts. The final section offers some guidelines to be considered when extending attachment work into new arenas.

Bowlby's Attachment Concept

Attachment Relationships

Attachment refers to a very particular kind of close relationship (Bowlby, 1969, 1973). Human babies are born vulnerable and relatively helpless and remain so for a number of years. For their survival, a system and process were needed that would insure their proximity to a more capable partner who would defend them and/or take them to safety. The attachment system serves this function. Infants, for their part, are disposed to organize a collection of behaviors (e.g., looking, crying, clinging, calling, reaching) around an adult who has been consistently present and interactive with them over time. They discriminate attachment figures from all others and seek them out in particular circumstances.

Continually present adults, because of their own built-in emotional dispositions, have the necessary complementary responsiveness to infants and encourage this proximity, especially in conditions of threat. Attachment is a powerful emotion-based relationship system, without which humans would not have survived.

Attachment is distinctive from "bonding" in two ways. Historically, "bonding" (Klaus & Kennell, 1976) referred to the tie of the parent to the infant and was thought to occur in the early hours of life. Subsequent research, however, including one of our studies, showed that even infants separated from their parents for the first two weeks of life were just as likely to have secure relationships with their parents by the end of the first year (Rode, Fisch, Chang, & Sroufe, 1981). In addition, bonding has a trait connotation, implying that one can be too tightly or too loosely bonded (Sroufe & Waters, 1977). Attachment refers to the evolving emotional connection of the infant to its caregiver and to the relationship that develops between them over a considerable period of time. In fact, Bowlby did not speak of attachment proper in the first few months of life. Bowlby (1969) described a series of phases in the development of infant-caregiver attachment in the early years, culminating in what he called the "goal-corrected partnership." Bowlby distinguished his attachment relationship concept from trait concepts, arguing that all infants are attached, even those who are mistreated, and that differences in attachment are differences in quality not differences in amount (Sroufe & Waters, 1977). Moreover, Bowlby (1969) used the term "specific attachments," because attachment applies to the relationship with a particular caregiver. Attachment quality refers to the relationship, not to a characteristic of the infant, even though attachment measures typically focus on and assess the infant's behavior with the parent.

Ample research has supported this relationship position. Thus, quality of attachment with two parents can vary, and these differences reflect differences in the history of interaction with each parent (Main & Weston, 1981; Sroufe, 1983). While one assesses infant behavior in Ainsworth's standard attachment assessment (Ainsworth, Blehar, Waters, & Wall, 1978), observed differences are predicted by earlier parent behavior and not by infant temperament (Sroufe, 1983). Moreover, assessments of the infant attachment relationship predict later parent behavior (even with another sibling), as well as later child behavior (Sroufe, 1983). Finally, as discussed in a subsequent section, children's later relationships, including both how they behave toward teachers and peers and how these social partners behave toward them, are predicted by infant attachment relationship assessments (Sroufe & Fleeson, 1988). In the end, the attachment relationship construct gives coherence to this array of findings.

The three defining features of an attachment relationship are (a) secure base behavior, (b) preferential treatment under stress, and (c) profound reactions to loss (Bowlby, 1969; Sroufe & Waters, 1977). Secure base behavior refers to the way infants center their exploration of the environment around the caregiver, ranging away and returning (especially if frightened or uncertain), always monitoring the whereabouts and movements of the caregiver. Secure base behavior also refers to the generally greater comfort young children feel in the presence of their caregiver, and to the fact that, when distressed, infants can rather easily be reassured by the caregiver and can thus return to play. In a related way, preferential treatment means that in particular circumstances—when ill or tired, frightened, or distressed—the young child will specifically want contact with the attachment figure and will be much more readily reassured by them. Finally, loss of an attachment figure is followed by a unique sequence of protest, despair, and detachment, which at various times includes anger, numbing, and profound longing that simply do not occur when other relationships end (Bowlby, 1980). This sequence is further testimony to the centrality of attachment relationships in human adaptation.

Given these criteria, it is clear that only a small subset of human relationships can be thought of as attachments. Many other social relationships, while quite important in their own right, are not attachments. Bowlby (1969) argued that children have a "small hierarchy" of attachment figures. Generally, children in many cultures are attached to their mothers and, unless their involvement is minimal, their fathers. Again, based on involvement, children may be attached to their grandparents, nannies, or other adults, or even to older children in very particular circumstances. Adult love relationships, over a period of time, also become attachments. But many romantic relationships and most friendships, even close ones, are not attachments, nor are the majority of relationships with daycare providers. Likewise, while our research shows that relationships with teachers are very important, even distinguishing those who drop out of school from those who do not (Sroufe et al., 2005a), child teacher relationships are almost never attachments. Children do not typically grieve for a lost teacher when they go to a new school, although they may certainly miss them, nor do they generally wish to go to school when they are sick. Finally, it is not appropriate to speak of an attachment to an institution or a cause. Attachment, as defined by Bowlby and Ainsworth, is a relationship between two people wherein at least one provides a secure base for the other and is vital to their sense of safety and well-being. Bowlby (1973, 1980) was clear in distinguishing affectional, affiliative, and attachment systems (see also Bischof, 1975).

Distinguishing between attachments and other relationships is not a trivial or simply semantic matter. Maintaining such distinctions allows one to explore connections among relationships, to discover their unique functions, and to describe how they work together to promote development. The importance of relationships with teachers, peers, and others are worthy of study in their own right (Jimerson, Campos, & Greif, 2003), but not because these relationships are attachments. As described more fully below, child-caregiver attachments predict a number of important aspects of later functioning, while other aspects of functioning are better predicted by other features of parenting, or by peer relationships, or by school experiences. Moreover, when taken together all of these influences are much more powerful than any single one, including attachment (Sroufe et al., 2005a; Sroufe, Egeland, Carlson, & Collins, 2005b). Finally, the fact that teacher-child relationships are not attachments does not mean that attachment concepts cannot be utilized when attempting to enhance teacher-child relationships, as discussed in the final section.

Attachment Assessment and Attachment Intervention

Not all measures, even those focused on social interactions or the topic of parental relationships, qualify as attachment measures. Aside from reactions to loss, the key criterion for an attachment assessment is that it is related to observed attachment/exploration balance (secure base behavior) in the child's natural environment. This can be done directly with, for example, many hours of observation in the home. Alternatively, there is a laboratory procedure, known as the Strange Situation (Ainsworth et al., 1978), that allows one to classify attachment relationships into categories (see also Kennedy & Kennedy, this volume). Secure relationships are those wherein the infant is confident in the responsiveness and availability of the caregiver. Anxious/resistant relationships are those in which the infant is preoccupied with an inconsistently available caregiver. Avoidant attachments are those wherein infants fail to turn to their emotionally unavailable caregivers when such approach would be expected. Finally, in the face of frightening or unfathomable caregiving practices, infants may show disorganized attachment (Main & Hesse, 1990).

The Strange Situation procedure has been extensively validated against home observations (e.g., NICHD, 1997; Pederson, Gleason, Moran, & Bento, 1998; Posada et al., 1999). This well replicated connection to infant signals and caregiver responses in the home justifies the claim that the Strange Situation procedure and scoring system yields an assessment of attachment. Certain representation measures (see Kennedy & Kennedy, this volume) can lay claim to being measures of attachment because they relate to such direct observations in the home or to Strange Situation assessments. Thus, the Adult Attachment Interview (AAI; George, Kaplan, & Main, 1985; Hesse, 1999; Main & Goldwyn, 1994), which takes an hour to administer and about 6 hours to score, can claim to yield a measure of attachment representation because it predicts Strange Situation assessments of that individual with their infant and because infant attachment predicts adult AAI in low risk samples (e.g., Waters, Merrick, Treboux, Crowell, & Albersheim, 2000). The AAI also predicts secure base behavior in adult love relationships; further, these links are not due to extraneous factors such as IQ or verbal ability (Crowell & Waters, 2005). Many other measures of representation in the field have not been validated as measures of attachment, nor do they predict secure base behavior. To date, there is no validated measure of attachment that is brief and simple to score.

Again, choice of measure is not a trivial matter. If a simple measure, called an "attachment" measure, is actually a measure of self-esteem, verbal ability, or social desirability, then its correlation with other such measures reveals nothing about the role of attachment in development. Further, any measure of representation will always be influenced by multiple factors, not all of which pertain to attachment experiences. As an example, if a group of disturbed psychiatric patients responds in a certain way on a representation measure, does this mean that a particular attachment problem led to this disorder or that the disorder leads to a distortion in this measure of representation? Determining the answer to this question is not possible based on contemporaneous measures.

Only certain kinds of interventions follow from attachment considerations. Not all work with parents constitutes attachment treatments. For example, teaching parents to be more consistent in their discipline, to set and maintain clear limits, or to provide supervision to their teenagers, as valuable as all of these are, would not per se be attachment interventions. Attachment interventions center on the secure base concept; that is, they specifically aim to enhance detection of the child's signals of need for closeness, and sensitive responsiveness to those signals, which are the keys for promoting a secure attachment (e.g., Cooper, Hoffman, Powell & Marvin, (2005)). As attachment figures become more reliable, infants become more confident in this responsiveness and evolve deeper beliefs in themselves as worthy of care and as effective in eliciting care (see also Kennedy & Kennedy, this volume). Less direct approaches, such as increasing parental awareness of their own attachment feelings and helping them build a solid social support system are attachment interventions to the degree that they enhance parent secure base provision. Attachment interveners learned early on that the most effective interventions were comprehensive, multifaceted, and of considerable duration (Meisels & Shonkoff, 1995). As with assessment, there is no fast, simple intervention that follows from attachment principles.

Attachment concepts can also be applied more broadly to an array of social situations, certainly including the schools. Robert Marvin, a longtime associate of Mary Ainsworth, has articulated the rationale for such interventions (see Circle of Security website http://www.circleofsecurity.org/). In discussing secure base relationships, Marvin points out that "when children feel threatened, exposed, criticized, or vulnerable to attack, their exploratory system terminates and their attachment system is activated." He goes on to point out that no one, including adults can "adequately learn and defend themselves at the same time." Thus, interventions that enhance the child's sense of safety and acceptance may be considered attachment interventions. This would include work that helps teachers be more responsive to the emotional needs of children and to provide a generally safe classroom environment. The judicious use of attachment concepts, especially in concert with other approaches to effective classroom design and management, is an important direction for future work.

Key Findings From the Minnesota Study of Parents and Children

Many tests and elaborations of attachment theory derive from longitudinal studies, because, in such studies, the later affects of actual infant attachment experiences are captured. The Minnesota Study of Parents and Children, the most extensive of these studies, has followed the same individuals prospectively from pre-birth to the present, now age 32 years. Validated observational measures of the infant-caregiver attachment relationship were obtained at both 12 and 18 months of age. The consequences of variations in these early attachments were tracked age by age in various ways, including observation, interviews, and standardized questionnaires and tests. Numerous reporters included participants, parents, teachers, romantic partners, and friends. The study has been summarized in two books (Sroufe, 1996; Sroufe et al., 2005a) and more than 100 scientific articles. Only a few key findings can be summarized here, and these will emphasize social behavior and school-related outcomes.

Collectively, findings from the Minnesota study amply support Bowlby's attachment relationship construct and his proposition that early caregiving history is internalized and carried forward. Variations in infant-caregiver attachment predict later individual characteristics, such as curiosity, self-esteem, and self-confidence (Sroufe, 1983), emotional regulation (Sroufe, Schork, Motti, Lawroski, & LaFreniere, 1984), and dependency (Sroufe, Fox, & Pancake, 1983; Urban, Carlson, Egeland, & Sroufe, 1991). Consistent with predictions, insecure attachment history was related to higher dependency scores measured through teacher ratings and independent observations. Ideally, children are neither rigidly independent nor wholly reliant on others. Rather, they can discriminate and evaluate their needs to seek support when their capabilities are insufficient to resolve presenting problems. Our research suggests that attachment history shapes this developing capacity.

Beyond such individual capacities and more germane to this mini-series, early attachment history predicts later relational capacities and social relationship qualities as well (see also Kehle, Bray, & Grigerick, this volume). For example, those who are secure in their attachments, having experienced sensitive, empathic care, later show notably more empathy with peers. Those with avoidant attachment histories (who have experienced chronic rebuff when seeking care and affection) are notably non-empathic; that is they are observed to do precisely the thing that makes a distressed child feel worse (Kestenbaum, Farber, & Sroufe, 1989). In general, positive regard from peers and social competence are strongly related to attachment history from the peer play of preschoolers (Sroufe, 1983), to effective functioning in the middle childhood peer group (Elicker, Englund, &

Sroufe, 1992; Shulman, Elicker, & Sroufe, 1994), to the complex intimate relationships of adolescence (Sroufe, Carlson, & Shulman, 1993; Sroufe et al., 2005a). Those with secure attachment histories more often select friends with secure histories, and they more readily form close friendships. Moreover, they are better able to balance demands of friendship and functioning in the peer group. All of these are germane to adjustment at school.

Qualities of the relationships that children form are also predictable. Repeatedly, our study has shown that attachment is a powerful predictor of peer, romantic, and teacher-student relationships across time (Collins & Madsen, 2006; Sroufe et al., 2005a). One striking finding concerns victimization in relationships. For example, in preschool play pairs, victimization only occurred when two children with insecure histories were partnered (Troy & Sroufe, 1987). The bullies were always children with avoidant histories, while the victims also had an insecure classification (avoidant or resistant). Children with secure histories were neither exploitative nor victims. Rather, they became nurturing to children with resistant histories and took strategies to confront or avoid bullies.

Attachment variations predict not only the quality of peer relationships, but relationships with teachers as well. Children elicit certain reactions from relational partners. In this way, the quality of early interactions forecasts later social functioning. Using extensive observational data, preschool teacher behavior was rated for each child (Sroufe & Fleeson, 1988). Overall, when interacting with children with secure histories, teachers were affectionate and engaged, holding high expectations of them. They had age-appropriate standards for these children. In contrast, for children with resistant histories, the teachers were highly nurturing but had low expectations and treated these children as younger than their age. The teachers also had low expectations for children with avoidant histories but they were low on nurturance and high on anger with them. These early findings evidence how developmental pathways are constrained. Not only is attachment history internalized, but ongoing experience with teachers parallels and reaffirms expectations of relational partners. Guiding teachers to disconfirm maladaptive expectations that children have could be a powerful intervention.

Turning now to school, attachment security (behaviorally assessed in infancy) predicts a number of school outcomes, including work habits, reading achievement, math achievement, highest level of education obtained by early adulthood, and dropping out (Egeland, Pianta, & O'Brien, 1993; Egeland & Sroufe, 1986; Englund et al., 2003; Jimerson, Egeland, Sroufe, & Carlson, 2000). Moreover, these relationships hold with key variables such as IQ and SES controlled. Beyond these basic findings, there were several important lessons from this comprehensive study. First, other aspects of parenting (e.g., quality of support and overall guidance provided in a problem solving situation) predicted these educational outcomes as well as the attachment assessments. Second, taken together, several indicators of parental support were stronger than any single measure. With this composite variable, dropping out of high school was predicted with 77% accuracy by age 3 ½ years (Jimerson et al., 2000). This prediction was stronger than that for IQ, and clearly it is not confounded by the fact that the child is already failing at school. Finally, later parenting measures, both in and outside of the attachment arena, and measures of peer relationships in middle childhood, also add to the prediction of educational outcomes and to changes in trajectories (Englund et al., 2003). Although powerful, early attachment is not destiny, and change is possible throughout childhood.

In sum, an early observed, secure infant-caregiver attachment relationship has demonstrable implications for later individual competence, relationship functioning, and school success, among other things. Findings are especially strong when attachment measures are combined with assessments of other features of parenting and other social supports. Such findings provide the evidence base so aptly called for by Cook, Little, and Akin-Little (this volume), needed for guiding interventions.

Implications of Attachment Theory and Research for Intervention

This final section includes a discussion of some of the clearest implications from attachment work for school-based intervention. The following suggestions are in close accord with those of Lovett, Eckert, Talge, and Akin-Little, 2007 (this volume). These authors discuss general issues in attachment interventions in the preschool years, describing the details of three such interventions conducted by investigators well versed in attachment theory and research. In addition, as noted by Cook et al. (this volume), it is important that further research examine treatment integrity, social validity, and whether risk factors are associated with the effectiveness of attachment-based interventions.

Foci for Intervention

Two related central foci for attachment-based intervention are provision of secure-base support and responsiveness to child signals of emotional need. The secure base concept is directly relevant to attachment-based interventions in general and school based interventions in particular (Pianta, 1999). The reciprocal relationship between attachment behavior and exploration indicates that when children feel safe, they will explore and engage their environment. Conversely, when children feel threatened, comfort seeking takes precedence, and exploration and mastery will be compromised. A parent-figure who provides reassurance and safety in moments of threat or uncertainty facilitates the child's reengagement with exploration; this is the secure base concept. Therefore, attachment interventions should retain measures of secure base behavior; that is, they should consider the balance between exploration and comfort seeking rather than either one in isolation.

Interventions can target the parent-child dyad directly (e.g., The Circle of Security) and foster secure base functioning by enhancing the caregiver's responsivity and the interactional synchrony between parent and child (Cooper et al., 2005). Additionally, more general interventions can integrate the secure base concept. For instance, a classroom management plan that seeks to provide a non-threatening, supportive environment optimizes the likelihood that children will be engaged.

Responsiveness to children's signals increases children's confidence in the availability of a caring adult should emotional needs arise, thus increasing their sense of security. Attachment based interventions should acknowledge the distinct needs of children with different attachment histories and how those needs may be expressed differently. Disrupted or inefficient signaling of emotional needs is a correlate of insecure attachments (see Sroufe et al., 2005a, for review). Distortions in signals are a lawful and coherent response to insufficiency in caregiver response earlier in infancy (Ainsworth et al., 1978). For example, if caregivers are routinely rejecting when the infant signals a need for closeness, the infant typically stops signaling such needs. However, when carried forward to other relationships and situations, these altered signals compromise a child's capacity to garner support. That is, inefficient communication poses an obstacle to interactions with teachers, classmates, and friends.

One result is that relational partners may be challenged in determining the child's underlying needs. For example, a child with an avoidant attachment history, who has learned to contain expressions of need based on rejecting caregiving, will extend these expectations or "internal working models of relationships" (Bowlby, 1969) to others. Therefore, in the school setting this child is unlikely to solicit help from the teacher when ill, disappointed, and/or distressed. Rather, this child would most likely require that the teacher approaches rather than the child contacting the teacher. What was adaptive behavior in the parent-child dyad is not adaptive in the school setting; indeed, this maladaptive behavior impedes a child's developing capacity to take advantage of available resources. In practical terms, interventions that foster accurate emotional interpretation by adults and clear signaling by children may modify these maladaptive relational patterns (e.g., Slade et al., 2005).

Contextualizing Attachment Interventions

How attachment relationships are coordinated with other important relationships is an important issue to consider. For example, school psychologists and other potential intervention professionals may need to consider how attachment-based interventions and other interventions can be mutually supportive. In this context, how individual attachment histories interact with various intervention approaches are important aspects of conceptualizing, developing, and implementing attachment interventions.

Adaptation and competence are not solely dependent upon the child. Rather, mastery depends on the child, the context, and the interaction between the child and the context. Pianta and Walsh (1996) present the contextual systems model as a framework that views adaptation as a process that is distributed across child and context. This dynamic interplay between child and context suggests that a child's potential relies on optimal environmental scaffolding. Optimal intervention is child specific and acknowledges that particular developmental histories warrant particular interventions.

Treatment efficacy may be enhanced if attachment interventions are combined with other interventions. Extensive empirical work indicates that contextual factors (e.g., life stress, social support) interact with parent-child functioning in general and attachment history in particular. For instance, in our study, change in attachment classification between 12 and 18 months was accounted for by changes in the mothers' lives (Sroufe et al., 2005a). When attachments changed from insecure to secure, this shift was associated with decreases in stress and increased social support for the caregiver. Thus, comprehensive interventions, which include attachment based goals, can have impressive results (e.g., Bakersmans-Kranenburg, van Ijzendoorn, & Juffer, 2003, 2005; Slade et al., 2005). These interventions suggest that treatment components can impact parenting and attachment, as well as general health and well-being. In the end, the parent-child dyad does not exist in isolation. Therefore, targeting individual, dyadic, family, school and community level variables in combination is optimal.

Attachment interventions should consider early history as a factor that initiates pathways rather than one that determines outcomes. Development is a transactional process between individuals and their environments whereby these components mutually influence each other (Cicchetti & Toth, 1995). Children do not simply experience environmental input; rather, they are active participants in their own developmental course. Based on early interactions with caregivers, children arrive at subsequent developmental stages with a repertoire of behaviors. Children actively maintain a familiar course of development; whether or not children's behavior evokes positive responses, they tend to act in such a way that promotes their understanding of their environment. Children consequently elicit certain responses from caregivers, teachers, and peers that mirror earlier patterns of interactions with caregivers. Viewing development as a transactional process suggests that the responses of relational partners may enlighten an understanding of a child's history. The reactions a child evokes from others inform us about the treatment the child received over time. Understanding this pathway perspective allows us to embrace change that may be initiated by caregivers as well as by teachers, friends or partners. This reciprocal shaping between a child and relational partners has the potential to influence the reorganization of behavioral functions throughout development.

Conclusion

Extending and advancing scholarship that explores the implications of attachment as related to the school context is vitally important. The authors of articles in this mini-series have done an important service in helping to launch this discussion. Moreover, by bringing in more broadly considerations of relationships with teachers and peers, and the child's sense of connection to the school, they emphasize the critical role of psychosocial factors in academic performance and school adjustment. With further scholarship, the unique contributions of attachment concepts within this broader picture will become clear. Our perspective is that attachment-based interventions are a circumscribed subset of the many school-based interventions that may be undertaken. This view neither trivializes attachment-based interventions nor those that we do not view as following directly from attachment research and theory. In fact, by keeping the array of potential interventions conceptually separate it will be possible to explore how they supplement and mutually support one another.

References

Ainsworth, M. D. S., Blehar, M. C., Waters, E., & Wall, S. (1978). *Patterns of attachment: A psychological study of the strange situation.* Hillsdale, New Jersey: Erlbaum.

Bakersmans-Kranenburg, M. J., van Ijzendoorn, M. H., & Juffer, F. (2003). Less is more: Meta-analysis of sensitivity and attachment interventions in early childhood. *Psychological Bulletin, 129,* 195-215.

Bakersmans-Kranenburg, M. J., van Ijzendoorn, M. H., & Juffer, F. (2005). Disorganized infant attachment and preventive interventions: A review and meta-analysis. *Infant Mental Health Journal, 26,* 191-216.

Bischof, N. (1975). A systems approach towards the functional connections of fear and attachment. *Child Development, 46,* 801-817.

Bowlby, J. (1969/1982). *Attachment: Vol. 1 of Attachment and loss.* New York: Basic Books.

Bowlby, J. (1973). *Separation: Anxiety & anger. Vol. 2 of Attachment and loss.* New York: Basic Books.

Bowlby, J. (1980) *Loss: Sadness & depression, Vol. 3 of Attachment and loss.* New York: Basic Books.

Cassidy, J., & Shaver, P. (in press). *Handbook of Attachment, 2nd ed.* New York: Guilford Press.

Cicchetti, D., & Toth, S. (1995). Developmental psychopathology and disorders of affect. In D. Cicchetti & D. Cohen (Eds.), *Developmental psychopathology and disorders of affect* (pp. 369-420). Oxford, England: John Wiley & Sons.

Collins, W. A., & Madsen, S. D. (2006). Close relationships in adolescence and early adulthood. In D. Perlman & A. Vangelisti (Eds.), *Handbook of personal relationships* (pp. 191-209). New York: Cambridge University Press.

Cook, C., Little, S. G., & Akin-Little, K. A. (2007). Interventions based on attachment theory: A critical analysis. *Journal of Early Childhood and Infant Psychology*.

Cooper, G., Hoffman, K., Powell, B., & Marvin, R. (2005). The circle of security intervention: differential diagnosis and differential treatment. In L. Berlin, Y. Ziv & M. Greenberg (Eds). Enhancing Early Attachments. New York: Guilford.

Crowell, J., & Waters, E. (2005). Attachment representations, secure-base behavior and the evolution of adult relationships: The Stony Brook Adult Relationship Project. In K. E. Grossmann, K. Grossmann, & E. Waters (Eds.), *The power of longitudinal attachment research: From infancy and childhood to adulthood* (pp. 48-70). New York: Guilford.

Egeland, B., Pianta, R. C., & O'Brien, M. A. (1993). Maternal intrusiveness in infancy and child maladaptation in early school years. *Development and Psychopathology, 5*(3), 359-370.

Egeland, B., & Sroufe, L. A. (1986). *Stressful life events and school outcomes: A study of protective factors.* Paper presented at the meeting of the American Psychological Association, Washington, DC.

Elicker, J., Englund, M., & Sroufe, L. A. (1992). Predicting peer competence and peer relationships in childhood from early parent-child relationships. In R. Parke & G. Ladd (Eds.), *Family-peer relationships: Modes of linkage* (pp. 77-106). Hillsdale, NJ: Erlbaum.

Englund, M., Forman, D., Quevedo, K., Morales, J., Johnson, L., & Sroufe, L. A. (2003). *Early adolescents' interactions with parents and educational outcomes in a poverty sample.* Paper presented at the meeting of the Society for Research on Adolescence, Baltimore, MD.

George, C., Kaplan, N., & Main, M. (1985). *The Adult Attachment Interview.* Unpublished manuscript, University of California at Berkeley.

Grossman, K. E., Grossman, K., & Waters, E. (2005). *Attachment from infancy to adulthood: The major longitudinal studies.* New York: Guilford Press.

Hesse, E. (1999). The Adult Attachment Interview: Historical and current perspectives. In J. Cassidy & P. R. Shaver (Eds.), *Handbook of attachment* (pp. 395-433). New York: Guilford Press.

Jimerson, S. R., Campos, E., & Greif, J. (2003). Towards an understanding of definitions and measures of school engagement and related terms. *The California School Psychologist, 8,* 7-28.

Jimerson, S. R., Egeland, B., Sroufe, L. A., & Carlson, E. (2000). A prospective longitudinal study of high school dropouts: Examining multiple predictors across development. *Journal of School Psychology, 38* (6), 525-549.

Kehle, T. J., Bray, M. A., & Grigerick, S. E. (2007). Attachment and friendship formation as they relate to school-based outcomes. *Journal of Early Childhood and Infant Psychology.*

Kennedy, J. H., & Kennedy, C. E. (2007). Applications of attachment theory in school psychology. *Journal of Early Childhood and Infant Psychology.*

Kestenbaum, R., Farber, E., & Sroufe, L. A. (1989). Individual differences in empathy among preschoolers: Concurrent and predictive validity. In N. Eisenberg (Ed.), *Empathy and related emotional responses* (pp. 51-56). San Francisco: Jossey-Bass.

Klaus, M., & Kennell, J. (1976). *Maternal infant bonding.* St. Louis: Mosby.

Lovett, B. J., Eckert, T. L., Talge, N. M., & Akin-Little, K. A. (2007). Attachment intervention programs: A guide for school psychologists. *Journal of Early Childhood and Infant Psychology.*

Main, M., & Goldwyn, R. (1994). *Adult attachment rating and classification system* (Version 6.0). Unpublished manuscript, University of California, Berkeley.

Main, M., & Hesse, E. (1990). Parents' unresolved traumatic experiences are related to infant disorganized attachment status: Is frightened or frightening parental behavior the linking mechanism? In M. Greenberg, D. Cicchetti, & E. M. Cummings (Eds.), *Attachment in the preschool years* (pp. 161-182). Chicago, IL: University of Chicago Press.

Main, M., & Weston, D. (1981). The quality of the toddlers' relationship to mother and to father: Related to conflict behavior and the readiness to establish new relationships. *Child Development, 52,* 932-940.

Meisels, S., & Shonkoff, J. (Eds.) (1995). *Handbook of early childhood intervention.* New York: Cambridge University Press.

NICHD Early Child Care Research Network. (1997). The effects of infant child care on infant-mother attachment security: Results of the NICHD study of early child care. *Child Development, 68,* 860-879.

Pederson, D., Gleason, K., Moran, G., & Bento, S. (1998). Maternal attachment representations, maternal sensitivity, and the infant-mother attachment relationships. *Developmental Psychology, 34,* 925-933.

Pianta, R. (1999). *Enhancing relationships between teachers and children.* Washington, D.C.: American Psychological Association.

Pianta, R. C., & Walsh D. J. (1996). *High-risk children in schools: Constructing sustaining relationships.* New York: Routledge.

Posada, G., Jacobs, A., Carbonell, O. A., Alzate, G., Bustamante, M., & Arenas, A. (1999). Maternal care and attachment security in ordinary and emergency contexts. *Developmental Psychopathology, 35,* 1379-1388.

Rode, S., Fisch, R., Chang, P., & Sroufe, L. A. (1981). Attachment patterns of infants separated at birth. *Developmental Psychology, 17,* 188-191.

Shulman, S., Elicker, J., & Sroufe, L. A. (1994). Stages of friendship growth in preadolescence as related to attachment history. *Journal of Social and Personal Relationships, 11,* 341-361.

Slade, A., Sadler, L., De Dios-Kenn, C., Webb, D. Currier-Ezepchick, J., & Mayes, L. (2005). Minding the baby: A reflective parenting program. *The Psychoanalytic Study of the Child, 60,* 74-100.

Sroufe, L. A. (1983). Infant-caregiver attachment and patterns of adaptation in preschool. In M. Perlmutter (Ed.), *Minnesota symposia in child psychology: Vol. 16. The roots of maladaptation and competence* (pp. 129-135). Hillsdale, NJ: Erlbaum.

Sroufe, L. A. (1996). *Emotional development: The organization of emotional life in the early years.* New York, NY: Cambridge University Press.

Sroufe, L. A., Carlson, E., & Shulman, S. (1993). Individuals in relationships: Development from infancy through adolescence. In D. C. Funder, R. Parke, C. Tomlinson-Keesey, & K. Widaman (Eds.), *Studying lives through time: Approaches to personality and development* (pp. 315-342). Washington, DC: American Psychological Association.

Sroufe, L. A., Egeland, B., Carlson, E. A., & Collins, W. A. (2005a). *The development of the person: The Minnesota study of risk and adaptation from birth to adulthood.* New York: Guilford Press.

Sroufe, L. A., Egeland, B., Carlson, E., & Collins, W. A. (2005b). The place of early attachment in developmental context. In K. E. Grossmann, K. Grossmann, & E. Waters (Eds.), *The power of longitudinal attachment research: From infancy and childhood to adulthood* (pp. 48-70). New York: Guilford.

Sroufe, L. A., & Fleeson, J. (1988). The coherence of family relationships. In R. A. H. J. Stevenson-Hinde (Ed.), *Relationships within families: Mutual influences* (pp. 27-47). Oxford: Oxford University Press.

Sroufe, L. A., Fox, N., & Pancake, V. (1983). Attachment and dependency in developmental perspective. *Child Development, 54*(6), 1615-1627.

Sroufe, L. A., Schork, E., Motti, F., Lawroski, N., & LaFreniere, P. (1984). The role of affect in social competence. In C. E. Izard, J. Kagan, & R. Zajonc

(Eds.), *Emotions, cognition, and behavior* (pp. 289-319). New York: Plenum.

Sroufe, L. A., & Waters, E. (1977). Attachment as an organizational construct. *Child Development, 48*, 1184-1199.

Troy, M., & Sroufe, L. A. (1987). Victimization among preschoolers: The role of attachment relationship history. *Journal of the American Academy of Child and Adolescent Psychiatry, 26*(2), 166-172.

Urban, J., Carlson, E., Egeland, B., & Sroufe, L. A. (1991). Patterns of individual adaptation across childhood. *Development and Psychopathology, 3*, 445-460.

Waters, E., Merrick, S., Treboux, D., Crowell, J., & Albersheim, L. (2000). Attachment security in infancy and early adulthood. *Child Development, 71*, 684-689.

Attachment in the Schools: Toward Attachment-Based Curricula

Chantal Cyr
Centre for Child and Family Studies, Leiden University,
The Netherlands
Université du Québec à Montréal

Marinus H. van IJzendoorn
Centre for Child and Family Studies, Leiden University,
The Netherlands

Since the first publications on child attachment, researchers have mainly focused on the role of the mother as the primary caregiver to understand the development of child attachment. However, when reading Bowlby's trilogy, it is clear that more than one person may play the role of the attachment figure. Although an important body of work has been conducted on the teacher-child relationship and its implication for school outcomes, few studies have examined the role of the teacher as a potential secure base for children or for future attachment-based intervention in the schools. A major question is: How can attachment theory and research guide teachers' and school psychologists' work with pupils? Or, in other words, how can attachment-based interventions promote children's functioning within the school setting? Studies have found that attachment impacts various motivational, social, and cognitive conditions of learning and teaching, which in turn influences children's academic performance and social adaptation within the school setting. Based on a review of these studies and those concerning attachment-based intervention studies, our paper presents a model of attachment-based curricula.

All correspondence should be addressed to Chantal Cyr, Department of Psychology, Université du Québec à Montréal, Case Postale 8888, Succ. Centre-ville, Montréal (QC) H3C 3P8, Canada, e-mail: chantal.cyr.psy@videotron.ca ; or to Marinus H. van IJzendoorn, Centre for Child and Family Studies, Leiden University, The Netherlands, e-mail: vanijzen@fsw.leidenuniv.nl.

Research on child attachment during the school-age years is a relatively new area of research. As children get older, they depend less on behavioral proximity to express their attachment needs. Not only are older children better able to tolerate separations from their attachment figure, but the significant expansion of cognitive abilities enables them to express attachment needs through verbal communication. Increasingly, they also use other adults or peers instead of their parents to protect them from potential dangers or as secure bases from which to explore and learn (Marvin & Britner, 1999). The complex cognitive and emotional changes that arise during the school-age years, including the social networks that are extending, bring about important methodological challenges that render the study of attachment more difficult. Studies examining how attachment continues to develop within the school context, as well as those investigating the contribution of child attachment to school functioning, may provide crucial information on the relational and individual processes involved in children's development of attachment during the school age years.

During the last decade, more researchers have been investigating this unexplored developmental period of attachment in relation to children's emerging cognitive abilities and extended social life (see Kerns & Richardson, 2005, for a review). In conjunction with a growing number of studies testing the effectiveness of attachment-based interventions, attachment theory and research provide a focus for the development of future interventions within the school settings. A major question has been raised by a series of articles on attachment (Cook, Little, Akin-Little, 2007; Kehle, Bray, & Grigerick, 2007; Kennedy & Kennedy, 2007; Lovett, Eckert, Talge, & Akin-Little, 2007): How can attachment theory and research guide teachers' and school psychologists' work with students? Or, in other words, how can attachment-based interventions promote children's functioning within the school environment? Attachment may affect the conditions of teaching and learning in several ways. Numerous studies have found that attachment impacts the various motivational, social, and cognitive conditions of learning and teaching, which in turn influences children's academic performance and social adaptation. Based on a review of these studies and of those concerning attachment-based interventions, our paper proposes an attachment-based model of school curricula.

What is Attachment?

Attachment may be defined as the inborn bias of each human being to seek proximity to a stronger or wiser person in times of stress or distress. Attachments support the child in his or her regulation of (negative) emotions, in particular during infancy but also during later stages of development: Attachment is a universal and life-span phenomenon (Cassidy & Shaver, 1999). In his famous 1951 report for the World Health Organization, child psychiatrist John Bowlby somewhat rhetorically stated attachment to be as important for the psychological development as proteins and vitamins are for the physical development. With this metaphor he placed the "bias" of children to become attached among other primary needs such as the need for food. The way to a child's heart is not through the stomach but through continuous and sensitive interactions with a protective parent or caregiver. Attachment theory is built upon the assumption that children come to this world with an inborn inclination to show attachment behavior – and this inclination would have had survival (or 'inclusive fitness') value in the environment in which human evolution originally took place (Bowlby, 1969/1982, 1973, 1980).

Attachment Network

   Attachment theory is quite clear-cut about the role of the biological mother, and one of the most important experiments in the history of attachment theory – Harlow's rhesus monkey experiments with wire-mesh and terry clothed artificial mother figures – shows how the biological functions of child-bearing and feeding are separate from that of protection (Harlow, 1958). For Bowlby (1969/1982), the biological mother is not necessarily the most important attachment figure and, early in his work on attachment, he remarks that whenever he uses the term mother, "it is to be understood that in every case reference is to the person who mothers the child and to whom he becomes attached" (p. 29). From his trilogy it

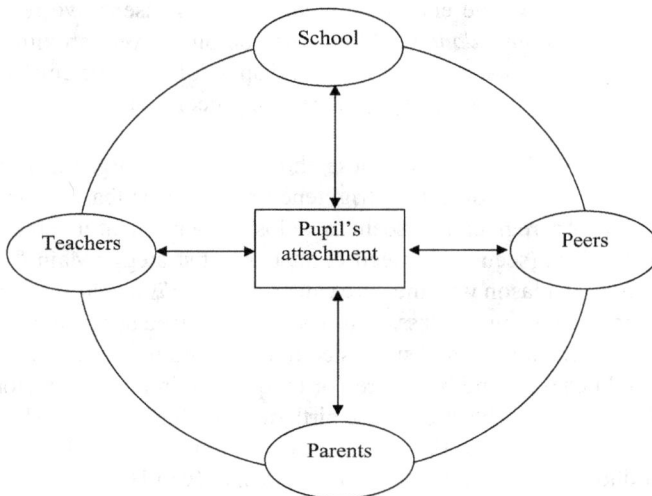

Figure 1. Attachment networks in the schools.

is also clear that more than one person may play the role of attachment figure. Therefore, it is somewhat disappointing that attachment theory still is mostly interpreted as dyadic, monotropic, and mother-fixated. In contrast, children are raised in networks of attachment, with the parents, grandparents, professional caregivers, and teachers being important nodes in the network (Goossens & van IJzendoorn, 1990; Howes, 1999; Tavecchio & van IJzendoorn, 1987). In fact, attachment to persons may evolve into attachment to institutions such as nations or society (Marris, 1991), religions (Kirkpatrick, 1999), and schools (Hirschi, 1969). In Figure 1, the network of attachment relationships in school-aged children is presented schematically.

Attachment Classifications

Although attachment is inborn, large differences in quality of attachment relationships emerge during the first years of life, due to environmental differences, in particular related to parenting. In stressful situations attachment behaviors are elicited and, on the basis of children's use of the parent or professional caregiver (Ainsworth, Blehar, Waters, & Wall, 1978; Goossens & van IJzendoorn, 1990; Howes & Hamilton, 1992) in coping with this stress, three patterns of attachment can be distinguished. Children who actively seek proximity to and support from their caregiver in times of stress, communicate their feelings openly, and are readily comforted, are classified as *secure* in their attachment to that person. Children who seem not distressed in stressful circumstances (but who nevertheless show physiological signs of stress), ignore or avoid the caregiver, and suppress their negative emotions (being afraid of insensitive rejection) are classified as *insecure-avoidant*. Children who combine strong proximity seeking with angry contact resistance, maximize the display of negative emotions (afraid of being insensitively neglected), and remain inconsolable are classified as *insecure-resistant*.

Some children from each of these three so-called 'organized attachment strategies' also display momentary frightened behavior or fearful facial expressions toward their caregiver, and seem to be lost for a moment in a breakdown of the usual, organized (secure or insecure) attachment strategy (Main & Solomon, 1990), which is the reason why they are categorized as *disorganized* on top of one of the three main attachment classifications. Disorganized attachment is the most anxious type of attachment, and suggested to be caused by frightening (or frightened) parental behavior and by (shared or unique) environmental factors such as loss or trauma in the parents around the birth of their child (Main & Hesse, 1990). Disorganized children are at risk for displaying externalizing behavior problems later in childhood, and for a tendency to dissociate (van IJzendoorn, Schuengel, & Bakermans-Kranenburg, 1999).

As an attempt to resolve the paradox presented by the frightened/frightening parent, most disorganized children develop during the preschool period a controlling strategy, with which they try to organize the parent's unpredictable frightening interactive behavior (Cassidy & Marvin, 1992 for coding system, Moss, Cyr, Bureau, Tarabulsy, & Dubois-Comtois, 2005; Teti, 1999). By the time disorganized children reach school age, two basic forms of controlling behavior can be observed (Main & Cassidy, 1988; Moss, Cyr, & Dubois-Comtois, 2004). Children who show *controlling-punitive* attachment behavior use hostile and directive behavior with the caregiver that may include harsh commands, verbal threats, and physical aggression. Children who manifest *controlling-caregiving* behavior structure the caregiver's interaction by being excessively cheery, polite, or helpful toward the caregiver. Although controlling children tend to organize their attachment behavior toward mother, they still manifest disorganization at the level of representation (Solomon, George, & De Jong, 1995) and therefore are considered a subcategory of disorganization (Moss, Cyr, & Dubois-Comtois, 2004). This role-reversal pattern may be well-suited to reassure or punish out of anger a helpless or frightening parent, and momentarily regulate the child's fear and distress, however it becomes quite inappropriate and problematic outside the family context when engaging with peers or teachers.

How is Attachment Related to Learning and Teaching?

Attachment may affect learning and teaching processes and outcomes in various ways. Although attachment security has been shown to be independent of intelligence as measured by IQ tests (van IJzendoorn, Dijkstra, & Bus, 1995), it is the crucial counterpart of exploration in the balance between exploring the uncharted territory and remaining close to a protective caregiver. The secure-base concept (Ainsworth et al., 1978) makes clear that children cannot explore without being able to return to their safe haven at regular intervals. In infancy and early childhood, secure-base behavior mainly involves play and physical proximity seeking, whereas in older children problem solving and support seeking at a more abstract level are predominant. Attachment may affect the conditions of teaching and learning in the following ways.

Motivation and Self-Esteem

First, attachment influences the *motivational* conditions of the learning process. Secure attachments involve trust in significant others, and as a corollary also trust in the self as worthy of the attachment figure's support and capable of having impact on the world around. Mastery motivation develops when the infant experiences sensitive reactions from the outside world in response to his or her manipulations and signals. As attachment relationships enable the child to regulate his or her negative emotions, the persistence or focus on the task or problem at hand becomes possible ('ego-control') as well as the ability to cope with the unavoidable frustrations of trying to solve difficult problems such as learning to read or write. The widely cited study of Matas, Arend, and Sroufe (1978) clearly demonstrated that securely attached children were more enthusiastic, compliant, and persistent, and exhibited fewer frustration behaviors during problem-solving tasks. The contribution of attachment to mastery motivation has also been replicated in other studies including children of different developmental ages (Moss & St-Laurent, 2001; Oppenheim, Sagi, & Lamb, 1988; van IJzendoorn, van der Veer, & van Vliet-Visser, 1987).

Research conducted in middle childhood also supports the view that self-worth or academic self-esteem, as influenced by the child's own attachment history, has a major impact on his or her academic performance during childhood and adolescence (Jacobsen, Edelstein, & Hofmann, 1994; Moss, St-Laurent, & Parent, 1999). Based on early experiences with the caregiver, children develop an internal working model of their attachment relationship that influences their perceptions of self and others (Bretherton & Munholland, 1999). Early parent-child relationships that compromise the child's balance of attachment and exploration needs may foster the development of internal working models of self as incompetent, which in turn interfere with the child's academic achievement goals and social adaptation with teachers and peers.

Kehle et al. (2007) emphasize the role of peer relationships for school outcomes. Children who are socially rejected from their peers are less likely to be academically motivated. Based on an integration of attachment and social pain theories, Kehle et al. argue that social support networks are important predictors of school success. As mentioned by the authors, social pain theory stresses that social exclusion may be as much of a threat to human survival as physical danger. In other words, people's reactions to social threats are very similar to those of physical threats. In this perspective, Kehle et al.'s argument is greatly relevant to our understanding of the maintenance of disorganized and controlling attachment behaviors within the school setting. The emotion of fear experienced by disorganized children toward their caregiver may elicit feelings of social or physical pain, further increasing the likelihood of peer rejection, which in turn may contribute to the stability of disorganization over time.

Collaboration

Attachment also affects the *social* conditions of learning and teaching. As secure children enter the preschool period, they engage in a goal-corrected partnership with the caregiver, in which each partner interacts on the basis of shared goals and plans (Bowlby, 1969/1982; Marvin & Britner, 1999). With the development of language and more sophisticated cognitive abilities, the older child can better communicate his or her own intentions and plans, understand those of the caregiver, and achieve with the caregiver mutual and common goals. Book-reading studies showed that securely attached children are able to cooperate with the parent or teacher, and are willing to be led through a new story more easily than insecure children (Bus & van IJzendoorn, 1988, 1991). Secure children accept the necessary support from their parents or teachers in coping with difficult tasks. They ask for help when they need it and openly communicate their distress when the task demands become overwhelming. Book-reading research also documented the fluency in the interactions between the parent/teacher and the secure child. They lose less time compared to their insecurely attached peers with resolving interpersonal conflicts and other off-task issues. During a collaborative problem-solving task, mothers of secure children are also more likely to share responsibility for task management, and secure children more easily accept being monitored (Moss, Gosselin, Parent, Rousseau, & Dumont, 1997). Research utilizing joint problem-solving activity has shown that mothers and children involved in a secure relationship demonstrated high levels of reciprocal exchanges and affective interactive quality (Cyr & Moss, 2001).

Parents with a securely attached child are better able to discipline the problematic or distracted behavior of their child and to structure the problem setting in a sensitive way (Bus & van IJzendoorn, 1991). In particular, mothers of secure children are effectively able to scaffold the emergence of cognitive functions of the child. During a joint problem-solving task, not only did mothers of secure children adjust their demands to the cognitive abilities of their child, but they also raised the level of cognitive demands slightly beyond the child's actual level by structuring more difficult tasks and allowing autonomy when the child was able to perform the activity (Moss, Parent, Gosselin, & Dumont, 1993; Moss et al., 1997). However, mothers of insecure children were far apart in structuring tasks appropriate to their child's level of cognitive development. Moss et al. (1997) also reported that adult strangers were less structuring with insecure children than with secure children. Possibly, the collaborative style of the teacher, especially toward insecure children, plays an important role in learning processes. In support of this argument, Hamre and Pianta (2005) recently demonstrated that teachers' high-quality instructional and emotional support are important factors that enable young children to make academic progress in early elementary school. Adequate teaching strategies with children showing clinical behavior problems, anxious/insecure attachments or controlling behaviors may be different from strategies used with other children. As mentioned by Dozier, Cue, and Barnett (1994), each attachment style reflects different needs and emotion regulation strategies. Researchers need to develop assessments reflective of teachers' work within high-risk schools, involving such factors as overcrowded classrooms and children with a variety of emotional problems, who also display (meta)cognitive deficits and learning disabilities. In the end, sensitive discipline and scaffolding are important keywords to successful teaching and learning processes in infancy and early childhood (Biringen, Matheny, Bretherton, Renouf, & Sherman, 2000; Moss et al., 1997) and these may remain important prerequisites of learning throughout the school years.

(Meta)cognition

Third, attachment may influence the *cognitive* conditions of learning. Secure attachment may facilitate attention to problem solving and to exploring new domains of knowledge. Undisturbed attention to cognitive problems implies being free of worries and anxieties about the self and significant others. Numerous experimental dot-probe and Stroop studies documented the susceptibility of anxious individuals to supra- or sub-liminal interferences with attentional processes to negative emotional stimuli (see Bar-Haim, Lamy, Pergamin, Bakermans-Kranenburg, & van IJzendoorn, 2007, for a meta-analyses and fuller descriptions of these procedures). Emotions may facilitate but also hamper the efficient processing of information, and insecure attachments may lead to less efficient attention to and decoding of information because attention has to be divided between cognitive exploration and attachment needs (De Ruiter & van IJzendoorn, 1993).

Research on attachment and children's execution of different theory of mind tasks has shown that children who were securely attached in infancy performed better than their insecure peers on a false-belief task at age 4 (Meins, Fernyhough, Russell, & Clark-Carter, 1998) and a belief-desire reasoning task at age 6 (Fonagy, Redfern, & Charman, 1997). These results indicate that attachment security is a good predictor of children's perspective taking skills, which support the general agreement that the parent-child relationship contributes to the emergence of symbolic thought. Other research has shown that securely attached children may develop metacognitive skills earlier and more thoroughly than insecure children. In fact, by the age of 3.5, secure children are more likely to use self-regulated strategies in joint problem-solving tasks such as monitoring and evaluation (Moss et al., 1997). At school age, 6-year-old disorganized-controlling children were found to show the lowest levels of metacognitive skills (Moss et al., 1999). Specifically, during a mother-child collaborative activity involving task-specific rules (called the grocery task), disorganized children showed fewer planning behaviors than other children. According to the authors, the development of metacognitive strategies is related to appropriate scaffolding and monitoring by the mother. Since the interaction of disorganized children and their caregivers is characterized by a role reversal pattern, it is not surprising to find that these children show evident problems in exploring different possible options and in predicting consequences of plans. Difficulties in metacognitive monitoring have also been identified in adolescents and adults with an unresolved attachment state of mind with respect to loss or other traumatic childhood experiences (Main, 1991). Metacognitive skills may help generalize problem solving to new areas and issues, which impact both the social adaptation and academic achievement of the child (Loper & Murphy, 1985; Riggs, Blair, & Greenberg, 2003).

Thinking about one's thought processes and problem solving strategies has been found to be more prevalent among securely attached children, perhaps because these children have learned to openly communicate with their parents and teachers about the ways in which they address the demand characteristics of a new domain of learning. Recent research on mother-child conversation patterns indicates that securely attached preschoolers are more inclined than their insecure peers to self-reflect on personal experiences and share intentions and emotions when verbally engaging with their mother (Cyr, Dubois-Comtois, & Moss, in press; Newcombe & Reese, 2004; Thompson, Laible, & Ontai, 2003). This verbal pattern has been related to mothers' own abilities to elicit children's exploration and elaboration of thoughts and emotions during conversations, either by promoting self-reflection, supporting exploration by means of imaginary play, or encour-

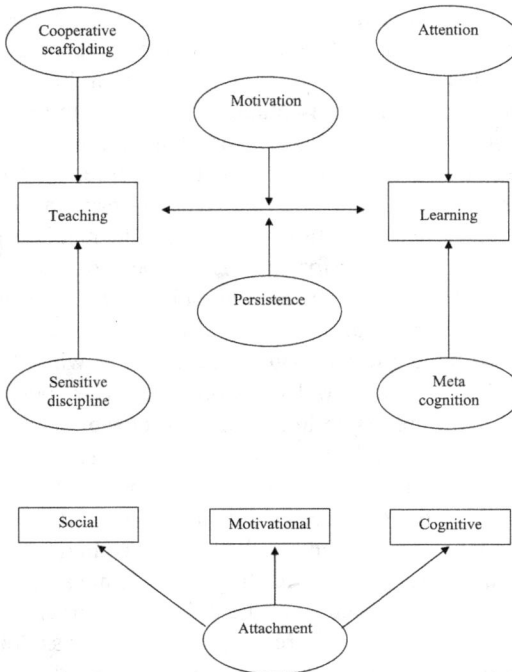

Figure 2. Attachment-based influences on the teaching-learning process.

aging sharing of personal experiences with others (Cyr et al., in press; Laible, 2004). Parents' and children's early communication styles can certainly facilitate learning and teaching processes. Our recent work even shows that conversational exchanges constitute a pathway through which security can be maintained or revised over the preschool and school-age years (Dubois-Comtois, Cyr, Bureau, & Moss, 2007). From this perspective, daily conversations with significant teachers may well be seen as contexts through which children shape representations of attachment relationships, self and others, and influence the way they approach both social and learning experiences within the school setting.

What Do We Know About the Relation Between Attachment and School Performance and Adaptation?

In the course of their longitudinal study, investigating the associations between attachment at school-age and child developmental outcomes, Moss and her colleagues have intensively examined the links between attachment, academic achievement and behavior problems of children in the school setting. Results of their studies revealed that, once child IQ and gender had been taken into account, children with disorganized-controlling attachment behavior at age 6 showed the greatest deficits in academic functioning two years later, especially in math performance (Moss et al., 1999). These results are in line with studies indicating that insecure attachment representations are related to poor academic performance (Jacobsen & Hofmann, 1997) and that children with disorganized attachment representation are showing the most difficulties on deductive reasoning tasks (Jacobsen et al., 1994). These two research teams have also tested the hypothesis that positive representations of self would mediate the link found between attachment and school performance. As expected, academic self-esteem or self-confidence explained the observed association between attachment and school performance (Jacobsen et al., 1994; Moss & St-Laurent, 2001). These findings are in line with the growing body of research showing that beyond children's cognitive abilities and overall classroom behavior, positive interaction between teachers and children is an important predictor of academic and behavioral school functioning in children, especially those at-risk for early academic failure (Hamre & Pianta, 2001, 2005; Morrison & Connor, 2002). At the moment, studies examining associations between child attachment and school performance are rare. More research on teacher-child relationships is therefore needed to clarify our understanding of the pathways leading to academic success. Such studies could also elucidate the risk trajectory of the different disorganized groups.

Disorganized or controlling children are not only at-risk for poor abstract reasoning. Their overall school functioning profile seems affected by the overwhelming relationship they have with their attachment figure. Our work has demonstrated that, already in kindergarten, disorganized children are more withdrawn or show more aggressive behaviors toward their peers than do secure or insecure organized children (Moss, Bureau, Cyr, Mongeau, & St-Laurent, 2004). The social behavior of insecure children certainly increases the likelihood of peer rejection and unsuccessful attempts to create and maintain friendships. According to Kehle et al. (2007), unsuccessful friendships may have an enduring negative impact on the achievement of academic goals and even on the capacity to benefit from social support. In support of Kehle et al.'s argument, our longitudinal work has also shown that the problematic social profile of disorganized children in kindergarten is maintained throughout the school-age years (Moss, Cyr, & Dubois-Contois, 2004). Specifically, we have found that among insecure disorganized children, those showing controlling-punitive attachment behavior were at greater risk to develop externalizing behavior problems than children showing controlling-caregiving attachment behavior. Although results regarding behavior problems of insecure organized children (avoidant or ambivalent) are mixed, some other studies have shown that these children are also at-risk for externalizing or internalizing behavior problems (Cohn, 1990; Moss, Bureau et al., 2004; Munson, McMahon, & Spieker, 2001; NICHD Early Child Care Research Network, 2001). As Marcus and Sanders-Reio (2001) suggest, insecure attachments may set an early path toward school drop-out through elevated aggression and anxiety in insecure pupils, and we suspect that, in particular, insecure-disorganized attachments are responsible for problem behavior in school and resulting school drop-out.

In their review of studies examining children's attachment and behavioral outcomes, Kennedy and Kennedy (2007) highlight the role of other potential risk factors for poor behavioral outcome such as biological and/or neurological vulnerabilities, family or community stressors, and poor parental management. However, as they suggest, children's own internal working model of attachment may be the process through which risk factors are increasing externalizing and internalizing behavior problems. This mediation hypothesis, brought up in the Kennedy and Kennedy paper, lies exactly at the heart of what constitutes attachment-based intervention programs. By aiming attachment representations or behavior involved in the development of attachment security, as targets of intervention, attachment-based interventions may help promote child attachment security and school outcomes, and buffer the negative consequences related to risk factors.

What Attachment-Based Interventions Might Work in (Pre-)schools?

More than 20 years ago, the Leiden Attachment Research Program started to develop an attachment-based intervention: Video-feedback Intervention to promote Positive Parenting (VIPP). The program aims at enhancing sensitive parenting behaviors through providing personal video feedback (Juffer,

Bakermans-Kranenburg, & van IJzendoorn, 2007). The program is short-term and home-based. Specific themes for each of the four to six sessions were developed, and guidelines for each session are described in a detailed protocol (see Juffer et al., 2007). The VIPP intervention indeed appeared to be effective in enhancing parental sensitivity. In one of our studies we found that some children may be more susceptible to the influence of parenting than other children, and that temperamental reactivity may be involved (see also Belsky, 2005). Furthermore, the VIPP intervention implemented in the baby's first year of life, significantly protected children from developing externalizing problem behaviors at preschool age (Klein Velderman, Bakermans-Kranenburg, Juffer, van IJzendoorn, Mangelsdorf, & Zevalkink, 2006).

Multiple Tests of VIPP

The VIPP programs have been successfully used in several intervention studies on various samples in different countries. In Italy, the VIPP program was implemented with two different clinical samples: preterm infants and infants affected by atopic dermatitis (Cassibba et al., in press). In the United Kingdom, Stein et al. (2006) used a VIPP-based intervention with video feedback to help mothers with postnatal eating disorders with their infants during the first year of life. Intervention results from these two research projects indicate that the VIPP was successful in improving maternal sensitivity and other key aspects of the mother-child interaction. Also, an intervention program was developed extending VIPP with components to enhance parental discipline strategies (promoting "Sensitive Discipline"). This VIPP-SD program is a synthesis of the Patterson and the Bowlbyan approach to parenting. The program was especially effective in families where children are at risk for externalizing behavior problems who, in addition, require structuring and limit-setting in a warm sensitive atmosphere. The VIPP-SD program was shown to be effective in a randomized case-control study of 1-, 2-, and 3-year-olds (Juffer et al., 2007; van Zeijl et al., 2006).

Most importantly, VIPP may also be adapted to work in classrooms. Research has shown that teachers who build positive relationships and use supportive learning techniques are better able to promote pupils' academic functioning and social skills within the classroom (Hamre & Pianta, 2005; Pianta, 1999). Elicker, Georgescu, and Bartsch (2007) translated VIPP into a program for professional childcare providers in the U.S.A. who work with groups of children from birth to 3 years. The principles and methods of VIPP were adapted to create a 4-week training program called *Tuning In*. In addition to reinforcing the caregiver's sensitivity and responsiveness, this program focuses on the caregiver's effectiveness in meeting children's individual needs. The pilot study shows the feasibility of the VIPP approach in the context of group care and preliminary results of the large-scale randomized controlled trial are promising. Moreover,

Elicker and his colleagues (2007) report that the caregivers involved in this trial show high consumer satisfaction. A recent meta-analysis has demonstrated that sensitivity-focused intervention programs, using the HOME inventory as an outcome measure, are also effective in enhancing the quality of the home environment, including learning materials provided to children (Bakermans-Kranenburg, van IJzendoorn, & Bradley, 2005). The HOME inventory has been known to be related to children's intellectual and academic performance (Belsky, Garduque, & Hrncir, 1984; Bradley, Caldwell, & Rock, 1988).

In line with this body of research, we expect the VIPP to be an effective technique for enhancing positive teacher-child relationships and school functioning in children. According to Pianta (1999), one of the best tools to use with teachers is videotape. Not only does it provide a neutral feedback on the child as well as the teacher's interactive behavior, but it also allows a focus on behaviors that are not subject to selective recall or lack of memory. Kennedy and Kennedy (2007) and Pianta (1999) have built a convincing argument that teachers' own representations of relationships (Internal Working Models) may influence teaching strategies and the quality of relationships teachers create with pupils. For example, teachers who minimize attachment information may appear rejecting to the needs of students, and their expectations for students' maturity and autonomy may be unrealistic. From this perspective, in order for teachers to become secure bases from which pupils explore academic and social environments, attachment intervention with teachers is highly recommended. However, as indicated by Kennedy and Kennedy, there have been relatively few studies testing such interventions in educational settings. Intervention with teachers may be conducted by school psychologists. Lovett et al. (2007) suggest that school psychologists should educate parents on the different general behavior management techniques that might promote children's functioning. In a similar fashion, school psychologists could educate teachers on attachment theory. Helping teachers recognize their own interpersonal strategies, expectations and goals, as well as those of their students, can promote academic achievement and peer relationships (Lovett et al., 2007).

Treatment Fidelity, Alliance, and Satisfaction

Studies on (preventive) parenting interventions in early childhood mainly focus on program outcome, determining whether an intervention results in the desired effects (Cook et al., 2007). As underscored by Cook et al. (2007) and Juffer et al. (in press), equally relevant but underreported are the processes of these programs that may be crucial to their outcomes such as the relationship between parent and intervener (alliance), parental satisfaction with the program, active implementation of skills, and program fidelity (Cook et al., 2007; Juffer et al., 2007).

Our results showed that the large majority of intervention participants found the video feedback informative (81%) and useful (76%). Furthermore, 93% of the intervention mothers rated their relationship with the home visitor as (very) good. Almost half of the mothers in the intervention group (49%) reported having practiced the advice given during the sessions (reasonably) often, and/or having read the booklet with advice after the intervention (47%). The large majority of mothers had discussed the advice with their partners (99%), with family members (83%), and/or with friends (75%). Finally, program fidelity was high: all participants received six home visits, each session was standardized in manuals, and interveners were extensively trained and supervised (see Stolk et al., in press, for a description of process assessment). The Nurse-Family Partnership program for first time mothers, developed by David Olds (2005), is probably the best example of how an intervention program can benefit from the assessment of treatment fidelity and consumer satisfaction. To date, this evidence-based intervention program, for which treatment integrity is respected, has been implemented in numerous clinical settings across the United-States.

Meta-Analytic Support for Brief Interventions with a Behavioral Focus

Meta-analytic results showed that randomized interventions that only focus on sensitive maternal behavior – like our VIPP approach – are most effective in changing insensitive parenting as well as infant attachment insecurity although the size of the combined effects remains in the small to modest range. Surprisingly, evidence was found for fewer contacts (up to 16 sessions) being somewhat more effective than longer interventions, and the same goes for interventions starting 6 months after birth or later. Effective intervention modalities were effective regardless of the presence or absence of multiple problems in the family (Bakermans-Kranenburg, van IJzendoorn, & Juffer, 2003).

What might explain the effectiveness of sensitivity-focused interventions such as the VIPP? First, long-term and broadly focused support of multi-problem families in coping with their daily hassles may take too much time and energy away from a potentially effective, goal-directed intervention approach. Second, in broad-band approaches with multiple goals it may be more difficult to bring about a significant effect on one of the many aspects that are included in the intervention. Third, the "average" intervener may more easily understand and learn the protocol of sensitivity-focused interventions. Interventions with broader aims and methods need intensively trained, highly qualified interveners (e.g., The Circle of Security Project; Marvin, Cooper, Hoffman, & Powell, 2002; see Lovett et al., 2007). Fourth, treatment fidelity may be problematic in long-term broadband interventions. Last, interveners may easily become overburdened, and staff-turnover may increase with the duration of the intervention (Lovett et al., 2007; Spieker, Nelson, DeKlyen, & Staerkel, 2005). Also, long-term interventions may create unfeasible obligations for the participating families, resulting in high attrition.

From a methodological perspective, the focused approach of VIPP and similar interventions may be preferred. As raised by Kennedy and Kennedy (2007), broad-band interventions may be very effective on certain outcome measures, but it remains unclear exactly what ingredients are responsible for such effects. For example, the TEEP project of Kagitcibasi, Sunar, and Bekman (1996) proved to be rather effective, even after 7 years, in terms of school performance. The 2-year long intervention was, however, a combination of center-based group parent training and home-based individual cognitive stimulation, and it was impossible to determine which component was effective. Here we argue for a piecemeal approach to constructing effective interventions, starting with testing the effectiveness of small building blocks or intervention "modules" such as VIPP that after successful evaluations should be combined into an even more effective overall program. We believe that studies using such research designs will be able to answer the questions addressed by Lovett and al. (2007), that is: (a) How individualized attachment interventions should be? (b) At which level should attachment interventions intervene? and (c) Who are the interventions designed for?

Conclusions: Toward Attachment-Based Curricula

Attachment-based interventions in the school are meant to enhance classroom management and teaching skills of the teachers and mentors who guide the pupils' cognitive development. Attachment research on infants and young children has documented the three basic conditions for establishing a secure base: open communication, continuity of relationships, and sensitive discipline. Translated to school curricula and the wider school environment these secure-base conditions imply (a) open communication between teacher and pupils about the negative emotions arising from learning to master new skills and from acquiring new knowledge; (b) stable classroom settings with the same peers and teachers across an extended period of time; (c) firm discipline and safely structured classroom activities in the context of a warm atmosphere, in the absence of rejecting and frightening feedback from teachers as well as peers.

In addition to these components of the regular classroom, attachment-based curricula should include school counselors and psychologists who frequently pay individualized attention to attachment-related conditions that may impair learning in pupils, such as divorce, major illnesses or other traumatic family events. These professionals may form the bridges between children's different social worlds. Children develop within multiple social contexts (Bronfenbrenner, 1979) and are involved in transactional processes within and across these contexts (Sameroff & Chandler, 1975). From the perspective of the child, therefore, the network of attachment relationships resists artificial boundaries among its various components, and open communication between the nodes of the attachment network may optimize teaching-learning processes.

References

Ainsworth, M. D. S., Blehar, M. C., Waters, E., & Wall, S. (1978). *Patterns of attachment: A psychological study of the strange situation.* Hillsdale, NJ, Erlbaum.

Bakermans-Kranenburg, M. J., van IJzendoorn, M. H., & Bradley, R. H. (2005). Those who have, receive: The Matthew effect in early childhood intervention in the home environment. *Review of Educational Research, 75,* 1-26

Bakermans-Kranenburg, M. J., van IJzendoorn, M. H., & Juffer, F. (2003). Less is more: Meta-analyses of sensitivity and attachment interventions in early childhood. *Psychological Bulletin, 129,* 195-215.

Bar-Haim, Y., Lamy, D., Pergamin, L., Bakermans-Kranenburg, M. J., & van IJzendoorn, M. H. (2007). Threat-related attentional bias in anxious and non-anxious individuals: A meta-analytic study. *Psychological Bulletin, 133,* 1-24.

Belsky, J. (2005). The developmental and evolutionary psychology of intergenerational transmission of attachment. In C. S. Carter, L. Ahnert, K. E. Grossmann, S. B. Hrdy, M. E. Lamb, S. W. Porges, & N. Sachser (Eds.), *Attachment and bonding: A new synthesis* (pp. 169–178). Cambridge, MA: MIT Press.

Belsky, J., Garduque, L., & Hrncir, E. (1984). Assessing performance, competence, and executive capacity in infant play: Relations to home environment and security of attachment. *Developmental Psychology, 20,* 406-417.

Biringen, Z., Matheny, A., Bretherton, I., Renouf, A., & Sherman, M. (2000). Maternal representation of the self as parent: Connections with maternal sensitivity and maternal structuring. *Attachment and Human Development, 2,* 218-232.

Bowlby, J. (1969/1982). *Attachment and loss: Vol.1. Attachment.* New York: Basic Books.

Bowlby, J. (1973). *Attachment and loss: Vol.2. Separation.* New York: Basic Books.

Bowlby, J. (1980). *Attachment and loss: Vol.3. Loss.* New York: Basic Books.

Bradley, R. H., Caldwell, B. M., & Rock, S. L. (1988). Home environment and school performance: A ten-year follow-up and examination of three models of environmental action. *Child Development, 59,* 852-867.

Bretherton, I., & Munholland, K. A. (1999). Internal working models in attachment relationships: A construct revisited. In J. Cassidy & P. R. Shaver
(Eds.), *Handbook of attachment: Theory, research and clinical applications* (pp. 89-111). NY: Guilford Press.

Bronfenbrenner, U. (1979). *The ecology of human development.* Cambridge, MA:
Harvard University Press.

Bus, A. G., & van IJzendoorn, M. H. (1988). Mother-child interactions, attachment, and emergent literacy: A cross-sectional study. *Child
Development, 59,* 1262-1272.

Bus, A. G., & van IJzendoorn, M. H. (1991). Patterns of attachment in frequently
and infrequently reading mother-child dyads. *The Journal of Genetic
Psychology, 153,* 395-403.

Cassibba, R., van IJzendoorn, M. H., Coppola, G., Bruno, S., Costantini, A.,
Gatto, S., et al. (200). Supporting families with preterm children and
children suffering from dermatitis. In F. Juffer, M. J. Bakermans-
Kranenburg, & M. H. van IJzendoorn (Eds.), *Promoting positive parenting: An attachment-based intervention.* Mahwah, NJ: Erlbaum.

Cassidy, J., & Marvin, R. S. (with the McArthur Working Group on Attachment)
(1992). *Attachment organization in 2 1/2 to 4 1/2 year olds. Coding
manual.* Unpublished coding manual, University of Virginia.

Cassidy J., & Shaver, P. R. (1999). *Handbook of attachment: Theory, research,
and clinical applications.* NY: Guilford Press.

Cohn, D. A. (1990). Child-mother attachment of six-year-olds and social competence at school. *Child Development, 61,* 152-162.

Cook, C. R., Little, S. G., & Akin-Little, A. (2007). Interventions based on attachment theory: A critical analysis. *Journal of Early Childhood and Infant
Psychology.*

Cyr, C., & Moss, E. (2001). The role of mother-child interactions and the maternal depression during the preschool period in the prediction of the
attachment of the child at school age. *Canadian Journal of Behavioral
Science, 33* (2), 77-87.

Cyr, C., Dubois-Comtois, K., & Moss, E. (in press). Mother-child conversation
and child attachment at preschool age. *Canadian Journal of Behavioral
Science.*

De Ruiter, C., & van IJzendoorn, M. H. (1993). Attachment and cognition: A
review of the literature. *International Journal of Educational Research,
19,* 525-540.

Dozier, M., Cue, K., & Barnett, L. (1994). Clinicians as caregivers: The role of
attachment organization in treatment. *Journal of Consulting and
Clinical Psychology, 62,* 793-800.

Dubois-Comtois, K., Cyr, C., Bureau, J.-F., & Moss, E. (2007, March).
Attachment behavior and mother-child conversations as predictors of

attachment representations in childhood: A longitudinal study. Poster presented at the Society for Research in Child Development. Boston, MA.

Elicker, J., Georgescu, O., & Bartsch, E. (2007). Increasing the sensitivity of childcare providers: Applying the video-feedback intervention in a group care setting. In F. Juffer, M. J. Bakermans-Kranenburg, & M. H. van IJzendoorn (Eds.), *Promoting positive parenting: An attachment-based intervention.* Mahwah, NJ: Erlbaum.

Fonagy, P., Redfern, S., & Charman, T. (1997). The relationship between belief-desire reasoning and a projective measure of attachment security (SAT). *British Journal of Developmental Psychology, 15,* 51-61.

Goossens, F. A., & van IJzendoorn, M. H. (1990). Quality of infants' attachments to professional caregivers: Relation to infant-parent attachment and day-care characteristics. *Child Development, 61,* 832-837.

Hamre, B. K., & Pianta, R. C. (2001). Early teacher-child relationships and the trajectory of children's school outcomes through eighth grade. *Child Development, 72,* 625-638.

Hamre, B. K., & Pianta, R. C. (2005). Can instructional and emotional support in the first-grade classroom make a difference for children at risk of school failure? *Child Development, 76,* 949-967

Harlow, H. F. (1958). The nature of love. *American Psychologist, 13,* 673-685.

Hirschi, T. (1969). *Causes of delinquency.* Berkeley, CA: University of California Press.

Howes, C. (1999). Attachment relationships in the context of multiple caregivers. In J. Cassidy & P. R. Shaver (Eds.), *Handbook of attachment: Theory, research and clinical applications* (pp. 671-687). NY: Guilford Press.

Howes, C., & Hamilton, C. (1992). Children's relationships with child care teachers: Stability and concordance with parental attachments. *Child Development, 63,* 867-878.

Jacobsen, T., Edelstein, W., & Hofmann, V. (1994). A longitudinal study of the relation between representations of attachment in childhood and cognitive functioning in childhood and adolescence. *Developmental Psychology, 30,* 112-124.

Jacobsen, T., & Hofmann, V. (1997). Children's attachment representations: Longitudinal relations to school behavior and academic competency in middle childhood and adolescence. *Developmental Psychology, 33,* 703-710.

Juffer, F., Bakermans-Kranenburg, M. J., & van IJzendoorn, M. H. (2007). *Promoting positive parenting: An attachment-based intervention.* Mahwah, NJ: Erlbaum.

Kagitcibasi, C., Sunar, D., & Bekman, S. (2001). Long-term effects of early intervention: Turkish low-income mothers and children. *Applied Developmental Psychology, 22*, 333-361.

Kehle, T. J., Bray, M. A., & Grigerick, S. E. (2007). Attachment and friendship formation as they relate to school-based outcomes. *Journal of Early Childhood and Infant Psychology*.

Kennedy, J. H., & Kennedy, C. E. (2007). Applications of attachment theory in school psychology. *Journal of Early Childhood and Infant Psychology*.

Kerns, K. A., & Richardson, R. A. (2005). *Attachment in middle childhood*. NY: Guilford Press

Kirkpatrick, L. A. (1999). Attachment and religious representations and behaviour. In J. Cassidy & P. R. Shaver (Eds.), *Handbook of attachment: Theory, research and clinical applications* (pp. 803-822). NY: Guilford Press.

Klein Velderman, M., Bakermans-Kranenburg, M. J., Juffer, F., van IJzendoorn, M. H., Mangelsdorf, S., & Zevalkink, J. (2006). Preventing preschool externalizing behavior problems through video-feedback intervention in infancy. *Infant Mental Health Journal, 27*, 466-493.

Laible, D. J. (2004). Mother-child discourse in two contexts: Links with child temperament, attachment security, and socioemotional competence. *Developmental Psychology, 40*, 979-992.

Loper, A. B., & Murphy, D. M. (1985). Cognitive self-regulatory training for underachieving children. In D. Forrest-Pressley, G. McKinnon, & T. Waller (Eds.), *Metacognition, cognition, and human performance: Vol. 2. Instructional practices* (pp. 223-266). Orlando, FL: Academic Press.

Lovett, B. J., Eckert, T. L., Talge, N. M., & Akin-Little, K. A. (2007). Attachment intervention programs: A guide for school psychologists. *Journal of Early Childhood and Infant Psychology*.

Main, M. (1991). Metacognitive knowledge, metacognitive monitoring, and singular (coherent) vs. multiple (incoherent) models of attachment: Findings and direction for future research. In C. M. Parkes, J. Stevenson-Hinde, & P. Marris (Eds.), *Attachment across the life cycle* (pp. 127-159). London: Routledge.

Main, M., & Cassidy, J. (1988). Categories of response to reunion with the parent at age six: Predictable from infant attachment classifications and stable over a 1-month period. *Developmental Psychology, 24*(3), 415-526.

Main, M., & Hesse, E. (1990). Parents' unresolved traumatic experiences are related to infant disorganized attachment status: Is frightened and/or frightening parental behavior the linking mechanism? In M. T. Greenberg, D. Cichetti, & M. Cummings (Eds.), *Attachment in the preschool years*. (pp. 161-182). Chicago: University of Chicago Press.

Main, M., & Solomon, J. (1990). Procedure for identifying infants as disorgan-
    ized/disoriented during the Ainsworth Strange Situation. In M.
    Greenberg, D. Cicchetti & M. Cummings (Eds.), *Attachment in the pre-
    school years: Theory, research, and intervention* (pp. 121-160).
    Chicago: University of Chicago Press.
Marcus, R. F., & Sanders-Reio, J. (2001). The influence of attachment on school
    completion. *School Psychology Quarterly, 16*, 427-444.
Marris, P. (1991). The social construction of uncertainty. In C. M. Parkes, J.
    Stevenson-Hinde, & P. Marris (Eds.), *Attachment across the life cycle*
    (pp. 77-90). London: Routledge.
Marvin, R. S., & Britner, P. A. (1999). Normative development: The ontogeny of
    attachment. In J. Cassidy & P. R. Shaver (Eds.), *Handbook of attach-
    ment: Theory, research and clinical applications* (pp. 44-67). New York:
    Guilford Press.
Marvin, R., Cooper, G., Hoffman, K., & Powell, B. (2002). The Circle of Security
    project: Attachment-based intervention with caregiver-pre-school child
    dyads. *Attachment and Human Development, 4*, 107-124.
Matas, L., Arend, R. A., & Sroufe, L. A. (1978). Continuity of adaptation in the
    second year: The relationship between quality of attachment and later
    competence. *Child Development, 49*, 547-556.
Meins, E., Fernyhough, C., Russell, J., & Clark-Carter, D. (1998). Security of
    attachment as a predictor of symbolic and mentalising abilities: A longi-
    tudinal study. *Social Development, 7*, 1-24.
Morrison, F. J., & Connor, C. M. (2002). Understanding schooling effects on
    early literacy: A working research strategy. *Journal of School
    Psychology, 40*, 493-500.
Moss, E., Bureau, J.-F., Cyr, C., Mongeau, C., & St-Laurent, D. (2004).
    Correlates of attachment at age 3: Construct validity of the Preschool
    Attachment Classification System. *Developmental Psychology, 40*, 323-
    334.
Moss, E., Cyr, C., Bureau, J.-F., Tarabulsy, G., & Dubois-Comtois, K. (2005).
    Correlates and stability of attachment between preschool and early
    school-age. *Developmental Psychology, 41*, 775-783.
Moss, E., Cyr, C., & Dubois-Comtois, K. (2004). Attachment at early school-age
    and developmental risk: Examining family contexts and behavior prob-
    lems of controlling caregiving, controlling-punitive, and behaviourally
    disorganised children. *Developmental Psychology, 40*, 519-532.
Moss, E., Gosselin, C., Parent, S., Rousseau, D., & Dumont, M. (1997).
    Attachment and joint problem-solving experiences during the preschool
    period. *Social Development, 6*, 1-17.

Moss, E., Parent, S., Gosselin, C., & Dumont, M. (1993). Attachment and the development of metacognitive and collaborative strategies. *International Journal of Educational Research, 16*, 555-571.

Moss, E., & St-Laurent, D. (2001). Attachment at school age and academic performance. *Developmental Psychology, 37*, 863-874.

Moss, E., St-Laurent, D., & Parent, S. (1999). Disorganized attachment and developmental risk at school age. In J. Solomon & C. George (Eds.), *Attachment disoganization* (pp. 160-187), NY: Guilford Press.

Munson, J. A., McMahon, R. J., & Spieker, S. J. (2001). Structure and variability in the developmental trajectory of children's externalizing problems: Impact of infant attachment, maternal depressive symptomatology, and child sex. *Development and Psychopathology, 13*, 277–296.

NICHD Early Child Care Research Network (2001). Child-care and family predictors of pre-school attachment and stability from infancy. *Developmental Psychology, 37,* 847-862.

Newcombe, R., & Reese, E. (2004). Evaluations and orientations in mother-child narratives as a function of attachment security: A longitudinal investigation. *International Journal of Behavioral Development, 28*, 230-245.

Olds, D. (2005). The Nurse-Family Partnership: Foundations in attachment theory and epidemiology. In L. J. Berlin, Y. Zir, L. Amaya-Jackson, & M. Greenberg (Eds.), *Enhancing early attachments: Theory, research, intervention, and policy* (pp. 217-249). NY: Guilford Press.

Oppenheim, D., Sagi, A., & Lamb, M. E. (1988). Infant-adult attachments on the kibbutz and their relation to socioemotional development 4 years later. *Developmental Psychology, 24*, 427-433.

Pianta, R. C. (1999). *Enhancing relationships between children and teachers.* Washington, DC: American Psychological Association.

Riggs, N. R., Blair, C. B., & Greenberg, M. T. (2003). Concurrent and 2-year longitudinal relations between executive function and the behavior of 1st and 2nd grade children. *Child Neuropsychology, 9*, 267-276.

Sameroff, A. J., & Chandler, M. J. (1975). Reproductive risk and the continuum of caretaking casualty. In F. D. Horowitz (Ed.), *Review of child development research* (Vol. 4, pp. 187-244). Chicago: University of Chicago Press.

Solomon, J., George, C., & De Jong, A. (1995). Children classified as controlling at age six: Evidence of disorganized representational strategies and aggression at home and at school. *Development and Psychopathology, 7*(3), 447-464.

Spieker, S., Nelson, D., DeKlyen, M., & Staerkel, F. (2005). Enhancing early attachments in the context of Early Head Start: Can programs emphasizing family support improve rates of secure infant-mother attachments in low-income families? In L. J. Berlin, Y. Ziv, L. Amaya-Jackson, & M. T.

Greenberg (Eds.), *Enhancing early attachments: Theory, research, intervention, and policy* (pp. 250-275). New York, NY: Guilford Press.

Stein, A., Woolley, H., Senior, R., Hertzmann, L., Lovel, M., Lee, J., et al. (2006). Treating disturbances in the relationship between mothers with bulimic eating disorders and their infants: A randomized, controlled trial of video feedback. *American Journal of Psychiatry, 163*, 899-906.

Stolk, M. N., Mesman, J., van Zeijl, J., Alink, L. R. A., Bakermans-Kranenburg, M. J., van IJzendoorn, M. H., et al. (in press). Early parenting intervention: Identifying predictors of treatment response. *Journal of Community Psychology.*

Tavecchio, L. W. C., & van IJzendoorn, M. H. (1987). *Attachment in social networks: Contributions to the Bowlby-Ainsworth attachment theory.* Amsterdam: North-Holland.

Teti, D. M. (1999). Conceptualizations of disorganization in the preschool years: An integration. In J. Solomon & C. George (Eds.), *Attachment disoganization* (pp. 216-242). NY: Guilford Press.

Thompson, R. A., Laible, D. J., & Ontai, L. L. (2003). Early understandings of emotion, morality, and self: Developing a working model. In R. V. Kail (Ed.), *Advances in child development and behavior* (Vol. 31, pp. 139-172). San Diego, CA: Academic Press.

van IJzendoorn, M. H., Dijkstra, J., & Bus, A. G. (1995). Attachment, intelligence, and language. *Social Development, 4*, 115-128.

van IJzendoorn, M. H., Schuengel, C., & Bakermans-Kranenburg, M. (1999). Disorganized attachment in early childhood: Meta-analysis of precursors, concomitants, and sequelae. *Development and Psychopathology, 11*, 225-249.

van IJzendoorn, M. H., van der Veer, R., & van Vliet-Visser, S. (1987). Attachment three years later: Relationships between quality of mother-infant attachment and emotional/cognitive development in kindergarten. In L. W. C. Tavecchio & M. H. van IJzendoorn (Eds.), *Attachment in social networks* (pp. 185-224). Amsterdam: Elsevier.

van Zeijl, J., Mesman, J., van IJzendoorn, M. H., Bakermans-Kranenburg, M. J., Juffer, F., Stolk, M. N., et al. (2006). Attachment-based intervention for enhancing sensitive discipline in mothers of 1- to 3-year-old children at risk for externalizing behavior problems: A randomized controlled trial. *Journal of Consulting and Clinical Psychology, 74*, 994-1005.

Author's Note

We gratefully acknowledge the support of the Social Sciences and Humanities Research Council of Canada (SSHRC) to Chantal Cyr. Marinus van IJzendoorn is supported by the NWO SPINOZA prize of the Netherlands Organization for Scientific Research.

Child Mental Representations of Attachment When Mothers Are Traumatized: The Relationship of Family-Drawings to Story-Stem Completion

Daniel S. Schechter, Annette Zygmunt, Kimberly A. Trabka, Mark Davies, & Elizabeth Colon
Department of Psychiatry, Columbia University College of Physicians & Surgeons

Ann Kolodji
Department of Education, Ithaca College

Jaime E. McCaw
Department of Psychiatry, Columbia University College of Physicians & Surgeons

This study examines the relationship between child play-narratives and family drawings by children of violence-exposed mothers with posttraumatic stress disorder (PTSD). The Family Attachment Drawing Task (FAD-T) and MacArthur Story Stem Battery (MSSB) were administered. Of the 23 children (ages 4-7 years), 16 (70%) created drawings that were coded as being representative of insecure attachment. Attachment insecurity and disorganization of child-caregiver attachment on the FAD-T were significantly associated with trauma-related dimensions of the MSSB, but not to other factors. This study suggests that the FAD-T provides access to child mental representations, which may affect intergenerational transmission of violent trauma.

All correspondence should be addressed to Daniel S. Schechter, M.D., Division of Developmental Neuroscience, New York State Psychiatric Institute – Unit 40, 1051 Riverside Drive, New York, NY 10032. Electronic mail may be sent to dss11@columbia.edu.

Clinicians have long relied on child drawings to inform psychiatric assessment (Burns & Kaufman, 1972; DiLeo, 1973; Koppitz, 1966; Shapiro & Stine, 1965; Zalsman et al., 2000). Children's drawings have often been used to provide access to the child's mental representations of self, others, and relationships with others, as well as to mark change in those representations with intervention (Coates & Moore, 1997; LeRoy & Derdeyn, 1976; Peterson, Hardin, & Nitsch, 1995; Schechter, 2003). Bowlby (1988) hypothesized that mental representations of attachment are the vehicles for intergenerational transmission of disturbances of attachment that support "cycles of violence" in families. Fraiberg, Adelson, and Shapiro (1975) furthermore observed that mental representations of traumatizing figures and relationship with those figures in the caregiver's early life often permeate the caregiver's mental representations of her child, and as "ghosts in the nursery," mysteriously haunt the caregiver and child's present interactions.

The empirical study of the role of mental representations, as embodied in the drawings and narratives of young children, may provide useful clues as to the psychological mechanisms by which intergenerational cycles of violence are perpetuated in the context of the caregiver-child relationship (Schechter, 2003; Schechter, Brunelli, Cunningham, Brown, & Baca, 2002). Crucial to demystifying intergenerational transmission of violent trauma is the understanding of how child mental representations of self and other develop, and how these mental representations are influenced by the caregiver's experience and psychological functioning in early childhood.

The ability to measure the content and quality of mental representations in different modalities provides the potential for a more comprehensive assessment of mental representations, in both verbal and non-verbal or visual realms. Multimodal measurement of child mental representations also allows for potential integration by the child and the clinician with respect to various aspects of mental representations of self and other, particularly in the context of disintegrating intergenerational cycles of trauma and disturbed attachments.

Kaplan and Main (1986) developed specific coding criteria to rate the quality of mental representations of attachment relationships through children's drawings of their families including themselves (ages 5-9 years). Kaplan and Main focused on size, location, degree of movement, individualized characteristics, completeness of figures, facial expression, context, and overall impression of vulnerability.

Since its development the measure has had a number of successful applications. Pianta, Longmaid, and Ferguson (1999) found via study of drawings of 200 five-year-old children that the Kaplan and Main (1986) coding system was significantly associated with previous and concurrent social and behavioral competence. Fury, Carlson, and Sroufe (1997) reported in a study of 171 eight-year-olds from a high-risk sample that infant attachment classifications based on observation of child behavior during the Strange Situation were significantly associated with coding categories of children's drawing of family including themselves. Recent studies have replicated this finding (Madigan, Goldberg, Moran, & Pederson, 2004; Madigan, Ladd, & Goldberg, 2003) and have found additional correlations with the quality of the home environment (Carlson, Sroufe, & Egeland, 2004).

Carlson et al. (2004) also found the following: (a) a moderate correlation (r = .43, p < .05) between the quality of mental representations derived using a semi-structured interview of preschoolers and the quality of mental representations coded on the task requiring children's drawing of family including themselves at age 8, namely, the Family Attachment Drawing Task; and, (b) a weak correlation (r = .22, p < .05) between the quality of mental representations on the Family Attachment Drawing Task at age 8, and those from a narrative measure at age 12. The Drawing Task showed continuity across time and modality. Yet the correlation between the quality of maternal representations with respect to attachment security on the FAD-T and the narrative measure at age 12 did not take into account properties of the narrative such as salient themes and coherence associated with attachment classifications. The question therefore remained: How do mental representations as coded on the Family Attachment Drawing Task relate to those mental representations coded on a narrative measure at the same time in the child's life.

In a previous paper (Schechter et al., in press), we found that child mental representations, as revealed by play narratives which were elicited from children ages 4-7 years in response to story stems on the MacArthur Story Stem Battery (MSSB), were significantly associated with maternal interpersonal violence exposure and related posttraumatic stress disorder (PTSD). Children of mothers who had filed for a restraining order because of domestic violence as well as children of mothers who had greater PTSD severity, created play narratives on the MSSB that displayed greater dysregulated aggression, spontaneous elaboration of danger and distress, as well as avoidance and withdrawal of emotionally-laden familial conflict. Indeed, these associations outshone the relationship of child interpersonal violence exposure and related PTSD to child responses on the MSSB. The MSSB dimensions that were significantly related to maternal exposure to domestic violence and PTSD have, in clinical samples, been both associated with disturbed parent-child relationship and disruptive child behavior (Warren, 2003).

The present study advances the hypothesis that insecure, more disorganized attachment representations as coded via the Family Attachment Drawing Task (FAD-T) would be:

1. Associated with greater levels of dysregulated aggression, danger and distress, and avoidance/withdrawal on the MSSB.

2. Secondarily, like the MSSB, associated with maternal interpersonal violence exposure and related PTSD symptoms. We additionally wanted

to explore any possible relationship between parallel child trauma and related symptom measures and ratings on the FAD-T.

Method

Permission was obtained from the Institutional Review Board of the New York State Psychiatric Institute/Columbia University Department of Psychiatry. The participants in this study represented a sub-sample of 25 children (ages 4 to 7 years) from 24 dyads that had participated in a larger study of 41 dyads two years prior when the children were ages 8 to 50 months. This larger "baseline study" focused on the relationship of maternal violence-related PTSD symptomatology to maternal perception and caregiving behavior (Schechter, 2003; Schechter et al., 2005; Schechter et al., 2004). No statistically significant differences were found between those participant dyads from the baseline study who returned (59%) and those who did not with respect to maternal or child age, maternal education, father's presence, or other measures of maternal adverse life events or symptomatology.

Exclusion criteria for the two-year follow-up visit were maternal or child mental or physical disability that would preclude performance on study-tasks. Further exclusion criteria included child receptive language functioning on the Peabody Picture Vocabulary Test (PPVT-III) (Dunn & Dunn, 1997) equal or greater than 1 standard deviation below the mean ($M = 100$, $SD = 15$). The PPVT has proven to be a reliable and valid measure of receptive language among low-income minority children (Qi, Kaiser, Milan, & Hancock, 2006). None of the children or their mothers had to be excluded on these bases.

Standard statistical methods were applied to test the a-priori hypotheses. Differences between groups of mothers were tested using a one-way analysis of variance; degree of association between continuous measures was estimated by Pearson's correlations (Type I error was unadjusted and set at $p = .05$, two-tailed tests).

Measures

Maternal trauma measures. As described in Schechter et al. (2005), maternal measures were obtained two years prior to acquisition of child mental representation data. Maternal interpersonal violent trauma history was assessed via a standard Demographic and Treatment History Questionnaire, the Life-Events Checklist (LEC) (Johnson & McCutcheon, 1980), and the Brief Physical and Sexual Abuse Questionnaire (BPSAQ) (Marshall, Jorm, Grayson, & O'Toole, 1998). Detailed information concerning the use and the scoring of the BPSAQ may be found in a previous paper by the authors of the present study (Schechter et al., 2005).

Maternal PTSD was assessed via the Structured Clinical Interview for the DSM-IV (SCID, including the PTSD Module with Chronology of Life Events) (First, Spitzer, Gibbon, & Williams, 1995), which has proven to be a consistently reliable and valid measure of Axis I psychiatric disorders (Schneider et al., 2004). Using the SCID, severity of disorder was marked by the total number of endorsed symptoms that followed disclosed interpersonal violent life experiences.

Child adverse events and dissociative symptoms. The Life-Events Checklist (LEC) (Johnson & McCutcheon, 1980), as noted above, was given to mothers about their children's adverse life experiences. This measure is a standard 17-item checklist that lists a range of potentially traumatogenic events from natural disasters to accidents, to combat and interpersonal violent events. The LEC classifies events as experienced directly, witnessed, or recounted by another individual.

The Child Dissociative Checklist (CDC) (Putnam, Helmers, & Horowitz, 1993) is a clinical screening instrument that assesses dissociation and other trauma-related symptoms on the basis of ratings given by caregivers or adults in close contact with the child. The CDC is a 20-item observer-report checklist with a 3-point scale (0 = not true, 1 = sometimes true, 2 = frequently true). A score of 6 or above is frequently found in the presence of child PTSD; whereas a score of 12 or higher suggests the possibility of a distinct dissociative condition (Putnam et al., 1993). The CDC shows good 1-year test-retest stability ($r = 0.65$) and internal consistency (Cronbach's alpha = 0.86). Good convergent and discriminant validity have been indicated (Putnam et al., 1993).

Family-attachment via child drawings. Children's mental representations of self and attachment figures were investigated in family drawings via the Family-Attachment Drawing Task (FAD-T) (Fury et al., 1997). At the start of the procedure, children were escorted into the playroom by the research psychologist. A sheet of 8" X 11" white paper was placed on the table with a packet of eight colored markers. Each child was then asked to "Draw a picture of your family including yourself." As the child drew, the psychologist asked the child to clarify which family member they were drawing, to identify any ambiguous features, and to tell what the family was doing and where they were. The entire drawing process was videotaped. Videotapes were reviewed by the coders to understand the order of figures drawn and anything else about the process that might affect coding, such as scratching out or tearing up a picture and starting over.

The drawing was coded using theoretically derived 7-point global ratings (Fury et al., 1997). Attachment classification as Secure, Insecure, including Avoidant and Resistant, and Other Insecure was based on (a) 7-point family relationship ratings that were designed to capture the child's expectations of family interaction and the child's sense of self in the context of the family, and (b) an overall impression that is guided by attachment classification descriptions. On the family relationship scale, high rating (i.e., "7") indicators included inclusion of all family members in the drawing, organized positioning of family members (e.g., not crowded together or randomly placed), complete figures (e.g., no gross distortions, disguises, or omissions of body parts or facial features), positive indices of family connection (e.g., figures holding hands, shared activity), and use of color and background elaboration. Process variables such as order of figures, time, effort, and detail spent on main figures versus the background or starting over were factored into the rating given.

The primary coder was completely naïve to details about the child or family; the secondary coder had been in contact with some of the families by phone and/or in the lab to assist in coordination of lab visits, but did not have access to other data that would have necessarily biased the coding. Kappa for the two raters was acceptable at .74, $p < .001$. Final classification was based on consensus.

Degree of disorganization was based on a 10-item checklist that collapsed signs of Anxious-Insecure and Disorganized/Disoriented attachment as conceptualized by Fury et al. (1997) based on the Kaplan and Main (1986) coding criteria. These signs included: lack of background detail, figures not grounded, incomplete figures, mother not feminized, undifferentiated gender in self and others, neutral or negative facial affect, false starts, scrunched figures, and unusual signs, symbols or scenes. A mixture of avoidant and resistant features (i.e., mother and child very far apart and child and sibling overlapping) also contributed to the disorganization score. Coders were asked to integrate the number of items coded as present on the 10-item checklist with their overall impression. The degree of disorganization consisted of a five-point scale based on the presence of three or more signs from the checklist. The scale ranged from "1" (e.g., "not at all") to "5" (e.g., "extremely"). Intraclass correlation coefficient of reliability for the two raters was excellent at .81, $p < .001$. The final score was the average of the two ratings.

Clinician-assessed child play narrative. Eight story stems from the MacArthur Story-Stem Battery (MSSB) (Bretherton, Prentiss, & Ridgeway, 1990) were administered by a female psychologist who was naive to any information about the index child and family. These 8 story stems were administered to all children after a positive emotionally charged story-stem about a birthday party was given as a model. The MSSB was conducted during individual video-taped sessions with examiner and child alone that lasted generally 25 to 30 minutes. The MSSB story stems chosen for this study protocol included a range of emotionally-charged family interactions that focused on parental conflict, child injury, separation, frightening situations, child temptation in the face of parental prohibition, parental emotional unavailability, child oppositionality, and child-triggered accidents. For example, in one story-stem, mother sets the breakfast table. After the family sits down, the child reaches for a glass of orange juice and spills it. The examiner then says to the child, "Show and tell me what happens next!"

The examiner introduced the cast of characters in the form of family dolls to each participant prior to each story-stem. The dolls were ethnically and gender matched to participants. Narratives were always presented in the same order. For each narrative, the child was asked to listen to the beginning of the story and then to show and tell the examiner what happened next. If the central theme or conflict in the story stem was not addressed by the participant, the examiner presented a standardized probe, such as, "What about the spilled juice?" or "What else happens after Johnny spilled the juice?"

For the purposes of testing the a-priori hypotheses of this study, the following selected subscale dimensions were used based on use in a prior study of story stem responses within an inner-city population (Robinson, Herot, Haynes, & Mantz-Simmons, 2000). The subscales of *aggression* (i.e., degree of hostile aggression noted in play-narrative content), *personal injury* (i.e., degree of preoccupation with bodily damage and integrity), and *escalation of conflict* (i.e., inflation of interpersonal conflict rather than resolution or lack thereof) were grouped as "Dysregulated aggression." The subscales *distress* (i.e., expression of helplessness, fear, and acute discomfort) and *new or clear worsening of danger* (i.e., introduction of or intensification of worries about lack of safety, threats, and impending disaster) were grouped together as "Danger and distress." And the subscales *exclusion of self* (i.e., degree of avoidance of representing the self/central child figure in the narrative), *repetition* (i.e., repeating the story stem or detail of the narrative that is not essential to the resolution of a conflict), *denial* (i.e., ignoring or minimizing the central conflict and associated negative affects), and *dissociation* (i.e., spacing out during the narration/play, derailing the narrative with non-sequiters, or otherwise odd, or bizarre verbalizations, voicings/devoicings, or other behavior at moments of tension in the narrative, as if to remove oneself from the assessment) were grouped together as "Avoidance/withdrawal." In addition to the three content dimensions, "Narrative coherence" as a qualitative dimension of the narrative was also coded (i.e., linking events in the narrative in a logical and understandable sequence, maintaining character, and maintaining a unifying or organizing topic/theme or set thereof).

Videotapes were coded independently by two experienced coders who were reliable on the MSSB and naïve to any information about the participant except for age and gender. Overall interrater reliability was excellent ($ICC = 0.94$). Interrater reliability on the subscales that were used to test hypotheses in this study was also quite good: Dysregulated aggression ($ICC = .86$), Danger/distress ($ICC = .79$), Avoidance/withdrawal ($ICC = .80$), and Narrative Coherence ($ICC = .98$).

Procedure

Mothers who had participated in the baseline study (i.e., when child was ages 8 to 50 months) were sent a letter asking them to contact research staff within 2 weeks if they would like to participate or if they did not want us to call them. Three weeks after the letters were sent, a female research assistant called the mothers to describe the study and set up an appointment if they were interested in participating.

Following informed consent, the research assistant obtained updated demographic and treatment history data as well as self-report and report of child symptoms from participant mothers. Children were escorted into the playroom by the clinical psychologist, who administered the Family Attachment Drawing Task followed by the PPVT and MSSB. This single videotaped "follow-up visit" lasted 1-2 hours. Mothers were financially compensated. The children received a toy or book.

Characteristics of the Sample

Demographic and descriptive measures. Thirteen boy and 12 girl participants were recruited from 24 mothers who had originally participated in the study. Two children were fraternal twins, a boy and a girl. The average age at the time of the visit was 71 months ($SD = 11.8$). The average age of the mothers was 32 years ($SD = 7.3$). The average number of years of mothers' education was 11 ($SD = 2$, range 7-16). Sixty-seven percent ($n = 16$) of the mothers were without male partners steadily living in the home and were eligible for public assistance; 51% ($n = 12$) received public assistance.

Maternal trauma and PTSD. All mothers reported a history of interpersonal violent trauma (physical and/or sexual abuse, and/or domestic violence exposure) prior to age 16 years on the BPSAQ. In total, the mean number of violent events experienced by each mother was 3 ($SD = 1.8$, range 1-7). Of the 24 mothers who returned for the follow-up study, the mean number of lifetime PTSD symptoms related specifically to the violent traumatic experience with which they were diagnosed on the SCID in the baseline study was 12.4 ($SD = 2.5$, range 8-15). All mothers met criteria for lifetime violence-related PTSD but not necessarily for current PTSD. In this sample of 24 mothers, 6 (25%) met criteria for current violence-related PTSD on the SCID.

Follow-up study of child sample. Twenty-three of the 25 child-participants who returned two years after maternal trauma and PTSD assessment completed the MSSB. Two children were not able to complete the MSSB. A 5-year-old boy became disorganized and disruptive 10 minutes into the procedure, and a mutual decision with the caregiver was made to terminate the MSSB. In the other case, a 5-year-old girl who had become selectively mute and separation anxious in the context of an acute family stressor would not participate in the task and became acutely distressed in the playroom in the company of her mother. In both cases, complete maternal reported data were obtained. No statistically significant differences were found between these two children and those children who were able to complete the task with respect to maternal or child age, maternal education, father's presence, or other measures of maternal adverse life events or symptomatology.

The results reported below thus pertain to the 23 children (e.g., 11 boys and 12 girls) of 22 mothers, who completed both the MSSB and the Family Attachment Drawing Task.

Results

Child Trauma and PTSD

The mean number of adverse life events across all types of trauma (e.g., accidents, medical/surgical procedures, and experienced and/or witnessed violence) meeting DSM-IV PTSD Criterion A on the LEC was 2.3 (SD = 2.3, range 0-10). Only 4 (16%) experienced no such event. The mean severity of the CDC was 9.4 (SD = 8.8; range 0-34). The correlation between the number of adverse life events on the child LEC and the CDC was robust: r = .59, p = .005.

Representational Measures: FAD-T and MSSB

Seven of those 23 children (30%) who completed both representational measures created drawings that were coded as "secure," with 16 (70%) children's drawings coded as "insecure." Of the 16 children whose drawings were classified as insecure, 14 (88%) were classified as "disorganized," 1 (6%) as avoidant, and 1 (6%) as resistant. When a continuous rating scale of disorganization was applied to the coding of all 23 children's drawings, the mean on a scale of 1-5 was 3.4 (SD = 1.5). Child age at time of the drawing task was, nevertheless, not significantly associated with the degree of disorganization (r = -.21, p = .34).

While maternal PTSD severity explained 36% of the variance of the aggregated MSSB subscales mentioned (Schechter et al., invited paper/submitted), the FAD-T was not significantly associated with any maternal factors including maternal PTSD severity. Nor was the FAD-T associated with child psychopathology measures based on maternal report.

Means and standard deviations for the three content dimensions and narrative coherence on the MSSB were measured. The means for dysregulated aggression (range 0-2), danger and distress (range 0-2), and avoidance/withdrawal (range -1 to 1) were .87 (SD = .58), .57 (SD = .40), and .48 (SD = .50), respectively. The mean for narrative coherence (range 0-2) was .47 (SD = .31).

The FAD-T was, however, robustly associated with child play behavior and narratives as coded along the MSSB dimensions that were of a priori interest given our hypotheses. Table 1 describes these results.

Table 1. Relationship of Selected MSSB Dimensions to Family Drawing-Attachment Classification and Disorganization (N=23)

MSSB Dimensions	ANOVA: Associations with Family Attachment Drawing Measure Classification (Secure vs. Insecure)							Correlations with degree of disorganization	
	Secure?	Mean	SD	N	Effect Size	F df=1,21	p	r	p
Aggregate of Content Dimensions Listed Below	Yes	.32	.67	7	1.33	8.75	.007	.54	.007
	No	1.66	1.11	16					
Dysregulated Aggression	Yes	.27	.22	7	1.13	6.24	.021	.44	.036
	No	.74	.45	6					
Danger and Distress	Yes	.23	.27	7	.40	.69	.420	.05	.828
	No	.34	.28	6					
Avoidance/ Withdrawal	Yes	-.35	.27	7	1.10	6.01	.023	.63	.001
	No	.15	.51	6					
Narrative Coherence	No	.65	.18	7	0.88	3.69	.068	-.40	.056
	Yes	.39	.33	16					

Discussion

In this study, we found that both security and disorganization of child-caregiver attachment as measured via the Family Attachment Drawing Task (FAD-T), within a sample of 23 referred children (ages 4-7 years) and their traumatized mothers, were significantly associated with key trauma-associated dimensions of child play-narrative and associated behavior as measured via the MacArthur Story Stem Battery (MSSB). This study supports the findings of several other studies that the FAD-T is a useful tool to assess child mental representations of the primary attachment relationship(s) in the context of psychosocial assessment and intervention (Carlson et al., 2004; Fury et al., 1997; Madigan et al., 2003; Madigan et al., 2004; Pianta et al., 1999).

The strongest effects measured in our study were those of the associations between the two measures of child mental representations. In support of our hypotheses, both categorical attachment insecurity and greater attachment disorganization on the continuous scoring of the FAD-T converged in inverse relationships with the three aggregated dimensions on the MSSB (i.e., dysregulated aggression; danger and distress; avoidance/withdrawal). Of these three dimensions, avoidance/withdrawal, an analog of "frightened" (i.e., helpless) content and behavior was most robustly associated with attachment security and degree of disorganization on the FAD-T. The analog of "frightening" (i.e., hostile/intrusive) content and behavior on the MSSB was also, by itself, significantly associated with attachment security and degree of attachment disorganization on the FAD-T. However, the MSSB dimension of danger and distress, by itself, was not. Attachment insecurity and the degree of attachment disorganization on the FAD-T were inversely associated with narrative coherence on the MSSB at trend-levels of significance as predicted.

It is noteworthy that both "helpless" and "hostile" states of mind (Lyons-Ruth, Bronfman, & Atwood, 1999) are already present in the representations of the young children of traumatized mothers, together with reduced narrative coherence (i.e., lack of integration), and that these characteristics of the child mental representations are associated with attachment insecurity and disorganization during early childhood.

The clinical usefulness of the FAD-T not withstanding, we were interested to note that trauma-related maternal factors, such as severity of PTSD, were not significantly associated with the results of the FAD-T as they had been in relation to the MSSB (Schechter et al., invited paper/submitted). We wondered whether this might have to do with one or more of the following factors: (a) the nature of the FAD-T, (b) limited power, and/or (c) lack of a non-violence-exposed control group of mothers and their children. As we were unable to have a control group in this pilot study, we cannot discount that if comparison to a non-traumatized group of mothers and children were possible, maternal trauma-related factors might have been more significantly associated with child performance on the FAD-T.

The lack of a significant relationship of results on the FAD-T with those of maternal-report measures of number of adverse events or child trauma-associated symptoms (e.g., the Child Dissociative Checklist) was, on the other hand, consistent with our findings with respect to the MSSB. In other words, maternal experience of trauma and related psychological symptoms were more salient to the development of the child's mental representations than the child's experience and related symptoms. This is not to say that the child's adverse experiences did not demonstrate any effect; but rather, it seems as if the impact of the child's experience can be buffered or exacerbated by the caregiver's response and, in turn, her contribution to the co-constructed meaning of the experience.

Bowlby's (1969) notion of the *internal working model* suggested that the mental representations that are based on early childhood attachment experiences with the primary caregiver form a template that guides parenting behavior during adulthood. Bowlby (1988) and later Bretherton and Munholland (1999) suggested the role of the dysregulated and dysregulating internal working model as a vector by which trauma may be communicated intergenerationally. Our studies have supported the existence of a clear link between maternal interpersonal violence-related PTSD and the content and quality of child mental representations as measured by the MSSB. This paper provides evidence specifically for a relationship between the MSSB as a well-established narrative measure of child mental representations and the FAD-T as a less well-established, but nonetheless useful drawing measure of child mental representations. This work thus extends our previous research linking maternal interpersonal violent trauma and related PTSD to maternal mental representations of her child as well as to child mental representations of self and other on the MSSB (Schechter, 2004; Schechter et al., 2005; Schechter et al., invited paper/submitted).

In addition to lack of a control group as mentioned, this study was limited by its small referred sample, hence potentially by unknown selection bias. Having been unable to recruit more than 59% of the original sample, attrition bias may also have limited replicability in this prospective study.

Clinical Example

To demonstrate the convergence and divergence of the MSSB and FAD-T in the assessment of child mental representations within our sample with respect to intergenerational communication of violent trauma in the context of attachment, we will present the following case of Libby and her mother Nancy.

The case of Nancy and Libby at the time of their initial assessment has been described in detail in a previously published paper (see Schechter, Kaminer, Grienenberger, & Amat, 2003). For the purposes of the present paper, we will provide therefore only a brief summary of that initial assessment, intervention at that time, and then describe more specifically Libby's follow-up using the MSSB and the FAD-T two years later.

Initial Assessment

This 29-year-old mother and her then 16-month-old daughter came to our clinical attention following mother's having been reported to child protective services by hospital pediatricians when it was found out that she had been having doctors prescribe sedating medications for her toddler with the understanding that her child had a seizure disorder. Closer neurological and psychiatric investigation confirmed that her daughter, Libby, was manifesting paroxysmal emotional distress that had been interpreted by Nancy as "seizures," or in her native Spanish "ataques." In colloquial English, "fits" was an additional term used by hospital staff to describe the events.

Nancy and her older daughter also suffered from a similar nervous condition and had been prescribed anti-seizure medications. It became clear in the course of the assessment that Nancy had suffered significant repeated physical and sexual abuse from an early age through her teen years, in the context of early maternal abandonment that followed probable domestic violence. We understood her paroxysmal falling to the floor, writhing, and headbanging as manifestations of severe affect regulation in the wake of trauma and her use of medication as a "chemical restraint" or external regulator in the absence of self-regulatory capacity. We thus understood that Nancy's disturbance of emotional regulation had very likely impacted needed mutual regulation in Libby and Nancy's attachment-relationship.

Observations of Nancy and Libby's interactive behavior during free-play and separation-reunion showed multiple examples of frightening-frightened behavior on Nancy's part and disorganized attachment behavior on Libby's part (see Schechter et al., 2003). Overt physical or sexual abuse, and domestic violence exposure was denied by Nancy. However, we know that Libby, at least, had witnessed her mother having "ataques" in which she fell to the floor screaming and banging her head against the floor. With this in mind, Libby had shown symptoms consistent with posttraumatic stress disorder (see Schechter et al., 2003). Yet the symptoms could not be validated by the child as relating to those witnessed events. Libby of note was delayed in her expressive language development at that time.

Intervention

Following a videotaped research assessment with a single videofeedback intervention (Schechter et al., 2003), the dyad entered child-parent psychotherapy (Lieberman & Van Horn, 2005). Despite many missed visits and a limited course of fewer than 10 sessions in 6 months as described by Hatzor (2005), the following changes were noted: Within one month, Nancy's trauma-related distress moved from somatic memory and symptoms (pseudo-seizures) to declarative memory and verbalized/symbolized emotional domain. She suffered no further somatoform relapses. An empathic focus on Nancy's traumatic life experiences, with a gentle confrontation of avoidance of painful affects and concommitant support and stimulation of reflective functioning, enabled Nancy to engage and maintain phone contact with the therapist despite missed visits.

A substantial portion of the therapeutic work involved helping Nancy follow Libby's lead, jointly attend to her interests with her, and maintain joint attention long enough to reflect upon Libby's perspective. A telling moment in the treatment occurred when the therapist Dr. Hatzor suggested that Nancy and Libby read a picture-book together before bedtime. Nancy returned the next day and said that they had "read together" for an hour! When Dr. Hatzor asked her to tell more about the experience, it became clear that Nancy had chosen to read a violent crime novel by herself while seated next to Libby, to whom Nancy had given a board-book. It was some days later that the mother and daughter would actually be looking at the same children's book from cover to cover. Only gradually could Nancy begin to take Libby's developmental and individual perspective.

In a parallel, simultaneous process, Libby's play, which had for weeks involved being the caregiver while playing with dolls or animal figures, reached a turning point. Libby during the last session turned over her precious dolls to the therapist for care, and hugged the therapist as if to say she could give up her reversed caregiver role and be the child. Overall, Libby's play became more reciprocal with her therapist and mother, and involved less of "reading her own book" to the exclusion of the therapist.

Efforts were made to explore the meaning of the missed visits and to reach out to the family. However, Nancy would not accept that her ambivalence towards the treatment and what it might bring up contributed to her avoiding the sessions. And when in session, Nancy often avoided making connections between her and her daughter's memories, affects, and actions, and in turn, reactions at many levels—which we also understood as defensive (Bion, 1959). This avoidance both prohibited full development of a meaningful narrative co-construction of the events that led to referral, yet it also frequently transmitted to her daughter and to the dyad's therapist the sense of meaninglessness, chaos, and isolation that haunted Nancy during her childhood (Laub, 2005).

Of note, Libby's father also never came into treatment despite many invitations and outreach. While we had suspected a stormy marriage bordering on domestic violence by both partners, physical violence had never been confirmed. Despite the family's elusiveness, Nancy responded to our recruitment call for the

Figure 1. When Libby entered the consultation room, she was asked to draw her family including herself. The picture that she drew is depicted in this figure. Going left to right, the black-crayon outlined smallish figure drawing first is Nancy. The next figure is Libby, followed by "Teta" her baby sister, and Alisa her older sister. Next to Alisa is depicted Libby's doll "Ti-ti," as a head without a body.

follow-up study. Nancy denied any new traumatic life events in the family with the possible exception of increased marital tension since her husband's unemployment began.

The following excerpts from the videotaped assessment of Libby include the narrative about her family-attachment drawing (see Figure 1) and the MacArthur Story-Stem Battery (MSSB) narrative that completes the story-stem entitled "Burn":

1. The Family-Attachment Drawing Task (Interviewer's words are in parentheses.)

(And now, you're going to draw me a picture of your family.)

But, I don't know how to draw the house.

(It's ok. It's ok, you draw whatever you know how to do.)

That's my mother.

(That's your mother, ok.)

. . . Oh! That's me. I'm bigger.

(You're bigger, bigger than who?)

Bigger than, than, than, my [older] sister! [NB: In reality, also bigger than her mother. . .]

(Bigger than your sister, ok)

But, I have these eyes. Cause that one don't have no eyes, but I do. Oh, look, look, look my mouth. My mouth looks like a tiny mouse.

(What looks like a tiny mouse?)

This, right there.

(Oh, your mouth looks like a tiny mouse.). . .

. . . (Which sister is this?)

Alisa.

(Your baby sister? Or your big sister?)

Yup. Sometimes! Sometimes!

(Is she a big sister?)

Yeah, but sometimes, sometimes she did hit me like this! *(slaps herself in the face)*

(Oh, that's not nice.)

Nope.

(That must make you feel bad.)

Every time I tell that to my mother. And. . . and, and, and my mother and my big sister, they smack each other.

(They what each other?)

They smack each other like this *(makes punching motions).*

(Who fights each other? Your mother and your sister.)

Sometimes.

(Your sister, she's bigger than you or smaller than you?)

No, bigger than me!

2. MSSB "Burn"

 (Ok, well here's the story. Mom and Susan are at the stove. Ok?)

And mom says, "Ow! I burned myself."

(Oh! Wait a minute, wait a minute. You almost. . . you, you, you have a good, uh, imagination . . . So, here's what happens. You ready? Hands on your lap, and we're going to start! Mom says, "We're going to have a good supper, but it's not ready yet, so don't get too close to the stove. And Susan says, "mmmm. . . that looks good. I don't want to wait, I want some now!" *(I. has doll reach for pan on stove and drop it)* "Ow, ow. Ow, I burned my hand, it hurts, it hurts!")

Now I go?

(Yes.)

And then, Susan says, she put her arm up and she say, "Ow!"

(She puts her arm up and says "ow.")

And then she says, "Ok mommy, I go sit at the table."

 (I'm going to the table.)

And they say, "What happened Susan?"

(They say what happened Susan.)

So, Susan says, "I, I burned myself"

. . . And then mommy said, "I will pick this up."

. . . And she says, "I, I will clean it."

. . . So she had to put more sauces inside.

. . . And then she turned on the grill, with that button and that button hot.

. . . And then she said, "I cooking, I cooking."

. . . And then she hold it. There.

. . . And then she says, "supper time!"

. . . And then, Susan says, "great." *(C. has mom putting sauce from pan into plates on the table.)*

(What about Susan's burned hand? What did they do about her burned hand, her hurt hand?)

(sighs) Dad, Mom says, "Susan, we're going to take you to the doctor."

. . . And Susan says, "oh mommy, watch out for my mom."

(And she says what?)

Watch out for my arm.

And then she says, "Oh no, I burnt my head."

(Who? Mommy burnt her head? What about Susan's hand. What did they do with Susan's hand?)

Oh. . . Oh. George said, "Whoa. I better cook." *(In aggressive voice)* *(has George (brother) kick down Mommy and Susan dolls to the floor)* And then he said, "thank you."

(George is kicking everybody?)

Uh huh. But, but, George and daddy gotta cook.

(Everybody's on the floor?)

Uh huh.

(Why, why is George kicking everybody?)

Cause, cause you say *(whispers)* "be a good girl."

(What?)

(looks around) "I wanna be a girl." *(still whispering)*

(he says, I wanna be a girl?)

Uh huh. But a magic girl came.

(What?)

A magic girl came.

. . . And then George said, "Eat your food. Let me make you a girl."

. . . And then he said "Ahh!" *(screams")*

(How does the story end?)

The mom says, "Ahhhh. . . . That was hot."

*(*Mommy burned her head. So, mommy has a burned head and Susan has a burned hand. . .)*

So, he has to burn hair.

. . . The dad go like that *(puts father doll near stove)*. Ah! I burned my foot!

(So, everybody's a little bit burned.)

Uh huh. So they says, "oh, wah, wah, wah." And they like this *(has them all laying down on the ground)*.

Clinical Discussion

These narratives share the theme of role-reversal in which a helpless parent and/or hostile parent imposes her needs on the child, and in which the child takes on the burden, with exaggerated, if not grandiose, and unrealistic expectations. Both drawing-related and story-stem completion narratives share prominent dys-regulated hostile-aggression between family members. More specifically, in the family drawing, we could not tell which figure represented the child and which, the mother. At one point, Libby speaks of her mouth appearing as a small help-less mouse, which is discrepant with her depicting herself as larger than her big sister and mother, and about which she is subsequently ambivalent and confused. Libby's inner world is one in which babies can become a powerful threat and adult caregivers engage in childlike fights.

In the "Burn" story, the little girl ("Susan") is left with a burn, unattended, only to tolerate the father-figure's aggression. When the interviewer brings back the concern about the injured child, the father says that she should see a doctor. But no sooner, father and mother themselves are burned and rendered helpless, and Susan never does receive medical attention. In the absence of any competent, available caregiver, a *deus-ex-machina* figure, "a magic girl" comes in to rescue the little girl. This concretization of Libby's narcissistic defenses as the "magic girl" seems to allow Libby to finish the story even as she begins to become dis-organized as noted by her making suddenly random sounds. Everyone in the story ends up "a little bit burned."

Thus, the family drawing's role-reversal and confusion is echoed in both story stems, which are consistent with Nancy's initial negative and distorted mental representations of Libby as "mean, likes to hit. . . " and thus confused with strong adult perpetrators of violent trauma in mother's own childhood (Schechter et al., 2003).

Summary

In conclusion, we have found to be consistent with one another two unrelated measures of child mental representations of self in relation to adult attachment figures, the Drawing Task and MSSB. Clinical implications of this study include the fact that these two measures, both of which involve direct-response from and observation of the child in very different modalities, are useful complementary methods for assessment of the young child's representational world in the wake of trauma affecting the caregiver. These measures, applied in this study to a referred sample, may also provide a clue to psychological processes underlying the intergenerational communication of violent trauma. Better understanding of such processes is crucial for the development of effective interventions to interrupt cycles of violence in families with very young children who are undergoing formative development of the capacity for emotional regulation and social cognition.

References

Bion, W. R. (1959). Attacks on linking. *International Journal of Psychoanalysis*, *40*, 308-315.

Bowlby, J. (1969). *Attachment and loss: Vol. 1. Attachment*. London: Hogarth Press and the Institute of Psycho-Analysis.

Bowlby, J. (1988). *A secure base*. New York: Basic Books, Inc.

Bretherton, I., & Munholland, K. A. (1999). Internal working models in attachment relationships: A construct revisited. In J. Cassidy & P. R. Shaver (Ed.), *Handbook of attachment* (pp. 89-114). New York: The Guilford Press.

Bretherton, I., Prentiss, C., & Ridgeway, D. (1990, Summer). Family relationships as represented in a story-completion task at thirty-seven and fifty-four months of age. *New Directions for Child Development, 48*, 85-105.

Burns, R. C., & Kaufman, S. H. (1972). *Actions, styles and symbols in kinetic family drawings (K-F-D)*. New York: Brunner/Mazel.

Carlson, E. A., Sroufe, L. A., & Egeland, B. (2004). The construction of experience: A longitudinal study of representation and behavior. *Child Development, 75(1)*, 66-83.

Coates, S. W., & Moore, M. S. (1997). The complexity of early trauma: Representation and transformation. *Psychoanalytic Inquiry, 17*, 286-311.

DiLeo, J. H. (1973). *Children's drawings as diagnostic aids*. New York: Brunner/Mazel.

Dunn, L. I. M., & Dunn, L. M. (1997). *Peabody Picture Vocabulary Test — Third Edition (PPVT—III)*. Circle Pines, Minnesota: America Guidance Service.

First, M. B., Spitzer, R. L., Gibbon, M., & Williams, J. B. (1995). *Structured Clinical Interview for DSM-IV Axis I Disorders.* Washington, DC: American Psychiatric Press, Inc.

Fraiberg, S., Adelson, E., & Shapiro, V. (1975). Ghosts in the nursery. A psychoanalytic approach to the problems of impaired infant-mother relationships. *Journal of the American Academy of Child and Adolescent Psychiatry, 14(3),* 387-421.

Fury, G., Carlson, E. A., & Sroufe, L. A. (1997). Children's representations of attachment relationships in family drawings. *Child Development, 68(6),* 1154-64.

Hatzor, T. (2005). *Anywhere I go, it's me and my girls: A parent-infant psychotherapy case of a severely traumatized mother and her 18-month old daughter.* Paper presented at the meeting of the Argentine Society for Psychotrauma. Buenos Aires, Argentina.

Johnson, J. H., & McCutcheon, S. M. (1980). Assessing the life stress in older children and adolescents: Preliminary findings with the Life Events Checklist. In I. G. Sarason & C. D. Spielberger (Eds.), *Stress and Anxiety, Vol. 7* (pp. 111-125). Washington, DC: Hemisphere.

Kaplan, N., & Main, M. (1986). *Instructions for the classification of children's family drawings in terms of representation of attachment.* Berkley: University of California.

Koppitz, E. M. (1966). Emotional indicators on human figure drawings of children: A validation study. *Journal of Clinical Psychology, 22(3),* 313-15.

Laub, D. (2005). Traumatic shutdown of narrative and symbolization: A death instinct derivative. *Contemporary Psychoanalysis, 41(2),* 307-26.

LeRoy, J. B., & Derdeyn, A. (1976). Drawings as a therapeutic medium. The treatment of separation anxiety in a 4-year-old boy. *Child Psychiatry and Human Dev*elopment, *6(3),* 155-69.

Lieberman, A. F., & Van Horn, P. (2005). *Don't hit my mommy!: A manual for child-parent psychotherapy with young witnesses of family violence.* Washington, DC: Zero-to-Three Press.

Lyons-Ruth L., Bronfman, E., & Atwood, G. (1999). A relational diathesis model of hostile-helpless states of mind: Expressions in mother-infant interaction. In J. Solomon & C. George (Eds.), *Attachment disorganization* (pp. 33-71). New York: The Guilford Press.

Madigan, S., Goldberg, S., Moran, G., & Pederson, D. R. (2004). Naive observers' perceptions of family drawings by 7-year-olds with disorganized attachment histories. *Attachment and Human Development, 6(3),* 223-39.

Madigan, S., Ladd, M., & Goldberg, S. (2003). One picture is worth a thousand words: Children's representations of family as indicators of early attachment. *Attachment and Human Development, 5,* 19-37.

Marshall, R. P., Jorm, A. F., Grayson, D. A., & O'Toole, B. I. (1998). Post-traumatic stress disorder and other predictors of health care consumption by Vietnam veterans. *Psychiatric Services, 49(12)*, 1609-11.

Peterson, L., Hardin, M., & Nitsch, M. (1995). The use of children's drawings in the evaluation and treatment of child sexual, emotional, and physical abuse. *Archives of Family Medicine, 4(5)*, 445-52.

Pianta, R. C., Longmaid, K., & Ferguson, K. E. (1999). Attachment-based classi-fications of children's family drawings: Psychometric properties and relations with children's adjustment in kindergarten. *Journal of Clinical Psychology, 28(2)*, 244-55.

Putnam, F. W., Helmers, K., & Horowitz, L. A. (1993). Development, reliability, and validity of a child dissociation scale. *Child Abuse and Neglect, 17(6)*, 731-41.

Qi, C. H., Kaiser, A. P., Milan, S., & Hancock, T. (2006). Language performance of low-income African American preschool children on the PPVT-III. *Language, Speech, and Hearing Services, 37(1)*, 5-16.

Robinson, J., Herot, C., Hayes, P., & Mantz-Simmons, L. (2000). Children's story stem responses: A measure of program impact on developmental risks associated with dysfunctional parenting. *Child Abuse and Neglect, 24(1)*, 99-110.

Schechter, D. S. (2003). Intergenerational communication of maternal violent trauma: Understanding the interplay of reflective functioning and post-traumatic psychopathology. In S. W. Coates, J. L. Rosenthal, & D. S. Schechter (Eds.), *September 11: Trauma and Human Bonds* (pp. 115-142). Hillside, NJ: The Analytic Press, Inc.

Schechter, D. S. (2004). Intergenerational communication of violent traumatic experience within and by the dyad: The case of a mother and her toddler. *Journal of Infant, Child, and Adolescent Psychotherapy, 3(2)*, 203-232.

Schechter, D. S., Brunelli, S. A., Cunningham, N., Brown, J., & Baca, P. (2002). Mother-daughter relationships and child sexual abuse: A pilot study of 35 mothers and daughters (ages 1-9 years). *Bulletin of the Menninger Clinic, 66*, 39-60.

Schechter, D. S., Coots, T., Zeanah, C. H., Davies, M., Coates, S. W., Trabka, K. A., et al. (2005). Maternal mental representations of the child in an inner-city clinical sample: Violence-related posttraumatic stress and reflective functioning. *Attachment and Human Development, 7(3)*, 313-31.

Schechter, D. S., Kaminer, T., Grienenberger, J., & Amat, J. (2003). Fits and starts: A mother-infant case-study involving pseudoseizures across 3 generations in the context of violent trauma history. *Infant Mental Health Journal, 24(5)*, 510-28.

Schechter, D. S., Zeanah, C. H., Myers, M. M., Brunelli, S. A., Liebowitz, M. R., Marshall, R. D., et al. (2004). Psychobiological dysregulation in violence-exposed mothers: Salivary cortisol of mothers with very young children pre- and post-separation stress. *Bulletin of the Menninger Clinic, 68(4),* 319-336.

Schechter, D. S., Zygmunt, A., Davies, M., Kolodji, A., Robinson, J., Trabka, K. A., & Colon, E. (Coates, S.W., in press). Caregiver traumatization adversely impacts young children's mental representations of self and others. *Attachment and Human Development.*

Schneider B., Maurer., K, Sargk, D., Heiskel, H., Weber, B., Frolich, L., et al. (2004). Concordance of DSM-IV Axis I and II diagnoses by personal and informant's interview. *Psychiatry Research, 127(1-2),* 121-136.

Shapiro, T., & Stine, J. (1965). Figure drawings of three-year-old children. A contribution to the early development of body image. *The Psychoanalytic Study of the Child, 20,* 298-309.

Warren, S. L. (2003). Narratives in risk and clinical populations. In R. N. Emde, D. P. Wolf, & D. Oppenheim (Eds.), *Revealing the inner worlds of young children: The MacArthur story-stem battery and child-parent narratives* (pp. 222-239). New York: Oxford University Press.

Zalsman, G., Netanel, R., Fischel, T., Freudenstein, O., Landau, E., Orbach, I., et al. (2000). Human figure drawings in the evaluation of severe adolescent suicidal behavior. *Journal of the American Academy of Child and Adolescent Psychiatry, 39(8),* 1024-31.

Author Note

This study was supported by grants from the International Psychoanalytical Association Research Advisory Board, the National Institute of Mental Health, and the Sackler Institute for Developmental Psychobiology at Columbia University. The authors thank Drs. Klaus and Karin Grossmann for their comments that inspired this research.

Young Selectively Mute English Language Learners: School-Based Intervention Strategies

Graciela Elizalde-Utnick
Brooklyn College,
City University of New York

Selective mutism (SM) is described in the research literature as an anxiety disorder characterized by a refusal to speak in anxiety-provoking, social settings, despite the ability to speak in other, anxiety-reduced settings. When diagnosing selective mutism in young English language learners (ELLs), one must differentiate between SM and the silent period, a normal process of second language acquisition. This article describes the etiology of SM and important considerations when working with selective mutism in ELLs. Early intervention is critical, especially implementation of school-based intervention strategies. A comprehensive intervention plan for the ELL with selective mutism should incorporate: (a) consultation with family and school personnel; (b) determination of language(s) of intervention; (c) behavioral strategies for decreasing social anxiety and increasing communicative behavior; (d) individual and group counseling; and (e) strategies for fostering skill and comfort with the second language, English. A case example illustrates the strategies and considerations described in the article.

Selective mutism (SM) is characterized by a refusal to speak in specific social settings, such as school, despite the ability to speak in other settings, such as the home (American Psychiatric Association, 2000). The extent to which a selectively mute child speaks in different contexts varies greatly (Freeman, Garcia, Miller, Dow, & Leonard, 2004). Often these children do not speak loudly in public, and there usually is a hierarchy of people with whom the child speaks (Freeman et al.). Schwartz and Shipon-Blum (2005) describe SM symptoms as falling along a continuum of severity. Children with *mild* SM only communicate

All correspondence should be addressed to Graciela Elizalde-Utnick, Ph.D., School of Education, Brooklyn College, 2900 Bedford Avenue, Brooklyn, NY 11210. Electronic mail may be sent to gutnick@brooklyn.cuny.edu.

with family and a select group of friends. These children use nonfluent language with gestures in settings in which they are less comfortable. Children with *moderate* SM communicate using sounds but not words. Children with *moderately severe* SM communicate using nonverbal means (e.g., gestures, head nod). With the most *severe* form, the children are nonverbal and do not use nonverbal communication.

The age of onset for SM is typically between two and four years of age, although it is typically not diagnosed until the start of school (Freeman et al., 2004). It affects about .71% of children in the United States (Bergman, Piacentini, & McCracken, 2002), with a higher incidence among children with speech and language delays. Studies report that the incidence of a speech and language delay in children with SM ranges from 11 to 68% (Dummit et al., 1997; Kristensen, 2000; Steinhausen & Juzi, 1996). However, the underlying cause of the mutism is anxiety rather than a delay in language.

There is also a higher incidence of SM in immigrant children (Elizur & Perednik, 2003; Toppelberg, Tabors, Coggins, Lum, & Burger, 2005). Elizur and Perednick (2003) found the prevalence of SM among the general population in Israel was .76%, but the rate among immigrants was 2.2%. In a Canadian study (Bradley & Sloman, 1975) the rate of SM was found to be 10 to 13 times greater in the immigrant population. In Germany and Switzerland, Steinhausen and Juzi (1996) found that 28 out of the 100 children with SM in their study were immigrants as well as language minorities. Toppelberg and colleagues (Toppelberg, Snow, & Tager-Flusberg, 1999; Toppelberg et al., 2005) suggest that the anxious immigrant child might be more likely to respond with SM than the anxious non-immigrant child because the immigrant child has to adjust to a new cultural environment. Similar to anxious immigrant youngsters, anxious English language learners (ELLs) have a greater likelihood than monolingual children to be selectively mute (Elizalde-Utnick, 2003; Shipon-Blum, 2002).

Etiology of Selective Mutism

Conceptualizations of SM have shifted over the last two decades. In the past, SM was considered to be related to several conditions, including trauma, family dysfunction, speech and language delays, and oppositional behavior (Anstendig, 1999; Bergman, Piacentini, & McCracken, 2002; Hayden, 1980). For instance, Hayden attributed one form of SM as resulting from a traumatic event, such as the start of school which may be particularly traumatic for those who are very shy.

From a family systems perspective, others have suggested that children with SM are living in families characterized by intense attachment patterns, fear of strangers and suspiciousness of the outer world, extreme shyness, faulty communication patterns, and tension among family members (see Meyers, 1999). It is thought that the relationship between the parent and the child with SM is charac-terized by dependency and ambivalence along with an extreme need to control (Anstendig, 1998). Such family dynamics are evidenced in the families of the SM sample of the current author's (Elizalde-Utnick) on-going, longitudinal, school-based research study. Many of the mothers report anxiety over their inability to control how their children are treated in school. Specifically, many of the moth-ers fear that their child will experience anxiety in the classroom as a result of teachers who "might say or do the wrong thing." Contrary to these mothers' fears, the teachers are so focused on not reacting the wrong way and putting undue pres-sure on the child that they often e-mail the researcher for feedback regarding inci-dents (e.g., how to respond when a peer announces to strangers who walk into the classroom that the child with SM does not speak) as they occur. These mothers have a difficult time relinquishing control, and even though they welcome input from the author who assists the teachers in differentiating instruction for the chil-dren with SM, they often express great concern regarding the day-to-day activi-ties of the classroom.

Another commonly used approach to understanding the etiology of SM is to examine the interaction between the child and the environment. Behavioral theo-rists view SM as a function of negatively reinforced learned responses (Kehle, Madaus, Baratta, & Bray, 1998; Porjes, 1999). Specifically, when a very shy child does not respond to a verbal request, the request is often withdrawn, thereby rein-forcing the mutism. Therefore, the nonverbal behavior of a child with SM is con-sidered a learned response which results in a decrease in anxiety. In other words, the child learns to avoid anxiety related to verbal interactions with others by refusing to speak in such settings. The child's refusal to speak in social settings is often misconstrued as being oppositional in nature. Freeman and colleagues (2004) suggest that it is anxiety rather than a resistant, oppositional nature that inhibits the children from speaking.

During this last decade, there has been an emphasis placed on the notion that SM is an anxiety disorder (Anstendig, 1999; Dummit et al., 1997; Freeman et al., 2004; Schwartz & Shipon-Blum, 2005). There is evidence for the familial trans-mission of anxiety disorders (Shamir-Essakow, Ungerer, & Rapee, 2005). First-degree relatives of children with SM tend to exhibit anxiety disorders and are often described as shy and reserved (Kristensen & Torgersen, 2001).

It has been suggested that SM is closely related to social phobia (Anstendig, 1999; Dummit et al., 1997; Stein, Chavira, & Jang, 2001), however, not all theo-rists agree with this suggestion (Bergman et al., 2002). Studies have found that the majority of children with SM also meet diagnostic criteria for social phobia or avoidant disorder (Black & Uhde, 1995; Yeganeh, Beidel, Turner, Pina, & Silverman, 2003). Black and Uhde found that 70% of parents of children with SM had a history of social phobia or avoidant behavior. However, Bergman and col-leagues (2002) point out an important distinction between SM and social phobia, namely that the age of onset for the two disorders is quite different. Whereas onset for social phobia is after 10 years of age, SM usually appears before the age of five. It has also been suggested that SM might be a subtype of social phobia, and that if left untreated, such individuals may continue to suffer from social phobia (Black & Uhde, 1995).

Like Black and Uhde (1995), Yeganeh and colleagues (2003) found that all the children with SM in their sample met the criteria for social phobia. However, there were conflicting findings regarding whether the children with SM were more socially anxious than children with social phobia alone. While clinicians rated the children with SM as being more socially anxious than the children with social phobia, these same children with SM did not score higher on self-report measures of anxiety than the children with social phobia. One interpretation to explain why the two groups of children do not differ in levels of anxiety is that once the children with SM avoid anxiety by not speaking, they then do not self-report "extreme fear" (Yeganeh et al., 2003, p. 1073). Alternatively, these authors suggested that the adults might have rated the children with SM high in terms of anxiety if the adults equated "not speaking" with being "frozen in fear" (Yeganeh et al., 2003, p. 1073), thereby perceiving greater distress in the children with SM in a social situation.

With reference to immigrant children, particularly ELLs, the higher incidence of SM in this population may be attributed to anxiety associated with adjustment to a new cultural and linguistic environment (Toppelberg et al., 1999, 2005). Young ELLs are in the process of learning two languages and often feel out of place in school. Furthermore, a shy ELL's temperament may compound the difficulty experienced in the new social context. Elizur and Perednick (2003) have suggested a diathesis-stress model as an explanation for the increased incidence of SM in bilingual children whereby

> . . . social disposition, family immigration status, and developmental delay were successfully tested as putative vulnerabilities… Risk-aversive behavior may affect normal second language acquisition in those children with a shy/inhibited temperamental disposition (Tabors, 1997). Oftentimes, other children will socially ostracize children learning a second language and are common in children with SM. (Toppelberg et al., 2005, p. 594).

Toppelberg and colleagues (2005) point out the difficulty in diagnosing SM in ELLs, since the DSM-IV stipulates that limited proficiency in the required language is an exclusionary criterion. However, such an exclusionary clause places ELLs with SM at risk for not receiving the proper intervention, which could worsen the condition and ultimately lead to social phobia (Bergman et al., 2002; Elizalde-Utnick, 2003; Toppelberg et al., 2005).

Young, Non-Speaking ELLs and Language Learning

Whenever considering a diagnosis of SM among ELLs, it is critical that school professionals understand the process of second language learning (Elizalde-Utnick, 2007). Learning a second language is similar in many ways to learning one's first language. The rate and pattern of language development are the same for monolinguals and bilinguals (Grosjean, 1982). Psychosocial factors (e.g., language usage in the home or school) strongly influence to what extent and for how long a child will remain bilingual. For example, a preschooler might decide to stop speaking the first language at home because his/her classmates at school are only speaking English, the second language.

There is a consistent developmental sequence exhibited by young ELLs in a monolingual English classroom (Tabors, 1997):

> 1. The young child continues to use the first language in the classroom for a short period of time, despite instruction being conducted primarily in the second language.
>
> 2. The child begins a nonverbal, or *silent period,* which lasts approximately four to five months. This occurs because the child realizes that the first language is ineffective in the classroom. During the silent period, the child focuses on listening and trying to comprehend. It should be noted that in a bilingual classroom, the silent period is characterized by the child attempting to talk with only those who speak the same first language and avoiding verbal interactions with speakers of the second language.
>
> 3. As the child's receptive language ability grows in the second language, he/she begins to speak in one- to two-word utterances in the second language.
>
> 4. The child begins to engage in conversations with others in the second language.

The Silent Period in English Language Learners

The silent period is a normal process of second language acquisition. It serves a specific purpose: to focus on listening strategies in order to facilitate comprehension of the second language. In a study of young ELLs, Tabors (1997) described two data gathering processes in the silent period: spectating and rehearsing. Spectating consists of active observations by the ELLs when they are in close proximity to English-speaking peers and focusing on the English language. Rehearsing consists of verbalizations by ELLs that do not appear to be communicative, but that indicate the child is practicing the English language.

During the silent period the child does not typically communicate verbally with others in the second language, but he or she communicates nonverbally. Examples of nonverbal communication include a head nod or shake and facial expressions that indicate a need/want. Children also might hand objects to adults for help (e.g., to fix a toy). It should be noted that there are social consequences of nonverbal communication. Young ELLs are often either ignored or infantilized by English-speaking peers.

Silent Period versus Selective Mutism

There are instances in which the silent period continues well beyond this four- to five-month period, and it becomes necessary to differentiate between the silent period and SM (Elizalde-Utnick, 2003, 2006). It is the presence of SM in *both* languages that helps differentiate SM from the silent period. In the silent period the child stops speaking because the child is in a linguistically different setting, and the child is not proficient enough in the second language to communicate. As a result, the child stops speaking and focuses on comprehension strategies. This same child placed in a setting in which the native language is spoken will speak the language he or she is fluent in. In contrast, the child with SM does not speak, regardless of the language being used in that setting, because of the anxiety he or she is experiencing (Elizalde-Utnick, 2003).

The Importance of Early Intervention

While many cases of SM in young children improve over time, shyness and anxiety may persist for several years (Freeman et al., 2004). However, some children do not improve when left to their own accord. According to Bergman and colleagues (2002), intervention is preferable to waiting for the child to speak. Freeman and colleagues (2004) suggest that children with symptoms lasting more than six months be evaluated and treated. Powell and Dalley (1999) describe persistent SM as occurring chronically for more than six months. Bergman and colleagues (2002) note that, "while persistent mutism may be related to more severe impairment, even a relatively short period of selective mutism may negatively impact functioning" (p. 940). The authors add that SM may be symptomatic of social anxiety and therefore needs intervention before the disorder worsens or other problems develop (e.g., low self-esteem, social phobia, school phobia).

Classroom Implications

SM interferes with school functioning and can be quite challenging and frustrating for school personnel. The inability to speak interferes with the ability to function in the classroom setting, including effective social interaction with peers and adults (Bergman et al., 2002; Dow, Sonies, Scheib, Moss, & Leonard, 1999;

Elizalde-Utnick, 2003). Typical school behaviors include: mutism, standing or sitting motionless and expressionless, staring into space when asked a question, heightened sensitivity to sensory input, difficulty with social routines involving expressive language, and difficulty with eye contact. Some children with SM may manifest noncompliant, manipulative behavior (Krohn, Weckstein, & Wright, 1992), although such behavior is considered secondary to anxiety (Dummit et al., 1996, 1997; Freeman et al., 2004; Wright, Cuccaro, Leonhardt, Kendall, & Anderson, 1995).

Since children with SM suffer from social anxiety (Black & Uhde, 1995; Yeganeh et al., 2003), it is critical that these children receive interventions that target the social anxiety. With ELLs, it is important to consider the language of instruction as well as the language used to implement the intervention, particularly since the process of making sense of a new linguistic environment can be anxiety-provoking (Elizalde-Utnick, 2006; Toppelberg et al., 2005). In addition to treating the social anxiety, it is equally critical to address the communicative behavior. The following section discusses intervention strategies that decrease social anxiety as well as increase communicative behavior.

School-Based Intervention Strategies

A multidisciplinary, school-based approach to treatment of children with SM is very effective (Dow et al., 1999). In order for an intervention to be effective, there needs to be collaboration between the school psychologist, family, classroom teacher, and other school personnel (Elizalde-Utnick, 2002). Preschool settings are ideal for developing and implementing intervention plans based on home-school collaboration, as parental involvement is greatest during the earlier years (Eccles & Harold, 1996).

The overall goal of a school-based intervention plan for treating SM is to decrease anxiety associated with speaking while encouraging the child to interact and communicate (Dow et al., 1999). When developing a comprehensive intervention plan for the selectively mute ELLs, the following should be incorporated: (a) consultation with family and school personnel; (b) determination of language(s) of intervention; (c) behavioral strategies for decreasing social anxiety and increasing communicative behavior; (d) individual and group counseling; and (e) strategies for fostering skill and comfort with the second language, English. Lopez (1995) notes that there needs to be on-going monitoring of interventions in order to determine their effectiveness and need for modifications.

Consultation with Families and School Personnel

School psychologists are in the position to be a bridge between the home and school (Elizalde-Utnick, 2002). The consultative process can enhance awareness

of the difficulties children with SM have across settings. In particular, it is critical to determine the hierarchy of individuals with whom the child speaks and the
conditions in which the child speaks or does not speak. Through the consultative
process, the school psychologist can also bridge the cultures of diverse families
and the culture of the school (Elizalde-Utnick, 2007). To do this, the school psychologist engages in a two-way process of information sharing and understanding. As consultants, school psychologists already engage in this two-way
communication process (Elizalde-Utnick, 2002). In addition to consulting with
families, school psychologists should consult with school personnel who work
with ELL preschoolers with SM. As a result, school professionals could learn to
alleviate the anxiety the young child with SM experiences, as well as to help maximize the learning potential of a given environment (e.g., classroom, counseling
session).

Language(s) of Intervention

Elizalde-Utnick (2007) suggests that the following factors need to be considered when selecting the language of intervention for the young ELL: (a) child's
proficiency in the first and second languages, (b) parent's preference and the
child's comfort level in each language, (c) nature of the child's disability, and (d)
availability of programs and bilingual personnel. It should be noted that a bilingual preschool class provides a special, nurturing environment for young ELLs.
However, if a bilingual classroom is unavailable, then a language-rich environment is a helpful alternative since it provides opportunities to verbally interact
with others and acquire skills in English (Tabors, 1997).

Behavioral Interventions

Behavioral interventions have been found to be very effective in treating SM
in children (Holmbeck & Lavigne, 1999; Porjes, 1999) and are considered the
first and primary intervention (Freeman et al., 2004). To this end, a behavior modification plan needs to be developed for the school setting. While it is time-
consuming and requires collaboration between family, teachers, and other school
professionals, it is quite effective in treating SM (Krysanski, 2003). Elizalde-
Utnick (2003) has used a two-prong approach to developing school-based behavioral interventions for preschoolers with selective mutism: 1) contingency
management techniques, which serve to increase communicative behavior; and 2)
exposure-based techniques, which serve to decrease social anxiety.

Contingency management involves the use of positive consequences in order
to increase the frequency of speech. Initially, communicative behavior, and ultimately speech are rewarded (Porjes, 1999). Contingency management incorporates several strategies: a) positive reinforcement, b) shaping, and c) stimulus

fading. With positive reinforcement, rewards are provided, contingent on the presence of some communicative behavior, in order to increase the frequency of speech. Rewards can vary in type, such as tangible rewards (stickers, stars, stamps, toys, edibles), social rewards (verbal recognition, verbal praise, first in line, note home, phone call home), and activities (spend time with teacher, read a story, feed class pet, use computer, bring toy to school). Furthermore, the reward system can be utilized across school settings (i.e., classroom and therapy sessions). For example, a whispered response can be reinforced with praise and a token; and the tokens can be traded in for prizes (Elizalde-Utnick, 2003, 2006).

The behavioral plan should also include shaping procedures, as there is a gradual building up of speech by reinforcing successive approximations (Elizalde-Utnick, 2003, 2006; Porjes, 1999). In other words, interactive and communicative behaviors (e.g., eye contact, hand raising) are reinforced initially, but eventually only speech is rewarded. For instance, mouth movements that increasingly approximate speech are reinforced until true speech is achieved. A sample hierarchy of communicative behaviors follows: 1) raising one's hand, 2) mouthing a single word, 3) whispering a single word, 4) whispering a phrase or sentence, and 5) speaking in an increasingly audible voice.

It should be noted that children with SM typically experience what Lysne (1999) describes as the "start barrier." The child with SM often worries about the first responding moment (i.e., anxiety related to the reaction of others when the child finally speaks) (Elizalde-Utnick, 2003; Lysne). The start barrier consists of this worrying and is described as "intrapsychic resistance to start speaking" (Lysne, 1999, p.83), which includes resistance to give up the role as the non-responding child. To overcome the start barrier, it is critical that a trusting relationship with an adult be established.

In addition to shaping, stimulus fading procedures are introduced once the child feels comfortable speaking in one school environment (e.g., the therapy room) (Elizalde-Utnick, 2003, 2006; Porjes, 1999). An attempt is made to generalize speech to other individuals or environments. In this procedure, stimuli from the safe environment are gradually faded out, while stimuli from the feared environment are faded in. One strategy that has been used in the research literature is to establish speech by having the caregiver(s) present in a neutral space where speaking is most likely to occur (e.g., therapist's office, away from the classroom) (Holmbeck & Lavigne, 1999). Then, the stimulus fading progresses gradually to situations that successively approximate the setting where speech is least likely to occur (i.e., the classroom). For example, the child can be rewarded when speaking to the mother in the therapist's presence. Next, the child could be rewarded when speaking to the therapist in the mother's presence. The next step would be to reward the child when speaking alone with the therapist. Subsequently, the child would be rewarded when speaking with the same therapist in another setting (e.g., another office). Then the teacher can be brought in and the child is rewarded for speaking with the therapist and the child's teacher. Finally, the child can be rewarded when speaking with one or two classmates.

In addition to contingency management procedures (i.e., positive reinforcement, shaping, stimulus fading) which help increase communicative behavior, exposure-based approaches should be implemented to decrease the anxiety surrounding speaking in school (Elizalde-Utnick, 2003, 2006; Freeman et al., 2004). Exposure-based approaches incorporate desensitization techniques in conjunction with alternative coping strategies (e.g., relaxation, presence of a trusted adult) (Freeman et al.). The child's environment is modified in such a way so that the child experiences a reduction in anxiety. As the child feels increasingly more relaxed in the presence of a trusted adult, the child is gradually exposed to increasingly anxiety-provoking situations. In preschool classrooms, the following anxiety hierarchy applies: 1) one-to-one interaction between the child and a trusted adult, 2) the child working with same adult and a peer, 3) the child working in small groups, 4) the child working in increasingly larger groups (Elizalde-Utnick, 2003).

Counseling Interventions

In addition to behavioral interventions both in and out of the classroom, children with SM benefit greatly from school-based counseling (Elizalde-Utnick, 2003, 2006b). The goals of counseling consist of: 1) decreasing the child's fear, including being able to identify such fear, 2) lowering anxiety, 3) increasing self-esteem, and 4) increasing confidence in social settings. The counseling sessions allow for practicing real-life scenarios so as to decrease social inhibition.

Initially, the sessions should be conducted individually. In order to facilitate talking, the parent(s) can be included in the sessions; over time, the parent(s) should be weaned. Once progress has been made between the child and the therapist on an individual basis, another child can be introduced (for the purpose of desensitization). Ultimately, "push-in" sessions (that is, the therapist working in the classroom with the child) can help generalize progress to the classroom.

Counseling is also effective for addressing the "start barrier" (Lysne, 1999). The child has an opportunity to discuss fears related to the first responding moment in the classroom and feelings about giving up the role as the non-speaking child. It should be noted that some children with SM think their voice sounds funny and that they may say the wrong thing (Dow, et al., 1999). Weckstein, Krohn, and Wright describe the use of counseling as a means of desensitization: "through role-playing and imagining what it might be like to talk" in the classroom, the child can experience a reduction in anxiety (1999, p. 243). Children's books related to SM and public speaking are also helpful resources when discussing the start barrier with the child (Elizalde-Utnick, 2003).

Elizalde-Utnick (2003) points out that the gender of the therapist should be considered when selecting therapists. It has been the author's experience that female preschoolers who are selectively mute respond better to female therapists. That is not to say that male therapists might not be just as effective. However, the critical variable is providing an environment in which the child feels comfortable, and, at times, the gender of adults makes a difference.

With ELLs, a bilingual therapist is critical (Elizalde-Utnick, 2003). There is extensive literature documenting the importance of providing counseling in the native language (Pérez Foster, 1998). Javier and Munoz (1993) found that bilinguals' languages influence the recollection of experiences. Discussing experiences in the same language that events were experienced in results in more vivid and more detailed descriptions compared with such discussions occurring in a different language (not the language used during the original event being discussed). Furthermore, Javier (1989) emphasized that when counseling ELLs, giving them a choice of language provides them with a coping mechanism when under psychic distress. In other words, use of a given language can bring one closer to one's feelings. However, with painful feelings and memories, the bilingual client might choose to speak in a language that provides more psychological distance from such feelings and memories, and this can sometimes be accomplished using the second language (Pérez Foster, 1998).

With young children, the primary language used at home is typically the child's "emotional language" or the language from which the young child derives comfort (Elizalde-Utnick, 2003). An interesting phenomenon of childhood bilingualism is the person-language bond (Fantini, 1978). Young children often attach a particular language to a person. If that person addresses the child in the other language, it may cause some distress and the child might pretend to not understand what is being said. Given the salience of language in the life of the young ELL, it is critical to provide the opportunity to use the various languages in the child's repertoire during counseling. In addition, given the heightened anxiety level of ELLs with SM, providing a linguistic environment in which anxiety is reduced helps foster a therapeutic alliance (Elizalde-Utnick, 2003). A case example that will be discussed will illustrate this.

Classroom Interventions to Promote Skill and Comfort with the Second Language

The increased incidence of SM in ELLs (Steinhausen & Juzi, 1996; Toppelberg et al., 2005) compared with monolinguals points to the importance of addressing second language acquisition processes when striving to reduce the anxiety experienced by such children in school. Elizalde-Utnick (2007) recommends that school professionals consider the following when differentiating instruction for young ELLs: (a) organization of the classroom, (b) communication strategies, and (c) instructional strategies.

Organization of the classroom. The preschool classroom should have "safe havens"; that is, there should be activities (e.g., manipulatives such as building blocks, legos, puzzles, playdough) available that allow ELLs to pursue an activity without requiring verbal interaction (Elizalde-Utnick, 2007). Such safe havens help to decrease anxiety because the ELLs do not have to ask anyone for help or negotiate play with other children. Eventually, when they are ready, the ELLs move into the rest of the classroom activities.

In addition to providing safe havens, classroom routines should be implemented in ways that are sensitive to the ELL's needs (Elizalde-Utnick, 2007). Such routines are typical of the preschool classroom (e.g., daily schedule of arrival, circle time, free play, clean-up, snack time, gym time) and allow ELLs to pick up cues as to what to do next. A visual display of the schedule with pictures is very helpful not only for the ELL but also for helping to alleviate anxiety in the child with SM, as the need for verbal interaction is minimized.

Communication strategies. A number of strategies can be used to foster ELL preschoolers' learning in the classroom. ELLs need time to become familiar and comfortable with the classroom and a new cultural and linguistic setting before being approached with questions and directives in English. Tabors (1997) emphasized the notion of buttressing communication, reiteration, and repetition when speaking to the young child in the second language. Buttressing communication involves using words together with some type of gesture, action, or directed gaze. With reiteration, the teacher restates a message in a form that is more understandable. Repetition involves the teacher repeating his/her statements in order to facilitate understanding in young ELLs. For example, teachers can re-read and re-tell particular stories (Morrow, 2005). Brice (2002) recommends that ELLs be allowed to switch between languages with bilingual peers in the classroom because it "will allow students to practice speaking and transition into using English at their readiness level" (p. 139).

Instructional strategies. As is true for young children in general, ELLs benefit from experiences that include: (a) hands-on activities, (b) literacy activities, (c) circle time, and (d) playground/gym (Tabors, 1997). Hands-on activities promote the acquisition of vocabulary and conceptual knowledge as well as social interaction. Such acquisition of language skills is enhanced further when the preschool teacher provides a "running commentary," which entails explaining his/her actions and the actions of others as an activity occurs (Tabors). ELLs also benefit from being paired with other ELLs as well as with English speakers (Kagan & McGroarty, 1993). Pairing ELLs with English-speaking "buddies" helps to decrease their isolation and to foster the development of English as a second language (Ovando, Collier, & Combs, 2003).

Case Example

Miguel was a bilingual (Spanish/English) four-year-old boy with moderately severe SM attending a special education preschool. He was initially referred to the Preschool Committee on Special Education (CPSE) by his pediatrician who was concerned about his delayed speech and language development. The bilingual evaluations reported that Miguel, a Spanish-dominant child (although skills in English were present), exhibited delays in cognitive functioning and speech and language development. As a result, he was placed in a center-based, half-day (two-and-one-half hours per day, five days per week) program where he received special instruction and speech therapy.

A closer inspection of the evaluation reports revealed that Miguel had not spoken during the evaluation, and therefore, his expressive language and pragmatic development could not be directly assessed. Instead, the evaluators relied on parent report and assumptions. Whereas nonverbal reasoning was found within the average range of cognitive functioning, there was scatter in terms of his verbal comprehension. Pre-academic skills were also delayed. Expressive language could not be assessed. Whether or not this child truly qualified for placement in a center-based program was unclear. Nevertheless, he was a child with SM who could greatly benefit from a language-rich preschool setting. Miguel was not placed into a bilingual classroom, as the special educator spoke only English. However, the two teaching assistants working in the classroom were fluent Spanish speakers. There was a total of 12 children in the class.

As Miguel's presenting problem was a cognitive and speech/language delay, counseling services were not offered at the time the individualized education plan (IEP) was developed. The school team working with Miguel perceived him as an extremely shy child "who would eventually come out of his shell." When the other school psychologist (monolingual English) consulted with the author regarding Miguel, the author raised the possibility of SM. After several observations, administration of Achenbach's Caregiver-Teacher Report Form, and consultation with the school team (teacher, teaching assistants, therapists) and the family, the diagnosis of SM was made. On the Achenbach, Miguel's Internalizing score was clinically significant, as were his Anxious/Depressed and Withdrawn scores. Children with SM typically earn such scores on this measure (Bergman et al., 2002). Bilingual counseling was recommended and the CPSE approved individual counseling for one session (30 minutes) weekly. Due to the limited time allotted for counseling, the author (who provided the bilingual counseling) spent additional time each week in the classroom, working with Miguel both individually and in small groups.

Background Information

Miguel's parents were born and raised in a South American country and immigrated to the United States a year before Miguel's birth. Spanish was the primary language spoken in the home. Miguel's parents were monolingual Spanish; however, English was spoken to Miguel by his 10-year-old sister, who had learned English in school.

Family history was significant for Miguel as his mother was selectively mute as a child. Miguel's mother suffered from a severe form of SM and she did not begin talking in school until 15 years of age. Unlike her son, she never received any intervention for her disorder. As an adult she continued to suffer from anxiety and a mild form of social phobia. Although she would attend school meetings when requested of her, she was quite soft-spoken during these meetings and did not speak in a spontaneous manner. Miguel's father reportedly did not suffer from an anxiety disorder, nor was there any history of an anxiety disorder in his family.

Miguel's medical and developmental history was uneventful, with the exception of the SM. At home with his immediate family, Miguel was quite boisterous and loud. However, when extended family visited on weekends, he was described as "muy timido" (very shy) and was often compared to his mother, who had been very similar to Miguel as a child. Outside of the home, Miguel never spoke in front of others, even with his mother beside him.

Miguel behaved similarly at school. In the English-speaking classroom, Miguel was mute, but he exhibited nonverbal communication. He would indicate yes/no with a head nod/shake, and he would point when asked to make a choice. He had recently begun to vocalize (sighs, grunts) during the speech therapy sessions around the same time that individual counseling was introduced. Miguel met the DSM-IV criteria for SM. He was not undergoing the silent period, as he was somewhat skilled in English by the time counseling was introduced.

School-Based Intervention Plan

A school-based intervention plan was developed for Miguel. In addition to the individual counseling, an instructional intervention plan was created for implementation in the classroom as well as in the speech therapy sessions. The instructional plan incorporated both contingency management and exposure-based techniques. A communicative behavior hierarchy was established as well. In order to familiarize Miguel with the reinforcement system, the first behaviors listed were the head nod/shake – behaviors already present in his response repertoire. Beginning with an already existing behavior served to decrease the anxiety associated with verbal communication. The next behaviors on the response hierarchy were as follows: whisper yes/no, whisper other single words, whisper a sentence, and speak in an audible (louder) voice.

With respect to exposure-based approaches, these behaviors were to be shaped initially using one-to-one interactions (teaching assistant and Miguel). The teaching assistant, rather than the head teacher, was selected because Miguel seemed more comfortable with the teaching assistant. Over time, the shaping occurred within the context of a small group (teaching assistant, Miguel, and another child). Eventually it occurred in increasingly larger groups. The speech therapist used a similar shaping schedule during the speech therapy sessions.

The plan utilized the teacher's already existing classroom management system, whereby the children earned tokens (balloon-shaped cards) for appropriate behaviors targeted to each child (e.g., sharing with peer; completing a task; asking to play with a toy rather than snatching). For Miguel, his rewards were made contingent on communicative behavior. Each time a child earned a balloon, the child taped it onto a poster of a bear holding a bunch of large balloons. Each large balloon on the poster was personalized for each child. In this way, the act of filling up the large balloon with little balloons served as a visual cue and incentive to earn more balloons or tokens. The children accumulated balloons throughout the week and each Friday earned prizes that they selected from the prize bin.

The author met with the class team on a monthly basis to monitor progress and fine-tune the plan. Whenever needed, the team met more frequently if it was determined that progress was made and the behavior to be reinforced should be changed prior to the next scheduled meeting.

Counseling Sessions

During the first counseling session, Miguel was asked, in Spanish, which language – Spanish or English – would he prefer the therapist to speak in. The therapist (the author) had not expected him to respond, given his school behaviors thus far. He whispered, "Español." From that point on, Miguel whispered consistently in Spanish when he was asked a question; he did not yet volunteer a verbal response. It should be noted that because Miguel was bilingual and possessed skills in English, all of his other services were provided in English. This was the first time that he had been given the opportunity to respond in Spanish. His behavior was consistent with the clinical literature (see Pérez Foster, 1998) that indicates that providing counseling in the native language is critical for ELLs. It has been the author's experience with selectively mute ELLs that a therapeutic alliance is readily established when the therapist uses the child's emotional language – the primary language of the home.

During the first two months of counseling, Miguel continued whispering in Spanish, although only on demand. He still did not offer any spontaneous verbalizations. Around the time that he began laughing aloud (he used to laugh silently) in counseling, he started to crack a smile in the classroom. By the third month of counseling, Miguel began speaking on his own, mainly to make requests regarding play activities. This is when the "start barrier" was discussed. Miguel described his fear of others' reactions to hearing his voice for the first time. He had grown accustomed to hearing the other children inform newcomers to the classroom that "Miguel does not talk – he's shy." When asked if he wanted to eventually talk, he would nod his head. Reading children's books about selectively mute children and shyness proved helpful; he asked that the same books be read each session.

Soon after he began speaking on his own during the counseling sessions, Miguel began to whisper in English with the speech therapist (who was mono lingual English) and to laugh aloud for the first time in the classroom. One month later, the whispering generalized to the classroom. Interestingly, the counseling dynamic changed abruptly at that point. Miguel demanded that English be used exclusively. Whenever the author attempted to use Spanish, Miguel would shake his head and answer in English. From that moment on, only English was spoken in the sessions. It seemed that when Miguel was mute in the classroom he needed to hear Spanish, his preferred language at the time, a language which was his emotional language. As his anxiety decreased and he overcame the "start barrier," he preferred to use the classroom language – English (also the language used by his sister). The language of his parents provided a safety net when Miguel felt anxious, but as he became comfortable with the classroom language, he needed to speak that language in all settings, including in counseling.

There came a point in counseling when Miguel seemed quite at ease and no more progress could be made in the individualized setting. The sessions were continued in the classroom in an effort to assist in moving him from whispering to providing voiced responses (stimulus fading). At first, he seemed to regress in the author's presence. He did not want to interact with her in the classroom. When alone in the therapy room, Miguel revealed that he wanted to continue coming to this room and did not like that he had to remain in the classroom. As a result, the author and Miguel arrived at an agreement: The initial half of the session was conducted in the classroom, and the second half continued in the therapy room. Miguel responded favorably to this modification. The following week he began whispering to the author in the classroom setting. Several weeks later he progressed to voicing a response to yes/no questions posed by both the author and the teaching assistant. At this point, the school year was drawing to a close and there was not enough time left to work on providing voiced responses to the teacher. Post-treatment scores on the Achenbach demonstrated improvement. Overall Internalizing scores improved, as assessed by the author in the counseling sessions as well as by the teacher. Both the Anxious/Depressed and Withdrawn scores, based on the counseling sessions were now in the normal range. In terms of the classroom scores based on the teacher's ratings, the Anxious/Depressed score now fell within the normal range, whereas the Withdrawn score was in the borderline clinical range.

While Miguel had improved greatly, he had not yet achieved full-voice responses in the classroom. Unfortunately, Miguel had aged out of the preschool program and could not continue working with the school team. He was registered in a general education kindergarten class with counseling and speech services. A report of his progress along with the school-based intervention plan was sent to his school in September. In addition, the author spoke with his teacher and the school psychologist to go over the plan and strategies that helped during the previous year. The school psychologist indicated that he would work with Miguel and the school team to continue with what had been conducted at the preschool.

A follow-up interview with the mother and Miguel revealed that despite some initial regression at the beginning of kindergarten, the gains made the previous year continued. By mid-year of kindergarten, Miguel was whispering to the teacher, and by the end of the year he was speaking using an audible voice. While he continued to be a shy child, he nevertheless seemed to learn how to cope with his anxiety, as demonstrated by his volunteering to answer questions in front of the whole kindergarten class. Miguel told the author that he becomes nervous as soon as he is called on by the teacher, but quickly added that he is proud of himself when he gives the correct answer and everyone can hear him. With that statement, Miguel's mother told him how proud she was with him. Miguel's mother understood Miguel's achievement, particularly since she did not speak in school until the age of 15.

Conclusions

School-based interventions for preschoolers with SM are very effective. Behavioral classroom interventions in conjunction with school-based counseling allow for a gradual building of speech within the school setting. The shaping procedures utilized with Miguel provided a structure for eliciting increasing approximations of fully-voiced responses. It is critical that modifications aimed at reducing anxiety were implemented in the classroom; the desensitization that occurred in both the classroom and during counseling seemed to be a key variable in Miguel's progress. As demonstrated in Miguel's case, his progress along the response hierarchy was quicker in the individualized settings – counseling, speech therapy, and one-on-one interaction with the teaching assistant. Furthermore, as suggested in the case, the language used in counseling makes a difference when working with selectively mute ELLs.

While the case of Miguel supports previous work on the efficacy of behavioral interventions with selectively mute children (Dow et al., 1999; Krysanski, 2003), more systematic research is needed on school-based interventions. Furthermore, most of the research has been conducted on school-aged children, and very little is known about preschoolers with SM as well as ELLs who are selectively mute.

References

American Psychiatric Association. (2000). *Diagnostic and statistical manual of mental disorders* (4th ed., Text Revision). Washington, DC: Author.

Anstendig, K. D. (1998). Selective mutism: A review of the treatment literature by modality from 1980-1996. *Psychotherapy, 35,* 381-390.

Anstendig, K. D. (1999). Is selective mutism an anxiety disorder? Rethinking its DSM-IV classification. *Journal of Anxiety Disorders, 13,* 417-434.

Atoynatas, T. (1986). Elective mutism: Involvement of the mother in treatment of the child. *Child Psychiatry and Human Development, 17,* 15-17.

Bergman, R. L., Piacentini, J., & McCracken, J. T. (2002). Prevalence and description of selective mutism in a school-based sample. *Journal of the American Academy of Child and Adolescent Psychiatry, 41(8),* 938-946.

Black, B., & Uhde, T. W. (1995). Psychiatric characteristics of children with mutism: A pilot study. *Journal of the American Academy of Child and Adolescent Psychiatry, 34,* 847-856.

Brice, A. E. (2002). *The Hispanic child: Speech, language, culture and education.* Boston: Allyn & Bacon.

Dow, S. P., Sonies, B. C., Scheib, D., Moss, S. E., & Leonard, H. L. (1999). Practical guidelines for the assessment and treatment of selective mutism. In S. A. Spasaro & C. E. Schaefer (Eds.), *Refusal to speak: Treatment of selective mutism in children* (pp. 19-44). Lanham, MD: Rowman & Littlefield Publishers, Inc.

Dummit, E. S., Klein, R. G., Tancer, N. K., Asche, B., & Martin, J. (1996). Fluoxetine treatment of children with selective mutism: An open trial. *Journal of the American Academy of Child and Adolescent Psychiatry, 35(5),* 615-621.

Dummit, E. S., Klein, R. G., Tancer, N. K., Asche, B., Martin, J., & Fairbanks, J. A. (1997). Systematic assessment of 50 children with selective mutism. *Journal of the American Academy of Child and Adolescent Psychiatry, 36(5),* 653-660.

Eccles, J. S., & Harold, R. D. (1996). Family involvement in children's and adolescents' schooling. In A. Booth & J. F. Dunn (Eds.), *Family-school links: How do they affect educational outcomes?* (pp. 3-34). Mahwah, NJ: Erlbaum.

Elizalde-Utnick, G. (2002). Best practices in building partnerships with families. In A. Thomas & J. Grimes (Eds.), *Best practices in school psychology IV* (pp. 413-429). Washington, DC: National Association of School Psychologists.

Elizalde-Utnick, G. (2003, April). *Selective mutism and English language learners.* Paper presented at the meeting of the Long Island ESOL Conference, Rockville Centre, NY.

Elizalde-Utnick, G. (2006a). Culturally and linguistically diverse preschool children. In G. B. Esquivel, E. C. Lopez, & S. Nahari (Eds.), *Handbook of multicultural school psychology* (pp. 497-525). NY: Erlbaum Publishers.

Elizalde-Utnick, G. (2006, August). *School-based interventions with selectively mute English language learners.* Poster session presented at the annual meeting of the American Psychological Association, New Orleans, LA.

Elizur, Y., & Perednik, R. (2003). Prevalence and description of selective mutism in immigrant and native families: A controlled study. *Journal of the American Academy of Child and Adolescent Psychiatry, 42(12),* 1451-1459.

Fantini, A. (1978). Bilingual behavior and social cues: Case studies of two bilingual children. In M. Paradis (Ed.), *Aspects of bilingualism* (pp. 283-301). Columbus, SC: Hornbeam Press.

Freeman, J. B., Garcia, A. M., Miller, L. M., Dow, S. P., & Leonard, H. L. (2004). Selective mutism. In T. L. Morris & J. S. March (Eds.), *Anxiety disorders in children and adolescents* (2nd ed.) (pp. 280-301). NY: The Guilford Press.

Grosjean, F. (1982). *Life with two languages: An introduction to bilingualism.* Cambridge, MA: Harvard University Press.

Hayden, T. (1980). Classification of elective mutism. *Journal of the American Academy of Child & Adolescent Psychiatry, 19,* 118-133.

Holmbeck, G. N., & Lavigne, J. V. (1999). Combining self-modeling and stimulus fading in the treatment of an electively mute child. In S. A. Spasaro & C. E. Schaefer (Eds.), *Refusal to speak: Treatment of selective mutism in children* (pp. 91-108). Lanham, MD: Rowman & Littlefield Publishers, Inc.

Javier, R. A. (1989). Linguistic considerations in the treatment of bilinguals. *Journal of Psychoanalytic Psychology, 6,* 87-96.

Javier, R. A., & Munoz, M. A. (1993). Autobiographical memory in bilinguals. *Journal of Psycholinguistic Research, 22,* 319-338.

Kagan, S. & McGroarty, M. (1993). Principles of cooperative learning for language and content gains. In D. D. Holt (Ed.), *Cooperative learning: A response to linguistic and cultural diversity* (pp. 47-66). McHenry, IL: Delta Systems.

Kehle, T. J., Madaus, M. R., Baratta, V. S., & Bray, M. A. (1998). Augmented self-modeling as a treatment for children with selective mutism. *Journal of School Psychology, 36,* 247-260.

Kristensen, H. (2000). Selective mutism and comorbidity with developmental disorders/delay, anxiety disorder, and elimination disorder. *Journal of the American Academy of Child and Adolescent Psychiatry, 39(2),* 249-256.

Kristensen, H., & Torgersen, S. (2001). MCMI-II personality traits in parents of children with selective mutism: A case-control study. *Journal of Abnormal Psychology, 110(4),* 648-652.

Krohn, D. D., Weckstein, S. M., & Wright, H. L. (1992). A study of the effectiveness of a specific treatment for elective mutism. *Journal of the American Academy of Child & Adolescent Psychiatry, 31,* 711-718.

Krysanski, V. L. (2003). A brief review of selective mutism literature. *The Journal of Psychology, 137(1),* 29-40.

Lysne, A. (1999). Elective mutism: Special treatment of a special case. In S. A. Spasaro, & C. E. Schaefer (Eds.), *Refusal to speak: Treatment of selective mutism in children* (pp. 83-90). Lanham, MD: Rowman & Littlefield Publishers, Inc.

Lopez, E. C. (1995). Best practices in working with bilingual children. In A. Thomas & J. Grimes (Eds.), *Best practices in school psychology III* (pp. 1111-1121). Washington, DC: National Association of School Psychologists.

Meyers, S. V. (1999). Elective mutism in children: A family systems approach. In S. A. Spasaro & C. E. Schaefer (Eds.), *Refusal to speak: Treatment of selective mutism in children* (pp. 195-207). Lanham, MD: Rowman & Littlefield Publishers, Inc.

Morrow, L. M. (2005). *Literacy development in the early years: Helping children read and write* (5th ed.). Boston: Allyn & Bacon.

Ovando, C. J., Collier, V. P., & Combs, M. C. (2003). *Bilingual and ESL classrooms: Teaching in multicultural contexts* (3rd ed.). Boston: McGraw-Hill.

Pérez Foster, R. (1998). *The power of language in the clinical process: Assessing and treating the bilingual person.* Northvale, NJ: Jason Aronson, Inc.

Porjes, M. D. (1999). Intervention with the selectively mute child. In S. A. Spasaro & C. E. Schaefer (Eds.), *Refusal to speak: Treatment of selective mutism in children* (pp. 65-82). Lanham, MD: Rowman & Littlefield Publishers, Inc.

Powell, S., & Dalley, M. (1999). When to intervene in selective mutism: The multimodal treatment of a case of persistent selective mutism. In S. A. Spasaro & C. E. Schaefer (Eds.), *Refusal to speak: Treatment of selective mutism in children* (pp. 45-61). Lanham, MD: Rowman & Littlefield Publishers, Inc.

Porjes, M. D. (1999). Intervention with the selectively mute child. In S. A. Spasaro & C. E. Schaefer (Eds.), *Refusal to speak: Treatment of selec-

tive mutism in children (pp. 65-82). Lanham, MD: Rowman & Littlefield Publishers, Inc.

Schwartz, R. H., & Shipon-Blum, E. (2005). "Shy" child? Don't overlook selective mutism: Recognize this social anxiety disorder and treat it early to help prevent long-term dysfunction. *Contemporary Pediatrics, 22(7),* 30-35.

Shamir-Essakow, G., Ungerer, J. A., & Rapee, R. M. (2005). Attachment, behavioral inhibition, and anxiety in preschool children. *Journal of Abnormal Child Psychology, 33(2),* 131-143.

Shipon-Blum, E. (February 2002). "When the words just won't come out" – Understanding selective mutism. *Communiqué, 30* (5, insert).

Stein, M. B., Chavira, D. A., & Jang, K. L. (2001). Bringing up bashful baby: Developmental pathways to social phobia. *Psychiatric Clinics of North America, 24,* 661-675.

Steinhausen, H. C., & Juzi, C. (1996). Elective mutism: An analysis of 100 cases. *Journal of the American Academy of Child and Adolescent Psychiatry, 35(5),* 606-614.

Tabors, P. O. (1997). *One child, two languages: A guide for preschool educators of children learning English as a second language.* Baltimore: Paul H. Brookes.

Toppelberg, C.O., Snow, C., & Tager-Flusberg, H. (1999). Severe developmental disorders and bilingualism. *Journal of the American Academy of Child and Adolescent Psychiatry, 38(9),* 1197-1199.

Toppelberg, C. O., Tabors, P., Coggins, A., Lum, K., & Burger, C. (2005). Differential diagnosis of selective mutism in bilingual children. *Journal of the American Academy of Child and Adolescent Psychiatry, 44(6),* 592-595.

Weckstein, S. M., Krohn, D. D., & Wright, H. L. (1999). Elective mutism. In S. A. Spasaro & C. E. Schaefer (Eds.), *Refusal to speak: Treatment of selective mutism in children* (pp. 233-264). Lanham, MD: Rowman & Littlefield Publishers, Inc.

Wright, H. H., Cuccaro, M. L., Leonhardt, T. V., Kendall, D. F., & Anderson, J. H. (1995). Case study: Fluoxetine in the multimodal treatment of a preschool child with selective mutism. *Journal of the American Academy of Child and Adolescent Psychiatry, 34(7),* 857-862.

Yeganeh, R., Beidel, D. C., Turner, S. M., Pina, A. A., & Silverman, W. K. (2003). Clinical distinctions between selective mutism and social phobia: An investigation of childhood psychopathology. *Journal of the American Academy of Child and Adolescent Psychiatry, 42(9),* 1069-1075.

Mothers' Dependent and Self-Critical Depressive Experience is Related to Speech Content with Infants

Tammy Kaminer
Private Practice, New York City

Beatrice Beebe & Joseph Jaffe
New York State Psychiatric Institute & College of
Physicians and Surgeons, Columbia University

Kristen Kelly
Pennsylvania State University, State College

Lisa Marquette
Franklin Township, Board of Education

The relationships among maternal depressive experience, maternal speech content, and infant gaze at 4 months were examined in a community, non-clinical sample of 87 mother-infant dyads at 4 months postpartum. Depression was assessed using the Center for Epidemiologic Studies-Depression Scale (CES-D), which taps depressive symptoms, and the Depressive Experiences Questionnaire (DEQ), which assesses vulnerability to dependent and self-critical depressive experience. Maternal speech was related to DEQ dependent and self-critical depressive experiences but not to CES-D depressive symptoms. When infant gaze was controlled, dependent mothers used a greater amount of infant-focused speech and self-critical mothers used a greater amount of critical and less positive speech. When the DEQ variables were used in interaction with infant gaze, dependent and self-critical mothers verbally acknowledged infant Agency/Action more under the stress of interacting with a less visually available infant, suggesting difficulty in supporting infant exploration and agency separate from mother. Maternal speech content to infants is affected by dependent and self-critical depressive experiences.

All correspondence should be addressed to Beatrice Beebe, New York State Psychiatric Institute #108, 1051 Riverside Drive, New York, NY 10032. Electronic mail may be sent to beebebe@pi.cpmc.columbia.edu.

Maternal depression is associated with negative consequences for mother-infant interaction and infant development regardless of whether depression is defined by clinician-based diagnosis or by self-report (Gitlin & Pasnau, 1989; Murray & Cooper, 1997). Depressed mothers are more withdrawn, less contingent on infant behavior, more intrusive, less playful, and more negative than non-depressed mothers. Infants of depressed mothers are less positive, more distressed, less active, and more gaze averted (see for example Cohn, Campbell, Matias, & Hopkins, 1990; Cohn & Tronick, 1989; Field, 1995; Murray, Kempton, Woolgar, & Hooper, 1993).

However, depression is not a unitary phenomenon. Two important profiles of maternal interactive disturbance have been identified: (a) "disengaged," characterized by low levels of interaction and positive behavior, and associated with more infant protest; and (b) "intrusive," characterized by high levels of rough, angry behaviors and low levels of positive behavior, and associated with more infant gaze aversion (Cohn & Tronick, 1989; Field, 1995). Disengaged mothers improve after training in attention-getting techniques, while intrusive mothers do so after learning imitation strategies (Malphurs et al., 1996).

Most of the above work measured depression with a symptom approach based on self-report, clinical diagnostic interviews, or both. In this study, a different approach to measuring depression and its subtypes is utilized. A well-developed adult literature on personality characteristics mediating depression and interactive difficulties has remained separate from that on maternal depression and mother-infant interaction (Blatt, Quinlan, Chevron, McDonald, & Zuroff, 1982). This study applies Blatt's assessment of depression and compares it to a self-report symptom approach, the Center for Epidemiological Studies-Depression Scale (CES-D), in examining the impact of maternal depression on mother-infant interaction.

The Depressive Experiences Questionnaire (DEQ), a reliable, well-validated instrument (Blatt, D'Afflitti, & Quinlan, 1979; Blatt et al., 1982), measures two configurations of vulnerability to depressive experience: (a) Dependency, excessive concern with maintenance of interpersonal relatedness; and (b) Self-Criticism, excessive concern with achievement of self-defining goals. The two personality configurations are distinct in terms of triggering events, the nature of depressive experience, and associated interpersonal behavior (Alden & Bieling, 1996; Blaney & Kutcher, 1991; Coyne & Whiffen, 1995).

The excessive focus of dependent individuals on relatedness results in a selective vulnerability to depressive experience in response to ruptures in important relationships. Dependent individuals are less psychologically reflective and are likely to express dysphoria in somatic complaints. They avoid offending others for fear of losing support and their sense of well being. When separated from significant others they are more likely to experience distress; when challenged with the task of regulating negative affect they are less likely to spend time alone (Blatt, Hart, Quinlan, Leadbeater, & Auerbach, 1992; Blatt & Zuroff, 1992; Fichman, Koestner, Zuroff, & Gordon, 1999; Mongrain & Zuroff, 1989).

The excessive focus of self-critical individuals on self-definition results in a selective vulnerability to depressive experience in response to achievement failures. Self-critical individuals exhibit excessive personal demands for accomplishment and control and experience relentless self-criticism and inferiority when depressed. They exhibit more negative reactions during conflict resolution and tend toward a hostile, controlling interpersonal style and harsh criticism of others. They are less likely to turn to others for emotional support (Aube & Whiffen, 1996; Blatt & Zuroff, 1992; Mongrain & Zuroff, 1989; Zuroff & Fitzpatrick, 1995).

This approach, that links personality, depression, and adult-adult interaction, is likely to be useful in differentiating depressed mothers' interactive difficulties with their infants. According to Blatt and colleagues (1976), difficulty in maintaining a balance between pursuit of relational and self-defining goals is the vulnerability predisposing an individual to depressive experiences and interactive difficulty. Providing care for an infant presents many challenges to maintaining the balance between protecting and nurturing an infant, and pursuing other roles such as wife, employee, and friend. For mothers with difficulty balancing relational and self-defining goals, depressive affect may be triggered and interactive difficulties with the infant may emerge. Although parenting has been shown to be affected by excessive concerns with relatedness and self-definition in studies of parental attitudes and behavior with adolescents (Thompson & Zuroff, 1999), and the capacity of new mothers to obtain social support (Priel & Besser, 2000; Thompson & Zuroff, 1998), to date no study has examined mothers' Dependency and Self-Criticism in relation to mother-infant interaction.

Mother-infant play was chosen for study because it is the social conversational context for the infant, and 4-month-olds are capable of robust participation (Jaffe, Beebe, Feldstein, Crown, & Jasnow, 2001; Stern, 1985; Tronick, 1989). Depression is known to disturb mother-infant play, with consequences for infant development (Field, 1995; Murray & Cooper, 1997). Furthermore, this face-to-face context is analogous to situations used in DEQ studies on depression and adult-adult interaction. Additionally, face-to-face play with the infant in a laboratory setting is likely to trigger interactive difficulties for mothers focused excessively on either relational or self-defining goals. Infant gaze aversion, a frequent occurrence for all infants during face-to-face play, would likely be experienced by dependent mothers as an instance of relational loss, and by self-critical mothers as an instance of failure in mastery of the mothering role.

A modified version of Murray, Kempton, Woolgar and Hooper's (1993) maternal speech content coding system was used to measure maternal interaction with the infant. This system assesses three aspects of maternal speech: (a) Focus: concern with experience of the mother, the child, or another person; (b) Affect:

negative vs. positive; and (c) Recognition of Agency: verbal acknowledgment of ongoing infant activity. These features of speech tap the types of interpersonal difficulties associated with Dependency and Self-Criticism. Murray et al. showed that the speech of postpartum depressed mothers was more negative, somewhat less likely to include acknowledgment of infant agency, and, with male infants, less likely to include infant-focused utterances. Furthermore, mothers' greater use of infant-focused speech predicted better child cognitive performance at 18 months (Murray et al.). In a later study, Murray, Fiori-Cowley, Hooper, and Cooper (1996) reported that these speech patterns of depressed mothers are associated with an immediate increase in the rate of infant "breaks in ongoing activity," in which infants suddenly interrupt their ongoing behavior.

Assessing Maternal Speech Content: Predictions for Maternal Dependency, Self-Criticism and Depressive Symptoms

Hypothesis 1. Dependency

Hypothesis 1a: Increased maternal dependency is associated with higher levels of speech focused on infant experience, and lower levels focused on the mother's own experience. Rationale: Dependent individuals focus excessively on partners. Hypothesis 1b: Increased maternal dependency is associated with higher levels of positive/complimentary speech, and lower levels of negative/critical speech. Rationale: Dependent individuals avoid angering others for fear of loss of contact. Hypothesis 1c: Increased dependency is associated with increased recognition of infant physiological and emotional states (requiring maternal caretaking and interaction), and decreased recognition of intentional infant actions (which highlight the infant's emerging capacities for separateness). Rationale: Dependent individuals have difficulty with establishing a separate identity; increased dependency compromises the mother's ability to show recognition of her infant as a separate person by acknowledging infant agency.

Hypothesis 2. Self-Criticism

Hypothesis 2a: Increased maternal Self-Criticism is associated with more speech focused on the mother's own experience, and less focused on the infant's experience. Rationale: Self-critical individuals are overly invested in their own accomplishments and control. Hypothesis 2b: Increased maternal Self-Criticism is associated with more negative/critical speech and less positive/complimentary speech. Rationale: Self-critical individuals tend toward a hostile, controlling interpersonal style. Hypothesis 2c: Increased maternal Self-Criticism is associated with increased recognition of infant intentional actions, representing first steps toward independent functioning, and decreased recognition of infant physiological and emotional states, which call for greater maternal intimacy. Rationale: Self-critical individuals are invested in establishing competence and gaining respect, and they have lowered tolerance for intimacy.

Hypothesis 3. Depressive Symptoms

Hypothesis 3a: Increased depressive symptoms (CES-D) are associated with more speech focused on maternal experience and less on infant experience. Rationale: Depression is associated with high levels of self-focused attention (Ingram, 1990), and in mothers, with increased intrusiveness and a decreased tendency to use speech focused on the infant (Cohn & Tronick, 1989; Field, 1995; Murray et al., 1993). Hypothesis 3b: Increased depressive symptoms are associated with more negative/critical maternal speech, and less positive/complimentary speech. Rationale: Maternal depressive symptoms are associated with increased anger, negative behaviors, tone of voice, and speech; and decreased positive affect, play, compliments, and empathic responses (Cohn et al., 1990; Cohn & Tronick, 1989; Field, 1995; Murray et al., 1993, 1996). Hypothesis 3c: Higher depressive symptoms are associated with a decreased ability to recognize infant agency. Rationale: Maternal depression is associated with a decreased tendency to recognize infant intentional behavior (Feldman & Reznick, 1996) and to acknowledge infant agency verbally (Murray et al., 1993).

The Infant's Interactive Contribution: Decreased Infant Visual Engagement

We anticipated that the influence of maternal depressive experience on maternal speech would be intensified under the stressful interactive condition of decreased infant visual availability. Infant gaze aversion might represent an unwanted loss of contact by dependent mothers, who are vulnerable to depression with disruptions in important relationships; or a failure to perform by self-critical mothers, who are vulnerable to disruptions in the achievement of important goals (Blatt & Zuroff, 1992). Lowered infant visual engagement is expected to intensify speech patterns characteristic of mothers high on depressive symptoms (CES-D) (Murray et al., 1996).

Based on the above, the following hypotheses were developed. Hypothesis 1d: Under high stress conditions of decreasing Infant Gaze, more dependent mothers will show increased Infant-Focused, Positive, and Agency/State speech, and decreased Mother-Centered, Negative, and Agency/Action speech. Hypothesis 2d: Under high stress conditions of decreasing Infant Gaze, more self-critical mothers will show increased Mother-Focused, Negative, and Agency/Action speech, and decreased Infant-Focused, Positive, and Agency/State speech. Hypothesis 3d: Under high stress conditions of decreasing

Infant Gaze, mothers with higher CES-D sores will show increased Mother-Focused and Negative Speech; and decreased Infant-Focused, Positive, Agency/State and Agency/Action Speech.

Method

This study is part of a larger project on maternal depression and mother-infant interaction in a community, non-clinical sample of 132 new mothers and their first-born infants.

Participants

Primiparous women delivering full-term, healthy, singleton infants without major complications, who had a telephone in the home, were at least 18 years old, and were married or living with a partner, were included in the sample. Mothers were asked to participate in a study of infant social development involving periodic phone calls and a lab filming session at 4 months postpartum. Subjects were included only if the videotape sound quality allowed transcription of maternal speech, resulting in 87 dyads with adequate sound. Of those 87, CES-D data were available for 86 dyads, and DEQ data were available for 77 dyads. The first 2.5 minutes of uninterrupted play was coded from the videotape. For a substantial number of the dyads ($n = 45$), some portion of the maternal speech was not sufficiently clear to code the verbal content. For example, the speech might be garbled, there might be interference, and there were some failures of the vocal channel. Rather than use a portion of what the mother said, dyads were only used if the entire 2.5 minutes was codable. To ensure that this did not skew the data, the samples with and without adequate sound were compared. There were no significant differences in the CES-D, DEQ Dependency, and DEQ Self-Criticism scores between the 87 participants (86 for CES-D, 77 for DEQ) and the 45 non-participants. Demographic data were available for 78 of the 87 dyads. Mean maternal age was 29.37 years ($SD = 6.63$). The highest level of maternal education included: 6.4% grade school, 7.7% high school, 24.4% some college, 30.8% completed college, and 30.8% graduate education. Maternal ethnicity data were available for 84 mothers: 54.8% White, 19.0% Black, and 26.2% Latina. Infant gender data were available for 86 dyads: 51 male and 35 female.

Procedure

At 4 months postpartum, dyads came to the laboratory for a 10-min video-recording of mother-infant face-to-face play. Mothers were instructed to play with their infants as they would at home. After filming, mothers completed the CES-D and the DEQ scales and provided demographic information.

Measures of maternal depression. The CES-D (Radloff, 1977) is a 20-item, 4-point scale used to assess depressive symptoms in the general population (Husaini, Neff, & Hurrington, 1980; Radloff). Inquiring about symptoms experienced in the previous week, the CES-D identifies current rather than chronic depression. Internal consistency is high, with alpha of 0.84 for the general population and split-half reliability coefficients ranging from 0.77 to 0.92 (Corcoran & Fisher, 1987). Convergent validity and sensitivity are also high (Gotlib & Cane, 1990).

The DEQ (Blatt et al., 1979) is a 66-item, 7-point scale that does not assess the primary symptoms of depression (Blatt et al., 1976, 1982), but rather taps vulnerability to two types of depressive experience, Dependency and Self-Criticism. Factor loadings reported in Blatt et al. (1976) for the female sample were used. Test-retest reliabilities for Dependency range from .89 (5 weeks) to .81 (13 weeks); and for Self-Criticism from .83 (5 weeks) to .75 (13 weeks) (Zuroff, Moskowitz, Wielgus, Powers, & Franko, 1983). Internal consistency (coefficient alpha) is .81 for Dependency and .80 for Self-Criticism (Blatt et al., 1982). Regarding construct validity, in clinical populations, Dependency and Self-Criticism are related to scores on the Beck Depression Inventory. In college populations, Dependency and Self-Criticism are associated with depressive affect (Zuroff & Mongrain, 1987). Dependency and Self-Criticism are also related in theoretically expected ways to self-concept, self-esteem, interpersonal behavior, descriptions of parents, and dysfunctional attitudes (Blatt et al., 1976, 1982; Mongrain & Zuroff, 1989; Zuroff et al.).

Videotape coding of maternal speech content and infant gaze. For each dyad, the first 2.5 minutes of uninterrupted play was coded for infant gaze and maternal speech. Coders were blind to maternal depression status. Infant gaze was coded second-by-second "on" and "off" mother's face (timing rules from Tronick & Weinberg, 1990). Kappas ranged from .68 - .97; mean kappa .83. A per dyad score of percentage infant gaze time on mother's face was created.

Transcripts were coded using a revised version of Murray et al.'s (1993) system, the Maternal Utterance Measure (MUM; see Table 1), differentiating Agency speech into Agency/Action-Acknowledging and Agency/State-Acknowledging. To improve reliability, several minor changes were made to streamline the measure, a coding manual was developed (Kaminer, 1999), and chance-corrected reliability estimates provided.

The MUM has five exhaustive and mutually exclusive primary categories, defined in the Appendix: (a) Infant-Focused speech, (b) Mother-Focused speech, (c) Other-Focused speech, (d) Contentless/Affective/ Verse-Song/Game, and (e) Greet/Call for Attention. Infant-Focused speech is further divided into: (a) No Agency, (b) Agency/Action-Acknowledging, and (c) Agency/State-Acknowledging. Mother-Focused speech is further divided into: (a) Self-Referential/ Neutral-Positive, (b) Negative (Corrections, Criticisms, and Self-Referential/

Table 1

Schematic Summary of Maternal Utterance Measure (MUM) Coding System

Infant-Focused[a]			Mother-Focused			Other-Focused	Contentless /Affective/ Verse-Song/ Game	Greet/Call for Attention
No Agency	Agency		Self-Referential/ Neutral-Positive	Negative (=Corrections+Criticisms & Self-Referential/Critical)	Directive(=Directives, Prompt Qs, &Self-Referential/ Demanding)			
	Action	State						

Positive

[a]see Appendix for definitions.

Critical), and (c) Directive (Directives, Prompt Questions, and Self-Referential/Demand for Attention). A secondary category, Positive speech, can be assigned to the primary category whenever relevant. The Appendix presents the coding system. Six MUM speech categories were analyzed: (a) Infant-Focused, (b) Mother-Focused, (c) Negative, (d) Positive, (e) Agency/Action-Acknowledging, and (f) Agency/State-Acknowledging.

Maternal speech was transcribed verbatim from videotape and coded utterance-by-utterance. Utterance boundaries were defined by pauses, intonation, and syntax. Occasional reference to videotape clips was required to clarify affective tone and ambiguous utterances. Reliability was established on 12 dyads not included in data analysis. To prevent coding drift, a second reliability check on five additional dyads was conducted. A total of 17 reliability dyads were used, representing 20% of the sample. Because some speech categories did not occur within all reliability dyads, several reliability calculations were based on fewer than 17 reliability dyads. For Infant-Focused speech, the initial Cohen's kappa was .80 (the second .90); Mother-Focused speech .82 (.86); Positive speech, .94 (1.00); Negative speech .86 (.95); Agency/Action-Acknowledging speech .89 (.88); and Agency/State-Acknowledging speech .91 (.85).

Statistical Analyses

Multiple regression analyses were used to examine the effects of maternal DEQ Dependency, DEQ Self-Criticism, and CES-D on maternal speech. Because of demographic heterogeneity, three maternal covariates were included in all analyses: ethnicity, education, and age. The two infant covariates included were gender and percentage of gaze time on mother.

To examine the role of infant gaze in interaction with maternal depression, a second multiple regression model examined the influence of Maternal Dependency X Infant Gaze; Self-Criticism X Infant Gaze; and CES-D X Infant Gaze on maternal speech, with three maternal covariates (i.e., ethnicity, education, age), and the infant covariate of gender. Alpha was set at .05. Since specific hypotheses were tested, significant individual variables are reported, even when the whole set may not be significant.

Since it was unexpected that the interaction of Dependency with Infant Gaze on Agency/Action speech would be similar to the interaction predicted for Self-Criticism with Infant Gaze, post-hoc qualitative analyses were conducted to answer the question: "Why do high Dependency and high Self-Criticism mothers use more action speech with low gaze infants?" To accomplish this task, transcripts and videotape clips of Agency/Action speech patterns were explored to identify differences between high Dependency and high Self-Criticism mothers, compared to low Dependency and low Self-Criticism mothers. Nine types of dyads were established using equal terciles (i.e., low-, mid-, and high-scoring) of DEQ mothers cross-referenced with equal terciles of infant gaze. The groupings of interest included: (a) low DEQ and low infant gaze, (b) low DEQ and high infant gaze, (c) high DEQ and low infant gaze, and (d) high DEQ and high infant gaze. The goal was to determine whether or not high Dependency mothers adjusted their use of Agency/Action speech in response to infant gaze levels for different reasons than did high Self-Criticism mothers. The adjustments in use of Agency/Action speech among low Dependency and low Self-Criticism mothers were also examined, as a standard against which to compare the Agency/Action speech usage of the high Dependency and high Self-Criticism mothers.

Results

Descriptive statistics and the relationships of Dependency and Self-Criticism to current depressive symptoms (CES-D) are first reported. We then evaluate the effects of the DEQ and CES-D scales on maternal speech. Each depression scale is evaluated to determine whether it accounts for maternal speech patterns independently, or in interaction with level of infant visual engagement. We predict that decreased infant gaze intensifies maternal depression effects on maternal speech.

Descriptive Statistics

The CES-D mean was 9.01 (*SD* = 9.10); DEQ Dependency mean was -0.89 (*SD* = 0.83); DEQ Self-Criticism mean was -0.77 (*SD* = 1.09). Unlike the CES-D, the DEQ has not been normed on a large representative sample. Dependency and Self-Criticism scales were moderately correlated (*r* = .30, *p* < .01). The CES-D was moderately correlated with Dependency (*r* = .25, *p* < .05) but highly correlated with Self-Criticism (*r* = .71, *p* < .01) (see Goodman, 1999).

Main Effects of Maternal Depression on Maternal Speech

The first stage of analyses examined the effects of each depression scale on maternal speech, with three maternal covariates (i.e., ethnicity, education, age) and two infant covariates (i.e., gender, percentage of gaze time on the mother). Findings are summarized in Table 2.

Effects of maternal dependency. For hypothesis 1 on the effects of maternal Dependency, only Hypothesis 1a was partially upheld. Increased Dependency was associated with increased Infant-focused speech (*p* = .05, in a positive direction, *pr* (partial correlation) = .25, ß = .26[1]). There was no association with Mother-focused speech.

Effects of maternal self-criticism. For Hypothesis 2 on the effects of maternal Self-Criticism, only Hypothesis 2b was upheld. Higher Self-Criticism was associated with increased maternal Negative speech (*p* = .018, in a positive direction, *pr* = .30, ß = .28[2]) and decreased Positive speech (*p* = .05, in a negative direction, *pr* = -.25, ß = -.24[3]).

Effects of depressive symptoms. Maternal CES-D scores were not related to any of the maternal speech categories (i.e., Hypotheses 3a-c).

---

[1] The total predictor set of maternal Dependency, three maternal covariates, and two infant covariates was not related to Infant-Focused speech (*p* = .26).

[2] The total predictor set of maternal Self-Criticism, three maternal covariates, and two infant covariates was related to Negative speech, *p* < .01.

[3] The total predictor set of maternal Self-Criticism, three maternal covariates, and two infant covariates was not related to Positive speech, *p* = .06.

Table 2

Summary of Hypotheses and Findings

	Focus	Affect	Agency
	Self vs. Other	Positive vs. Critical	Action vs. State
Dependency			
Hypotheses 1a, 1b, & 1c	Other	Positive	State
Result	Other*	NS	NS
Self-Critical			
Hypotheses 2a, 2b, & 2c	Self	Critical	Action
Result	NS	Critical*	NS
CES-D			
Hypotheses 3a, 3b, & 3c	Self	Critical	Less Agency
Result	NS	NS	NS
Under High Stress Conditions - Decreased Infant Gaze			
Dependency			
Hypotheses 1d	Other	Positive	State
Result	NS	NS	NS
Self-Critical			
Hypotheses 2d	Self	Critical	Action
Result	NS	NS	Action*
CES-D			
Hypotheses 3d	Self	Critical	Action
Result	NS	NS	NS

Note. * = Significant, NS = Not significant

Interaction Effects of Maternal Depression and Infant Gaze on Maternal Speech

In the second stage of analyses, instead of controlling for infant gaze, we used it as a predictor variable that may interact with maternal depression in predicting maternal speech. None of the predicted relationships of Hypothesis 1d were found for dependent mothers. Instead, Agency/Action speech was related to the Dependency X Infant Gaze variable in a negative direction, opposite that predicted (p = .014, pr = -.32, ß = -.69[4]). As Dependency scores increased, mothers became increasingly likely to use Agency/Action speech in response to lower gaze infants and vice-versa.

One of the predicted relationships of Hypothesis 2d for maternal Self-Criticism was upheld. The percentage of Agency/Action speech was significantly related to the Self-Criticism X Infant gaze variable (p = .032, in a negative direction, pr = -.30, ß = -.72[5]). As Self-Criticism increased, mothers became increasingly likely to use Agency/Action speech in response to lower gaze infants and vice-versa. None of the predicted relationships of Hypothesis 3d were supported for mothers with more depressive symptoms (CES-D). The CES-D X Infant Gaze variable was not related to any of the maternal speech categories (Hypothesis 3d).

Exploratory Descriptive Analyses

As previously noted, it was unanticipated that the effects of maternal Dependency and Self-Criticism on Agency/Action speech would interact in a similar fashion with Infant Gaze. Transcripts and videotape clips of Agency/Action speech patterns were thus explored. However, all conclusions are highly tentative given the qualitative nature of the review, and small samples in each group.

Under high interactive stress (attempting to engage low gaze infants), statistical analyses (above) documented that both more dependent and self-critical mothers produced increases in Agency/Action speech. The qualitative review indicated that for both types of mothers, these increases reflected increased maternal concern with infant disengagement. For example, a mother might repeatedly ask "What are you looking at?", while her infant looked away. No differences were noted between the two types of mothers.

Under low interactive stress (attempting to engage high gaze infants), statistical analyses showed that both more dependent and self-critical mothers produced decreases in Agency/Action speech. Qualitative review indicated that instead of Agency/Action speech, both types of mothers were likely to mirror infant movements and vocalizations with similar affect and concern; for example, with laughter in response to infant vocalization, and "Are you tired?" as a response to infant stretching. In addition, Agency/Action speech decreased

---

[4] The total predictor set of maternal Dependency x Infant Gaze, three maternal covariates, and one infant covariate was related to Agency/Action speech, p < .01.

[5] The total predictor set of maternal Self-Criticism X Infant Gaze, three maternal covariates, and one infant covariate was related to Agency/Action speech, p = .01.

because mothers responded to infant movement and vocalization with criticism, warning, and re-direction, rather than Agency/Action commentary; for example, "You're gonna sit up? No. Why don't you sit back?" The latter pattern was particularly characteristic of self-critical mothers and the only one that distinguished dependent and self-critical mothers.

Mothers scoring low in depressive vulnerability followed different patterns. Under high interactive stress (attempting to engage low gaze infants), both less dependent and self-critical mothers produced decreases in Agency/Action speech (reported above). Qualitative review indicated that these mothers responded to infant gaze aversion with directive speech, rather than Agency/Action commentary, reflecting maternal efforts to convince the infant to display organized, skillful behavior; for example, "Why don't you talk? You talk so nicely at home."

Under low interactive stress (attempting to engage high gaze infants), both less dependent and self-critical mothers produced increases in Agency/Action speech (reported above). Qualitative review indicated that these increases reflected a burst of maternal pride and pleasure in emerging infant motor capacities; for example, "You're clapping," in response to movements bringing the hands together; "Are you bicycling?" in response to leg stretches; and "You're talking," in response to vocalizations. These qualitative assessments are presented as a possible basis for rigorous evaluation in future research.

Discussion

In addition to a standard self-report measure of depressive symptoms (CES-D), empirical tools from the adult personality and depression literature, Dependency and Self-Criticism measures, were used to examine the effects of maternal depressive experiences on maternal speech content in mother-infant interaction. The three measures of maternal depressive experience were related, similar to findings in the adult literature. Self-Criticism had a stronger association with the CES-D than Dependency, also consistent with adult literature (Blatt et al., 1982; Goodman, 1999; Mongrain & Zuroff, 1989). Despite these associations, in our study, the CES-D generated no significant findings, whereas the Dependency and Self-Criticism measures differentiated the Focus and Affect categories of maternal speech in predicted ways. Non-significant findings with the CES-D may be due to the fact that our group was a non-clinical sample. A possible explanation for the limited DEQ results is that prior DEQ studies have tended to examine college populations, whereas 83.8% of the women in this study had college or graduate education.

When the effects of maternal Dependency and Self-Criticism on maternal speech were examined controlling for infant gaze, increased Dependency was associated with increased Child-Centered speech, such as "There you go," "Are you still investigating?" and "You like it here." In contrast, increased Self-

Criticism was associated with fewer positive statements, such as "What's wrong, sweetie?" and "Such a handsome guy" and more negative statements, such as "Put your tongue in your mouth," and "We don't cry." Although these findings fit our predictions, the expected relationships between CES-D or DEQ with the third speech category, Agency, did not emerge. In Agency speech a mother recognizes her infant as an independent actor, with the intention and the capacity to organize behavior. Examples include "What can you see up there?" and "Are you still investigating?"

However, when effects of maternal Dependency and Self-Criticism on maternal speech were re-examined in interaction with the level of infant visual engagement, findings emerged for Agency/Action speech. As hypothesized, under the stress of interacting with a less visually available infant, more self-critical mothers used more Agency/Action speech. We reasoned that because these mothers prioritize achievement and self-control, they are likely to recognize and support their infants' intentional actions, even if the infant action is looking away. Reciprocally, less self-critical mothers used more Agency/Action speech as infant visual engagement increased.

Under the stress of interacting with a less visually available infant, we expected that dependent mothers' tendencies to use Agency/Action speech would decrease. We reasoned that, because these mothers have difficulty tolerating breaks in contact with significant partners, they might ignore their infants' intentional actions, viewing them as first steps toward separateness. Instead, dependent mothers were just like self-critical mothers: As infant visual engagement decreased, dependent mothers produced more Agency/Action speech. Thus, both self-critical and dependent mothers were more likely to comment on infant Agency/Action if their infants looked away more. Less self-critical and dependent mothers were both more likely to comment on infant Agency/Action if their infants looked at them more.

A post-hoc qualitative review of transcripts and videotape indicated that both high-scoring dependent and self-critical mothers were sensitive to the loss of infant visual engagement. It was at these moments, when the infants visually disengaged, that mothers commented on the infant's agency, for example, "What do you see?" Thus comments on infant agency were linked to infant visual disengagement. In contrast, less dependent and self-critical mothers acknowledged infant agency as part of the ongoing visual engagement. They commented on infant vocalizations, and trunk or limb movements. For example, when one infant brought her hands together, her mother commented, "Oh, you're clapping."

We speculate that infants of more dependent and self-critical mothers will eventually learn that their agency (as measured by our agency/action code) is interpreted by the mother as separate or away from her. In contrast, infants of less dependent and self-critical mothers will learn that their agency is endorsed by their mother as part of their ongoing visual engagement. Because these observations are entirely qualitative, they need empirical replication.

The Picture of Dependent Mothers and Their Infants

More dependent mothers, preoccupied with maintaining interpersonal relatedness, stayed more focused on their infants' experience. This focus is likely to support infant development, and it predicts better child cognitive performance at 18 months (Murray et al., 1993). This partner-focused orientation is consistent with previous adult research. For example, in relation to romantic partners, dependent women report greater feelings of love (Zuroff & Fitzpatrick, 1995) and exhibit positive biases during a conflict-resolution task (Mongrain, Vettese, Shuster, & Kendal, 1998). With their adolescent daughters, dependent mothers are supportive (Thompson & Zuroff, 1998).

However, this supportive picture is complicated by the findings of the qualitative review, which suggest that more dependent mothers tend to recognize infant agency/action with nervous concern, when it causes a break in visual contact. In contrast, less dependent mothers tend to respond to a range of infant agency/actions with proud commentary. We speculate that more dependent mothers may not be able to optimally support the infant's efforts to explore, particularly exploration visually separate from mother.

The Picture of Self-Critical Mothers and Their Infants

More self-critical mothers, preoccupied with achievement and self-definition, used more corrections and criticisms, and fewer compliments and terms of endearment, suggesting a tense, controlling relational environment, shown to have a negative impact on infant development (Murray et al., 1996). Our findings are consistent with previous adult DEQ research. For example, self-critical women report less satisfaction and more negative reactions with romantic partners (Zuroff & Duncan, 1999), and they use more commands and negative feedback when coaching adolescent daughters (Thompson & Zuroff, 1998). Similar to dependent mothers, self-critical mothers tend to recognize infant action when it causes breaks in visual contact, suggesting difficulty in supporting infant exploration and agency separate from mother.

Comparison with Murray et al. (1993)

This study partially replicates Murray et al.'s (1993) original study of maternal depression and maternal speech content. Murray et al. and the current study characterized the speech of mothers experiencing depression as more negative and less infant-focused (for male infants only in Murray et al.). Both studies found that depressed mothers were less likely to acknowledge infant agency through their speech content, but our results are somewhat more complex. The similarities in results were obtained with very different samples and methods of measuring depression. Our community sample was low-risk, and our DEQ measure of depression was self-report, based on personality characteristics rather than symptoms (with 18% of mothers classified in the depressed range of 16+ on the CES-D). The Murray et al. sample was clinical and 49% of the mothers received diagnoses of depression based on self-report as well as a follow-up standardized clinical interview.

In our study, the DEQ detected the effects of maternal depressive experiences on maternal speech and infant gaze, whereas the CES-D did not. Most likely we did not obtain the same associations as Murray et al. between depression and maternal speech content because we did not have a clinical sample. In addition, the DEQ may have been effective because it measures personality-based vulnerability to depressive experience, rather than current depressive symptoms. Thus the DEQ can identify individuals who are vulnerable to depressive experiences but not currently experiencing sufficient symptoms to score high on an instrument like the CES-D (Blatt et al., 1982; Blatt & Zuroff, 1992). Nevertheless, in other analyses of this sample, using other statistical methods, the CES-D was effective in differentiating action patterns (but not speech content) in depressed and nondepressed mothers (Beebe et al., in press).

Conclusion

Perhaps the hypotheses in this study were not more readily supported because depressive experience was assessed in a non-clinical sample with self-report measures. However, maternal postpartum depression is associated with infant difficulties when measured with both self-report and clinical approaches, in both community and high-risk samples (Beck, 1995; Gitlin & Pasnau, 1989; Murray & Cooper, 1997). The fact that a self-report measure of depression was used in a community sample is a potential strength of the study because (a) our study is comparable to the literature, where three-quarters of the studies use self-report measures of maternal depression (Beck, 1995); and (b) community samples are more reflective of difficulties in the general population. The fact that the current community sample turned out to be highly educated, and that this level of education was correlated with older maternal age, may be a limitation of the study. Field et al. (1988), for example, found that maternal depression was associated with younger maternal age. If the current sample had been younger and less educated, we may have found different associations.

This study is important, despite its mixed results, because the narrative level in mother-infant interaction is rarely explored. Instead, the procedural action dialogue is usually examined. Since we know so little about this aspect of the mother's functioning, any findings at the narrative level are potentially important. The narrative level rapidly becomes central as the child develops into the second year and will set the stage for the narrative between the mother and child as the child learns language.

The content of maternal speech is important to consider in early intervention, particularly mother-centered vs. infant-centered focus, and positive vs. negative affect. This work retrospectively validates Fraiberg's (1974) awareness of the clinical significance of speech content in baby games. Our findings imply that maternal support for infant exploration and agency, while visually separate from mother, may be important in early intervention efforts.

Further research is needed to explore the utility of the DEQ measures for mother-infant disturbance. Future research should explore whether a younger and less educated community sample might generate different findings. A specific testable hypothesis emerged from our qualitative exploration, that is, maternal acknowledgement of infant agency during infant visual gaze moments is more adaptive than such acknowledgement during infant gaze away moments.

References

Alden, L. E., & Bieling, P. J. (1996). Interpersonal convergence of personality constructs in dynamic and cognitive models of depression. *Journal of Research in Personality, 30,* 60-75.

Aube, J., & Whiffen, V. E. (1996). Depressive styles and social acuity: Further evidence for distinct interpersonal correlates of dependency and self-criticism. *Communication Research, 23,* 407-424.

Beck, C. (1995). The effects of postpartum depression on maternal-infant interaction: A meta-analysis. *Nursing Research, 44* (5), 298-304.

Beebe, B., Jaffe, J., Chen, H., Buck, K., Cohen, P., Feldstein, S., & Andrews, H. (in press). Six-week postpartum depressive symptoms predict 4-month mother-infant self- and interactive regulation. *Infant Mental Health Journal.*

Blaney, P. H., & Kutcher, G. S. (1991). Measures of depressive dimensions: Are they interchangeable? *Journal of Personality Assessment, 56,* 502-512.

Blatt, S. J., D'Afflitti, J. P., & Quinlan, D. M. (1976). Experiences of depression in normal young adults. *Journal of Abnormal Psychology, 85,* 383-389.

Blatt, S. J., D'Afflitti, J. P., & Quinlan, D. M. (1979). *Depressive Experiences Questionnaire.* Unpublished manuscript, Yale University, New Haven, CT.

Blatt, S. J., Hart, B., Quinlan, D. M., Leadbeater, B., & Auerbach, J. (1992). Interpersonal and self-critical dysphoria and behavior problems in adolescents. *Journal of Youth and Adolescence, 22,* 253-269.

Blatt, S. J., Quinlan, D. M., Chevron, E. S., McDonald, C., & Zuroff, D. (1982). Dependency and self-criticism: Psychological dimensions of depression. *Journal of Consulting and Clinical Psychology, 50,* 113-124.

Blatt, S. J., & Zuroff, D. C. (1992). Interpersonal relatedness and self-definition: Two prototypes for depression in normal young adults. *Clinical Psychology Review, 12,* 527-562.

Cohn, J. F., Campbell, S. B., Matias, R., & Hopkins, J. (1990). Face-to-face interactions of postpartum depressed and nondepressed mother-infant pairs at 2 months. *Developmental Psychology, 26,* 15-23.

Cohn, J. F., & Tronick, E. Z. (1989). Specificity of infants' response to mothers' affective behavior. *Journal of the American Academy of Child and Adolescent Psychiatry, 28,* 242-248.

Corcoran, K., & Fisher, J. (1987). *Measures for clinical practice: A sourcebook.* New York: The Free Press.

Coyne J. C., & Whiffen, V. E. (1995). Issues in personality as diathesis for depression: The case of sociotropy-dependency and autonomy-self-criticism. *Psychological Bulletin, 118,* 358-378.

Feldman, R., & Reznick, J. (1996). Maternal perception of infant intentionality at 4 and 8 months. *Infant Behavior and Development, 19,* 483-496.

Fichman, L., Koestner, R., Zuroff, D. C., & Gordon, L. (1999). Depressive styles and the regulation of negative affect: A daily experience study. *Cognitive Therapy and Research, 23,* 483-495.

Field, T. (1995). Infants of depressed mothers. *Infant Behavior and Development, 18,* 1-13.

Field, T., Healy, B., Goldstein, S., Bendell, D., Schanberg, S., Zimmerman, E., & Kuhn, C. (1988). Infants of depressed mothers show "depressed" behavior even with non-depressed adults. *Child Development, 59,* 1569-1579.

Fraiberg, S. (1974). The clinical dimension of baby games. *Journal of the American Society of Child Psychiatry, 13,* 202-220.

Gitlin, M. J., & Pasnau, R. O. (1989). Psychiatric syndromes linked to reproductive function in women: A review of current knowledge. *American Journal of Psychiatry, 146*(11), 1413-1422.

Goodman, P. (1999). *Postpartum distress and object relations: An empirical analysis.* Unpublished doctoral dissertation, Yeshiva University, New York.

Gotlib, I. H., & Cane, D. B. (1990). Self-report assessment of depression and anxiety. In P. Kendall & D. Watson (Eds.), *Anxiety and depression: Distinctive and overlapping features* (pp. 131-163). New York: Academic Press.

Husaini, B. A., Neff, T. A., & Hurrington, T. B. (1980). Depression in rural communities: Validating the CES-D Scale. *Journal of Community Psychology, 8,* 20-27.

Ingram, R. E. (1990). Self-focused attention in clinical disorders: Review and a conceptual model. *Psychological Bulletin, 107,* 156-176.

Jaffe, J., Beebe, B., Feldstein, S., Crown, C., & Jasnow, M. (2001). Rhythms of dialogue in infancy. *Monographs of the Society for Research in Child Development, 66* (2, Serial No. 265).

Kaminer, T. (1999). *Maternal depression, maternal speech, and infant gaze at four months.* Unpublished doctoral dissertation, St. John's University, New York.

Malphurs, J. E., Field, T. M., Larraine, C., Pickens, J., Pelaez-Nogueras, M., Yando, R., & Bendell, D. (1996). Altering withdrawn and intrusive interaction behaviors of depressed mothers. *Infant Mental Health Journal, 17,* 152-160.

Mongrain, M., Vettese, L. V., Shuster, B., & Kendal, N. (1998). Perceptual biases, affect, and behavior in the relationships of dependents and self-critics. *Journal of Personality and Social Psychology, 75,* 230-241.

Mongrain, M., & Zuroff, D. C. (1989). Cognitive vulnerability to depressed affect in dependent and self-critical college women. *Journal of Personality Disorders, 3,* 240-251.

Murray, L., & Cooper, P. J. (1997). The role of infant and maternal factors in postpartum depression, mother-infant interactions, and infant outcome. In L. Murray & P. J. Cooper (Eds.), *Postpartum depression and child development* (pp. 111-135). New York: The Guilford Press.

Murray, L., Fiori-Cowley, A., Hooper, R., & Cooper, P. (1996). The impact of postnatal depression and associated adversity on early mother-infant interactions and later infant outcome. *Child Development, 67,* 2512-2526.

Murray, L., Kempton, C., Woolgar, M., & Hooper, R. (1993). Depressed mothers' speech to their infants and its relation to infant gender and cognitive development. *Journal of Child Psychology and Psychiatry, 34,* 1083-1101.

Priel, B., & Besser, A. (2000). Dependency and self-criticism among first-time mothers: The roles of global and specific support. *Journal of Social & Clinical Psychology, 19*(4), 437-450.

Radloff, L. S. (1977). The CES-D scale: A self-report depression scale for research in the general population. *Applied Psychological Measurement, 1,* 385-401.

Stern, D. (1985). *The interpersonal world of the infant.* New York: Basic Books.

Thompson, R., & Zuroff, D. C. (1998). Dependent and self-critical mothers' responses to adolescent autonomy and competence. *Personality and Individual Differences, 24*, 311-324.

Thompson, R., & Zuroff, D. C. (1999). Development of self-criticism in adolescent girls: Roles of maternal dissatisfaction, maternal coldness, and insecure attachment. *Journal of Youth & Adolescence, 28*(2), 197-210.

Tronick, E. Z. (1989). Emotions and emotional communication in infants. *American Psychologist, 44*(2), 112-119.

Tronick, E. Z., & Weinberg, K. (1990*). Infant Regulatory Scoring System (IRSS).* Unpublished manuscript, The Child Development Unit, Children's Hospital, Boston.

Zuroff, D. C., & Duncan, N. (1999). Self-criticism and conflict resolution in romantic couples. *Canadian Journal of Behavioral Science, 31*(3), 137-149.

Zuroff, D. C., & Fitzpatrick, D. K. (1995). Depressive personality styles: Implications for adult attachment. *Personality and Individual Differences, 18*, 253-265.

Zuroff, D. C., & Mongrain, M. (1987). Dependency and self-criticism: Vulnerability factors for depressive affective states. *Journal of Abnormal Psychology, 96*, 14-22.

Zuroff, D. C., Moskowitz, D. S., Wielgus, M. S., Powers, T. A., & Franko, D. L. (1983). Construct validation of the dependency and self-criticism scales of the Depressive Experiences Questionnaire. *Journal of Research in Personality, 17*, 226-241.

Appendix

Coding the Maternal Utterance Measure (MUM)

Two coding passes are involved in using the MUM. In the first coding pass, the coder places each utterance in one of the five exhaustive and mutually exclusive primary categories: (a) Infant-Focused speech, (b) Mother-Focused speech, (c) Other-Focused speech, (d) Contentless/Affective/Verse-Song/Game, and (e) Greet/Call for Attention. In the second coding pass, the coder decides which utterances also meet criteria for the Positive speech category.

Because of the design of the coding system, Positive and Negative speech are not the inverse of one another. The Negative speech category is used when the mother's speech conveys criticism. Infant-Focused utterances cannot be coded as Negative because they are, by definition, neutral or positive in affective tone and <u>cannot</u> consist of criticism. Mother-Focused utterances can be coded as Negative because they are, by definition, neutral or negative in affective tone and <u>can</u> consist of criticism.

The Positive speech category is used whenever the mother compliments the infant or expresses affection through a term of endearment. It is assigned as a secondary code whenever these criteria are met, regardless of whether criticism is also conveyed. Thus, it is even possible for an utterance to be coded for both Negative and Positive speech. For example, "That's not a smile, sweetie", meets criteria for Negative speech because it is an example of a criticism, and meets criteria for Positive speech because it ends with a term of endearment.

<u>Five Primary MUM Speech Categories (exhaustive and mutually exclusive)</u>

1. <u>Infant-Focused Speech</u> – acknowledges infant's current state of attention and arousal, and reflects an attempt to engage infant by addressing his/her current experience. Utterances are coded in one of the two Agency sub-categories if the mother makes reference to a specific infant action or state, occurring in the moment.

   a. <u>No Agency</u>: *"There you go."*; *"You're a beautiful boy."*

   b. <u>Agency/Action-Acknowledging</u>: *"What can you see up there?"*; *"Are you still investigating?"*

   c. <u>Agency/State-Acknowledging</u>: *"You like it here."*; *"Are you tired?"*

2. <u>Mother-Focused Speech</u> – content is maternal assessments of her own experience with the infant, and requirements of him/her within the filming situation. Included are self-referential speech, neutral commentary; expressions of dissatisfaction with some aspect of the current situation with the infant, and wishes or intentions to change some aspect of the interaction.

   a. <u>Self Referential/Neutral-Positive</u>: *"My nose hurts too."*; *"You're my sweet heart."*

b. Negative Speech - all speech in which negative affect is expressed. Comprised of the following four sub-categories:
   (1) Corrections + Criticisms: *"Put your tongue in your mouth."; "Oh no, that's not a smile."*
   (2) Self-Referential/Critical of Infant: *"You're ignoring me again."; "We don't cry."*
   (3) Self-Referential/Critical of Self: *"I'm running out of conversation."*
   (4) Self-Referential/Critical of Other: *"I can't clap for you like I do at home."*
c. Directive Speech - speech in which mother becomes insistent on the infant accommodating her needs.
   (1) Directives: *"Sit up."; "Come on."*
   (2) Prompt Questions: *"You wanna play peek-a-boo?"; "Do you wanna sing?"*
   (3) Self-Referential/Demand for Attention: *"Talk to mommy."; "Can I have a smile?"*
3. Other-Focused Speech – content is objects or persons other than the infant or the mother; or focus is on the infant and/or mother; but removed in time. Examples: *"It's an interesting room."; "What would daddy think about this?"*
4. Contentless/Affective/Verse-Song/Game
5. Greet/Call for Attention – any greeting or calling of the infant's name.

Secondary Speech Category

Positive Speech – all speech in which positive and affectionate affect is expressed; comprised of compliments and terms of endearment. This speech category is distinct in that it is assigned as an additional code whenever relevant, and can be added to any primary code. Examples:
"What's wrong, sweetie?"; "Such a handsome guy."; "You're my sweetheart."; "We can't sing, honey."

Author's Note

We acknowledge the support of NIMH R01 MH 56130, the Koehler Foundation, the Edward Aldwell Fund; the assistance of Marc Glassman, Yehouda Soffer, Michelle Carfagna, and Alexandra Floratus in data coding and analysis; and the contributions of Michaela Hager-Budny, Elizabeth Helbraun, Shanee Stepakoff, Sandra Triggs Kano, Jill Putterman, Patricia Goodman, Lisa Marquette, Caroline Flaster, Lisa Nastasi in the collection of the sample. We owe special thanks to Donna Demetri-Friedman. We also thank Morris Eagle, Everett Waters, and Gary and Jenny Cox-Steiner of the Center for Mental Health Promotion.

Examining Attention Networks in Preschool Children Born with Very Low Birth Weights

Elizabeth H. Snyder
Department of Psychological and Brain Sciences
University of Louisville

Deborah Winders Davis
Department of Pediatrics
University of Louisville

Barbara M. Burns & Julia B. Robinson
Department of Psychological and Brain Sciences
University of Louisville

Reportedly, as many as 60% of very low birth weight (VLBW) children require some type of special education services and have school-related problems even in the absence of major disabilities. Attention problems may be associated with these poor academic outcomes, but more data are needed to identify specific attentional abilities that may differentiate these children from their normal birth weight (NBW) peers. The current study examined attentional abilities in the three attention networks identified by Posner and Petersen (1990) in children born with VLBW (n = 96) and children born with NBW (n = 67). Preschoolers performed three computerized tasks to assess orienting, vigilance, and executive attention networks. Results revealed significant differences between the groups on reaction times on all three attention network tasks. The current findings suggest that preschool-age VLBW children may have subtle, yet specific attention deficits compared to their NBW counterparts. Additional research is needed to better characterize the attention problems that may be specific to children born prematurely. Findings from such research would allow for earlier identification of these subtle attention deficits and the develop-

All correspondence should be addressed to Dr. Deborah Winders Davis, Neonatal Follow-up Program, 601 South Floyd Street, Suite 801, Louisville, Kentucky 40202. Electronic mail may be sent to dwdavis@louisville.edu.

ment of specific interventions to support optimal development of attention skills and school readiness in VLBW children before they fall behind in the classroom.

Children born prematurely are often at risk for cognitive and school-related problems (Botting, Powls, Cooke, & Marlow, 1998; Breslau & Chilcoat, 2000; Davis, Burns, Snyder, Dossett, & Wilkerson, 2004; Horwood, Mogridge, & Darlow, 1998; Marlow, Wolke, Bracewell, & Samara, 2005; Sykes et al., 1997; Taylor, Klein, Minich, & Hack, 2000; Whitfield, Grunau, & Holsti, 1997; Wolke & Meyer, 1999). It has been documented that as many as 60% of very low birth weight (VLBW; ≤ 1500 g) children require some type of special education services and have school-related problems even in the absence of major disabilities (Buck, Msall, Schisterman, Lyon, & Rogers, 2000; Hille et al., 2001; Saigal, Hoult, Streiner, Stoskopf, & Rosenbaum, 2000; Taylor et al., 2000; Wolke & Meyer, 1999). Studies aimed at identifying factors that may contribute to less than optimal academic performance have indicated that VLBW is associated with subtle deficits including general inattentiveness and attention problems, difficulty in shifting attention from one stimulus to another, and difficulty following directions (Breslau & Chilcoat; Davis et al., 2004; Emsley, Wardle, Sims, Chiswick, & D'Souza, 1998; Hoy, Bill, & Sykes, 1988; Teplin, Burchinal, Johnson-Martin, Humphry, & Kraybill, 1991).

Recently, Elgen, Lundervold, and Sommerfelt (2004) found that 25% of their sample of 11-year-old children who were born with low birth weight (LBW; < 2000 g) exhibited attention problems; however, only 7% met the criteria for a diagnosis of attention deficit/hyperactivity disorder (ADHD). This study supports the assertion by others that these subtle deficits in attention may remain unrecognized until after VLBW children have fallen behind their normal birth weight (NBW) peers in school (D'Agostino & Clifford, 1998). Thus, identification of such subtle attention problems, prior to school entry, in children born prematurely is of extreme importance.

However, researchers have had difficulties diagnosing specific attention problems in premature children during the preschool years (Saigal, Szatmari, & Rosenbaum, 1992; Sommerfelt, Troland, Ellertsen, & Markestad, 1996; Spiker, Kraemer, Constantine, & Bryant, 1992). While researchers have shown that children born prematurely differ from NBW children on a number of measures related to behavioral and cognitive functioning (Breslau & Chilcoat, 2000; Breslau, Chilcoat, Johnson, Andreski, & Lucia, 2000; Hack et al., 2002; Hack, Friedman, & Fanaroff, 1996; Halsey, Collin, & Anderson, 1996; Hille et al., 2001; Marlow et al., 2005; McGrath & Sullivan, 2002; O'Callaghan et al., 1996; Vohr et al., 2000; Whitfield et al., 1997; Wolke & Meyer, 1999), no consistent pattern of specific attention problems has been described. Attention problems are frequently described from parent and teacher reports that are often based on

ADHD diagnostic criteria. There is evidence suggesting that children born prematurely are at risk for ADHD and other psychiatric and behavior disorders (Horwood et al., 1998; Sommerfelt et al.; Sykes et al., 1997; Szatmari, Saigal, Rosenbaum, Campbell, & King, 1990). However, it has also been suggested that many children born prematurely may not meet the diagnostic criteria for ADHD, but may have unique attention deficits that differ in degree or in composition from that of ADHD (Davis, Burns, Snyder, & Robinson, in press; Elgen et al., 2004; Spiker et al.). Thus, it is evident that further research is needed in order to gain a better understanding of the exact nature and profile of these subtle attention deficits in young children born with VLBW.

Multiple advances in the area of cognitive neuroscience can provide new insights into the individual differences in developmental outcomes, especially those related to attentional abilities of children born prematurely (see also Rothbart, Posner, & Hershey, 1995). In particular, Posner and Petersen (1990) have identified three attention networks, each one having a specialized function and located in specific areas of the brain. Posner and Petersen's model has become the most referenced framework of attention development and functioning, and is based on both behavioral data and neurobiological and brain imaging data. Each network (orienting, executive, and vigilance) is related to specific attentional skills. The orienting network is responsible for focusing, shifting, and disengaging attention to a particular location. The vigilance network is responsible for the maintenance of an alert state and has been associated with ADHD (Posner & Petersen). The executive network is primarily responsible for goal-directed behavior, target detection, and spatial conflict resolution (Berger, Jones, Rothbart, & Posner, 2000).

The current study employed these new methods to examine possible differences in attentional abilities between children born with VLBW and those born with NBW. These methods were selected because they have been shown to be sensitive measures of subtle, but important, performance differences between normally developing children and other children who are at risk for attention problems (Chang & Burns, 2005; Snyder, Burns, & Davis, 2006). Performance differences in each of the three attention networks were examined in preschool-age children of VLBW and NBW. The goal of the current study was to provide a better understanding of specific attentional abilities in VLBW children that are believed to be important for cognitive outcomes and school success.

Method

Participants

Participants were 96 children who were born between 23 and 33 weeks of gestation and who weighed $\leq$ 1500 g at birth (VLBW) as well as a comparison group of children born at full-term ($n = 67$). All participating children were 4 or

5 years of age (range = 48 – 72 months rounded to the nearest month). As part of a larger study, the VLBW children and their parents were recruited through the high-risk neonatal follow-up programs at two large urban medical centers. All surviving children who were admitted to the neonatal intensive care unit and who met the inclusion criteria were asked to participate. Based on available data from the follow-up programs, only children who were free from major disabilities (i.e., diagnosed conditions or developmental delays, mental retardation, and sensory impairments) and whose birth weights had been appropriate for gestational age were included. Children who are small-for-gestational age have been shown to be at greater risk for poor developmental outcomes and the etiology may differ from that of other preterm infants. It is for those reasons that we did not include them in this study. In addition, parents were also asked before the session was scheduled if their child has any disabilities or limitations that might affect their performance on any or all of the tasks. Children in the comparison group (NBW) were recruited through a variety of community programs, schools, churches, and public agencies. Children were not included in the study if they scored below 75 on the Kaufman Brief Intelligence Test (K-BIT). For the preterm children, letters were sent to the parents of children who met the inclusion criteria. The parents returned a postcard if they wished to participate and were then contacted to schedule an appointment. The parents of NBW children responded to a flyer that was posted or sent home with their children. Parents received a stipend and the children received a small gift for their participation. All procedures were approved by the University Institutional Review Board at each institution and completed only after obtaining written parental consent.

The mean age of the children at testing was 61 months (SD = 6.3; range 48.00 – 72.00 months). The sample consisted of 55.2% females and 44.8% males with a racial composition as follows: 61.2% White, 29.1% African-American, and 8.5% of another race or biracial. Almost all of the parents had at least a high school education (97.6%). Demographic data for the two groups are presented in Table 1. The two groups of children did not significantly differ from each other on gender, race, or IQ (p > .05). However, significant differences in chronological age, $t(161)$ = 5.26, p < .01, and mother's education level were found, $t(160)$ = -3.06, p < .01. As such, child age and mother's education were used as covariates in all subsequent analyses.

Materials and Procedure

Children were assessed on three computerized attention tasks designed to assess performance on the three attention networks identified by Posner and Petersen (1990). These attention tasks were developed by Berger and colleagues in response to a lack of appropriate methodology to measure development in the three attention networks in young children (Berger et al., 2000). The current

Table 1

Demographic Information for the Participants (N = 163)

	Birth Weight Group	
Variable	VLBW (*n* = 96)	NBW (*n* = 67)
Mean Age in Months (SD)	63.3 (5.4)	58.4 (6.4)
Mean Birth Weight in Grams (SD)	1009.3 (261.9)	N/A
Mean Gestational Age in Weeks	27.75	N/A
Mean IQ Composite Score (SD)	100.6 (11.6)	102.5 (12.8)
Gender		
Female	55.2%	56.7%
Male	44.8%	43.3%
Race		
Black	19.8%	43.2%
White	70.8%	49.3%
Other	9.4%	7.5%
Maternal Education		
Less than High school degree	4.2%	0.0%
High school diploma	39.6%	11.9%
Vocational training		
or 1 year of college	6.3%	22.4%
College degree	38.6%	40.3%
Graduate/Professional degree	11.5%	23.9%

Note. VLBW = very low birth weight; NBW = normal birth weight.

attention tasks were based upon existing methodology suitable to measuring performance in the three attention networks for adults, but modified for use with toddler-age through school-age children. These tasks have been employed with typically developing children and hearing-impaired children from a wide range of ages, race/ethnicity, and socioeconomic backgrounds (Berger et al.; Chang & Burns, 2005; Mezzacappa, 2004; Snyder et al., 2006). The three tasks took a total of approximately 15 minutes to complete and consisted of an orienting task, a vigilance task, and an executive task (see Berger et al., 2000). The children were tested in a quiet room. All three attention tasks were run on a standard Pentium II computer with a 15" touch-screen monitor. Children sat in a chair located approximately 13 inches from the monitor. In order to control for the trajectory length of the reaching response, children were told to place their finger on a sticker in front of them between trials. For each task, reaction times (RT) in milliseconds (ms) and accuracy were automatically recorded into an ASCII data file. The session was videotaped. In a small percentage of the trials, contact between the child's finger and the touch-screen monitor was not detected. Using the videotapes, these trials were localized and deleted. A small number of trials were also identified and deleted when a child did not have his/her finger on the sticker in front of them at the start of each trial (i.e., a false alarm).

Orienting task. The orienting task was designed by Posner and colleagues to be analogous to a cuing paradigm for spatial orienting of attention (Posner & Rogers, 1978). The task was introduced to the children as a game in which they were asked to "feed the fish" as quickly as possible when a fish appeared in one of two fish bowls that appeared on the screen 10° to the left and 10° to the right of a central point on the touch-screen monitor.

Following a central fixation stimulus that appeared at the beginning of each trail, a cue consisting of a color change (from light blue to dark blue to light blue) in one of the fish bowls appeared. The cue lasted 500 ms, appeared in both fish bowls with equal chance, and was followed by the appearance of a fish in one of the bowls. The duration between the cue and the appearance of the fish was either 150 or 1000 ms (stimulus onset asynchrony, SOA) and the inter-trial interval was 1,000 ms. The fish remained visible for 5,000 ms or until the child touched it. The orienting task consisted of 3 practice and 32 test trials. There were 8 conditions (2 cue locations X 2 target locations X 2 SOA conditions).

Vigilance task. The vigilance task was a measure of the child's arousal system following an auditory warning signal. The task was introduced to the child as a game in which he/she was asked to "help the farmer catch the animals" by touching the animal's picture as quickly as possible after it appeared in the center of the screen.

The vigilance task consisted of 3 practice and 32 test trials. For half of the test trials, an auditory warning signal was presented at one of the following intervals before each target appeared: 400, 700, 1,200, or 2,700 ms. In order to measure the impact of the warning signal, reaction times during tone trials were compared to those during no-tone trials. In addition, the differences in reaction times for the different warning intervals were indicative of differences in phasic alertness. From target onset, the participant had 5,000 ms to respond before the next trial began. The inter-trial interval was 1,000 ms. In sum, there were 8 experimental conditions (tone/no tone X 4 intervals).

Executive task. The executive, or spatial conflict, task was designed to assess the executive network. In the task, the children were required to resolve a cognitive conflict between the location of the stimulus and the location of the response.

In other words, children had to pay attention to a stimulus in one spatial location, but respond to (touch) the opposite location. Following a central fixation cue at the start of each trial, two houses appeared on the left and right bottom corners of the screen. Each house contained a different picture. A picture that matched one of the two pictures contained in the houses then appeared randomly on either the left upper or right upper corner with equal chance. A compatible trial occurred when the picture and the "inside-the-house" picture were on corresponding sides of the screen. An incompatible trial occurred when the picture and the "inside-the-house" picture were on opposite sides of the screen. The child was asked to "help the picture find its home" by touching the corresponding house. There were 5 practice and 32 test trials. In sum, there were 2 conditions (compatible and incompatible trials).

Child cognitive ability. General cognitive ability was assessed using the Kaufman Brief Intelligence Test (K-BIT; Kaufman & Kaufman, 1990). The K-BIT is a commonly used, individually-administered screening measure of verbal and non-verbal intelligence that has been standardized for children and adults from 4 – 90 years of age. An overall score known as the K-BIT Composite was used as an indicator of the child's cognitive ability (IQ). Adequate reliability and validity have been reported, and concurrent validity was established by comparison with the WISC-R (Kaufman & Kaufman). Correction for degree of prematurity was not done because participants were 4-5 years of age. Although there is an ongoing debate regarding the issue of correcting for gestational age at birth, it is generally recommended that correction only continue until 3 years for the more immature children (Marlow, 2004), such as those born with VLBW.

Demographic data. A researcher-developed parent information questionnaire was used to obtain parent demographic information. Clinic records were used to obtain child demographic data such as birth weight and gestational age.

Results

Attention Network Tasks: Preliminary Analyses

Two measures from each task were used to indicate performance: median reaction times (MRT) for the correctly responded trials and percent correct (accuracy). The MRT and accuracy were calculated for each participant for each condition. The averaged MRT and accuracy from all three tasks were also added to create composite reaction time and accuracy scores. These were indicators of overall performance across the three tasks. Preliminary analyses were done to determine if demographic characteristics were related to the attention variables. The examination of gender showed that females and males did not significantly differ on overall MRT or overall accuracy ($p > .05$). No significant correlations were found between race or mother's educational level and overall MRT or accuracy (p > .05). Analyses revealed a significant negative correlation between children's age and overall MRT, $r(163)$ = -.177, p = .024, as well as significant correlations between children's IQ and overall MRT, $r(162)$ = -.164, p = .037, and overall accuracy, $r(162)$ = .300, p = .000. Therefore, in addition to children's chronological age and mothers' educational level, children's cognitive ability was also used as a covariate in all subsequent analyses.

Partial correlations between overall MRT and accuracy for VLBW children and NBW children demonstrated that there were significant negative correlations between MRT and accuracy (VLBW, $r(90)$ = -.56, p = .000; NBW, $r(61)$ = -.40, p = .001), and thus no evidence of speed-accuracy trade-offs. The MRT and accuracy for each participant in each condition were then separately analyzed as dependent variables using a univariate analysis of covariance (ANCOVA), with chronological age, mother's educational level, and IQ as covariates. The independent variable was birth weight group (VLBW and NBW).

Attention Network Task Accuracy

The NBW group, on average, completed the orienting, vigilance, and executive attention networks tasks with accuracy levels of 98.5%, 99.9%, and 93.2%, respectively, while the VLBW children, on average, completed the same tasks with 97.3%, 98.0%, and 91.1% accuracy. On the orienting task, VLBW children (M = 0.97, SE = 0.00) significantly differed from NBW children (M = 0.99, SE = 0.01) on accuracy, $F(1, 156)$ = 5.68, p = .018. Significant differences in accuracy on the vigilance task were also found between VLBW (M = 0.98, SE = 0.00) and NBW children (M = 0.99, SE = 0.00), $F(1, 156)$ = 4.95, p = .027. Lastly, the two birth weight groups did not differ in accuracy on the executive task (VLBW, M = 0.91, SE = 0.01; NBW, M = 0.94, SE = 0.02, p > .05). Although NBW children were found to have significantly better accuracy on the orienting and vigilance tasks, VLBW children still averaged above 95% in accuracy for both tasks.

Orienting Network Task: Median Reaction Time

MRT for the two groups of children did not significantly differ for the orienting network task (VLBW, M = 1148.77, SE = 24.12; NBW, M = 1080.04, SE = 29.58, p > .05). A 2 (valid cue, invalid cue) X 2 (SOA of 150 or 1,000 ms) repeated measure ANCOVA was also performed with age, mother's education, and IQ as covariates. There were no significant main effects for cue or SOA or a significant interaction between cue and group (p > .05). A significant interaction between SOA and group was found, $F(1, 154)$ = 11.38, p = .001 (see Figure 1). Although children with VLBW had slower MRT than NBW children on all trials, the MRT for the VLBW children was similar to the NBW children on trials where the SOA was 1,000 ms. Conversely, when the SOA was 150 ms, the NBW chil-

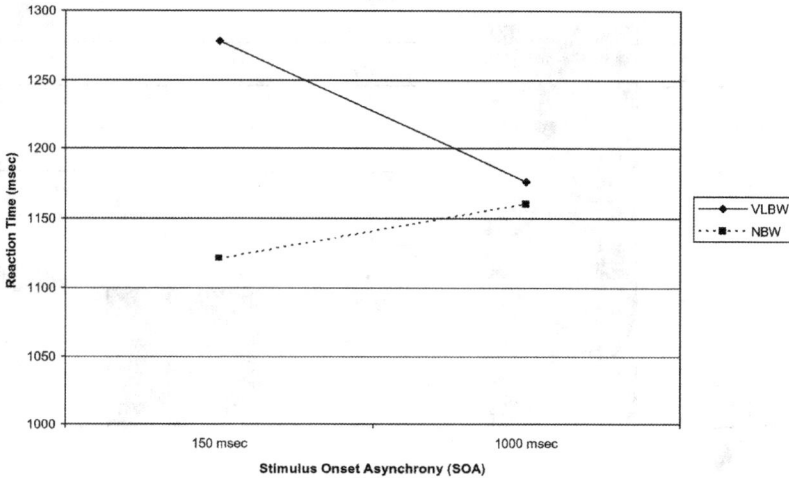

Note. N = 159 (*n* = 93 for VLBW; *n* = 66 for NBW). VLBW = very low birth weight; NBW = normal birth weight; ms = milliseconds.

Figure 1.   Speed on orienting attention network task by condition and birth weight group. Estimated marginal means for reaction times for two stimulus onset asynchrony (SOA) conditions (100 and 1000 ms) are presented. The two birth weight groups differed significantly after controlling for the effects of child age and IQ and mother's education, F (1, 154) = 11.38, p = .001.

dren were much faster than the VLBW children. In other words, when the VLBW children had more time to process the presentation of a visual cue, they performed in a manner similar to the NBW children. However, when the task demand required a more rapid response to the visual cue, the VLBW children, on average, were much slower to respond.

Vigilance Network Task: Median Reaction Time

For the vigilance network task, significant differences in reaction times were found between children with VLBW (M = 904.06, SE = 17.05) and children with NBW (M = 842.96, SE = 20.90), F(1, 156) = 4.60, p = .034 (see Figure 2). A 2 (tone, no tone) X 4 (400, 700, 1,200, or 2,700 ms intervals) ANCOVA was per-

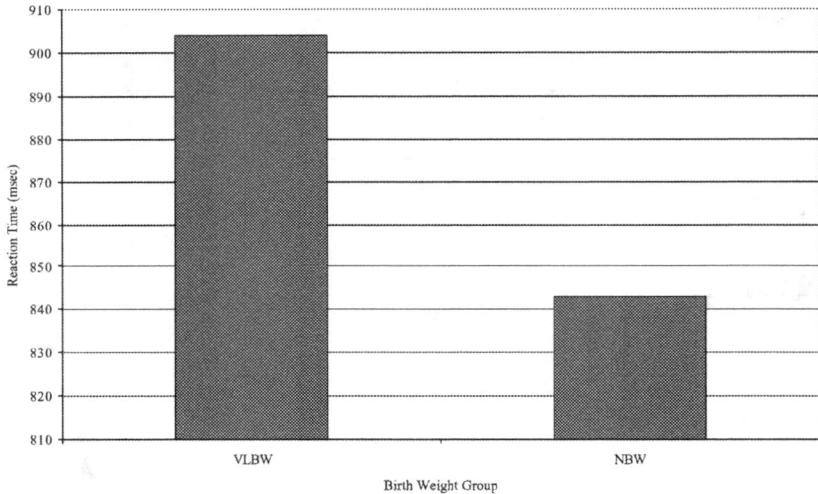

Note. N = 161 (*n* = 95 for VLBW; *n* = 66 for NBW). VLBW = very low birth weight;
NBW = normal birth weight; ms = milliseconds.
Standard errors (SE) = 17.5 for the VLBW group and 20.90 for the NBW group.

Figure 2.   Speed on vigilance attention network task by birth weight group. Estimated
marginal means for reaction times are presented. The two birth weight
groups differed significantly after controlling for the effects of child age
and IQ and mother's education, $F(1, 156) = 4.60$, $p = .034$.

formed with age, mother's education, and IQ as covariates. No significant main
effects for tone or interval were found ($p > .05$) and there were no significant
interactions between tone and group and interval ($p > .05$).

Executive Network Task: Median Reaction Time

For the spatial conflict task, significant differences in MRT were found
between VLBW children ($M = 1904.46$, $SE = 47.21$) and NBW children ($M = 1744.56$, $SE = 57.88$), $F(1, 156) = 4.11$, $p = .044$. A one-way repeated-measures
ANCOVA comparing compatible and incompatible trials with age, mother's edu-
cation and IQ as covariates was performed. Results showed no significant main
effect for spatial compatibility ($p > .05$), but a significant interaction was found
between compatibility and group, $F(1, 156) = 4.56$, $p = .034$ (see Figure 3).
Children with VLBW had slower MRT than children with NBW on both compat-

ible and incompatible trials. Both groups had slower MRT for the incompatible trials compared to the compatible trials. However, the VLBW children's MRT were significantly slower on the incompatible trials compared to those of the NBW children. In other words, both groups performed better when the picture and the "inside-the-house" picture were on corresponding sides of the screen; however, VLBW children performed much worse than NBW children when the picture and the "inside-the-house" picture were on opposite sides of the screen. Thus, VLBW children demonstrated much more difficulty than NBW children when asked to resolve a cognitive conflict.

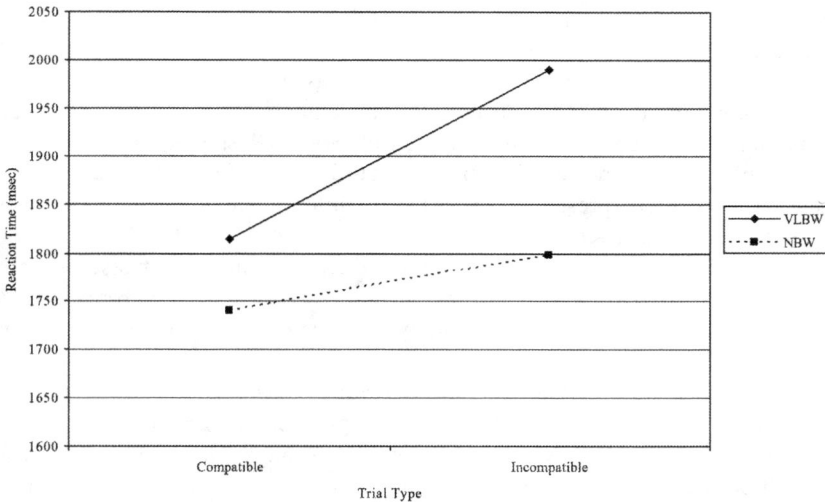

Note. N = 161 (*n* = 95 for VLBW; *n* = 66 for NBW). VLBW = very low birth weight; NBW = normal birth weight; ms = milliseconds.

Figure 3.   Speed on executive attention network task by condition and birth weight group. Estimated marginal means for reaction times for two stimulus types (compatible and incompatible) are presented. The two birth weight groups differed significantly after controlling for the effects of child age and IQ and mother's education, $F(1, 156) = 4.56, p = .034$.

Discussion

Research has consistently shown that children born prematurely are often at risk for cognitive and school-related problems, including higher rates of special education placement even in the absence of major disability (Botting et al., 1998; Breslau & Chilcoat, 2000; Buck et al., 2000; Davis et al., 2004; Horwood et al., 1998; Marlow et al., 2005; Saigal, Hoult, Streiner, Stoskopf, & Rosenbaum, 2000; Sykes et al., 1997; Taylor et al., 2000; Whitfield et al., 1997; Wolke & Meyer, 1999). Studies aimed at identifying factors that may contribute to less than optimal academic performance have indicated that VLBW is associated with attention problems. The goal of the current study was to better characterize differences in attentional abilities between preschool-age children who were born with VLBW and those born with NBW. Researchers have had difficulties with diagnosing specific attention problems in children born prematurely (Saigal et al., 1992; Sommerfelt et al., 1996; Spiker et al., 1992). In an attempt to provide further insight into the subtle attention problems of children born prematurely, the current study employed a new methodology based on recent cognitive neuroscience findings reported by Posner and colleagues, which characterizes attentional abilities in terms of three attention networks (Posner & Petersen, 1990). After accounting for the contributions of cognitive ability, chronological age, and maternal education, preschool-age VLBW children and NBW children were found to have significant differences in reaction times for all three attention networks. Overall, accuracy was very high for all attention network measures (above 90%) for both groups. The accuracy between the two birth weight groups was significantly different on the orienting and vigilance tasks, but not on the executive attention task.

In the orienting task, where a valid or invalid visual cue was presented at two different time intervals before the stimulus appeared, significant differences in overall MRT were not found between the two groups. However, a significant interaction was found between birth weight group and stimulus onset asynchrony (SOA). VLBW children had significantly slower reaction times than NBW children when the cue was presented 150 ms before the stimulus appeared (see Figure 1). Furthermore, although NBW children had faster reaction times for both conditions, reaction times for VLBW children were relatively faster when the cue was presented 1,000 ms before the stimulus appeared, while reaction times for NBW children became slower. These findings demonstrate that VLBW children may require more time than NBW children to orient and engage their attention to information in their environment.

In the vigilance task, significant differences in MRT were found between the two groups. Specifically, VLBW children had slower reaction times than NBW children on a task requiring children to maintain an alert state for varying lengths of time. This finding suggests that VLBW children have more difficulty sustaining attention compared to NBW children.

VLBW children were also found to have significantly slower reaction times than NBW children on the executive attention task. In addition, in the executive task, a significant interaction was found between birth weight group and trial compatibility. As Figure 3 illustrates, all children had faster reaction times for compatible trials than for incompatible trials. However, VLBW children, on average, were much slower in reacting when the picture and the "inside-the-house" picture were on opposite sides of the screen (incompatible trials) than NBW children were. Thus, it appears that VLBW children have greater difficulties (as evidenced by slower reaction times) with executive attention skills, including spatial conflict resolution, than do NBW children.

The current findings add to the growing body of literature that suggests that preschool-age children of VLBW may have a subtle, yet specific pattern of attention deficits compared to their counterparts of NBW. These particular differences found for each of the three attention networks are significant for several reasons. First, skills associated with each of the three attention networks (i.e., orienting and engaging attention, sustaining attention, and executive attention including resolving cognitive conflicts) are all necessary to succeed within the classroom environment (Burns et al., in press; Rueda et al., 2005). The school environment often requires the very skills that are difficult for those children with attention problems. For example, children must be able to orient and engage their attention to relevant information provided by their teachers in a time-efficient manner. When teachers are presenting new information, the speed with which children orient and engage their attention is critical to learning this new material. Delays in orienting and engaging their attention may result in children missing important components of the information being presented such that subsequent information does not make sense. Findings from the current study show that VLBW children are less effective on one specific task measuring orienting attention skills than NBW children, evidenced primarily by slower reaction times. In addition, VLBW children appear to have decreased sustained, selective, and executive attentional abilities, as measured by reaction times, which are all fundamental skills needed for success in an academic environment. These findings appear to shed some light as to why a large proportion of VLBW children receive special education services even in the absence of major disabilities (Buck et al., 2000; Hille et al., 2001; Saigal et al., 2000; Taylor et al., 2000; Wolke & Meyer, 1999). However, more data are needed to determine if these specific differences relate to classroom skills in this population of children who are at risk for poor achievement trajectories.

Limitations of the Current Study

It is important to note that age effects were found for reaction time on all three tasks. For both groups, younger children, on average, exhibited slower reaction times than older children suggesting that longitudinal studies are needed to better understand the development of these three attentional networks over time in children born prematurely. Researchers are only beginning to examine specific deficits in attentional abilities that may be unique to children born prematurely and little is known about how these abilities are expressed throughout childhood. Longitudinal methods will enhance our understanding of the stability or change in the expression of specific attentional deficits and how they relate to academic performance in particular areas. A limitation of the current study is that we did not assess parental history of attention disorders for either group of children. Research has shown that there is a hereditary tendency for attention difficulties, but as with all aspects of development, the environment also plays a significant role. The use of medications that could modify attention performance was also not assessed. Lastly, motor dexterity, eye-hand coordination, and visual motor skills were not assessed. However, given that the VLBW children performed similarly to the NBW children on one aspect of the orienting task suggests that they were not hindered by motor skill performance. In that task, the fish appear with equal chance in one of two fish bowls following a cue. Therefore, the difference in reaction time when there is a short SOA versus a long SOA should not be related to motor skill differences because the child does not know in which bowl the fish will appear. In other words, they cannot anticipate the appearance and begin to move their eyes to the appropriate bowl. In addition, there is a fixed finger position that the child must maintain at the beginning of each trial. Future research should obtain information regarding a family history of attention problems, the use of attention medications, and fine motor skills. Future research should also employ measures of pre-academic skills to gain a better understanding of the cognitive and developmental processes in early childhood that lead to poor academic achievement. Findings from such research would allow for earlier identification of these subtle attention deficits and the development of specific interventions to support optimal development of attention skills and school readiness in VLBW children before they fall behind in the classroom.

Conclusions

By employing Posner and Petersen's (1990) framework of attention networks, the current study provides a more systematic approach to measuring specific attentional abilities in children born prematurely. Attention skills require maturation and use of diverse areas of the brain. Yet, much of the previous research has tended to rely on parent and teacher reports, based on ADHD diagnostic criteria, to assess attention deficits in VLBW children. The current findings support the assertions made by others that the pattern of attention problems often exhibited by VLBW children may differ from that of other children with attention problems, especially ADHD (D'Agostino & Clifford, 1998; Davis et al., in press; Elgen et al., 2004; Indredavik et al., 2004; Spiker et al., 1992). The patterns of attention deficits described in the current study may be unique to this population. Previously, Elgen et al. have suggested that children born prematurely may have a disorder that is different from other attention disorders. However, in a group of 11-year-old children, they did not find differences between a sample of LBW (< 2000 g) children compared to a group of children born with NBW on measures of vigilance, selective attention, and alternating attention. Differences between our findings and those of Elgen et al. may be a reflection of the higher degree of prematurity and thus greater risk for attention problems in our sample of children weighing ≤ 1500 g. In addition, changes in the expression of attentional abilities over time may be another reason that our findings differed from those of Elgen et al. In another recent study, researchers found that 25% of a sample of VLBW children who were adolescents at the time of the study also had attention deficit symptoms, but only 7% met the criterion for a diagnosis of ADHD. They concluded that various psychiatric symptoms may relate to subtle deficits in comprehending environmental cues that compromise both cognitive and social developmental outcomes (Indredavik et al., 2004).

Since premature children have such high rates of academic problems (D'Agostino & Clifford, 1998; Davis, 2003; Hack et al., 2002; Hack et al., 1996; Halsey et al., 1996; Marlow et al., 2005; Whitfield et al., 1997), it may be that their attention problems interfere with academic success, but do not fit the model for ADHD. Attention problems may either be of insufficient quantity or may involve deficits in very specific attentional abilities such that they do not warrant a diagnosis of ADHD. More data are needed to clearly understand the nature of attention deficits in this population who is at such a high risk for school-related problems. Within the current framework, attention problems that do not meet the criteria for ADHD may be considered clinically insignificant when they may actually represent a new configuration of attention symptoms that are specific to children born prematurely. Thus, by examining multiple aspects of attention using this model, the current study has provided new knowledge of the nature and profile of subtle attention deficits in this population of children who are at risk for developmental and academic problems.

References

Berger, A., Jones, L., Rothbart, M. K., & Posner, M. I. (2000). Computerized games to study the development of attention in childhood. *Behavior Research Methods, Instruments & Computers, 32*(2), 297-303.

Botting, N., Powls, A., Cooke, R. W. I., & Marlow, N. (1998). Cognitive and educational outcome of very-low-birthweight children in early adolescence. *Developmental Medicine and Child Neurology, 40*, 652-660.

Breslau, N., & Chilcoat, H. D. (2000). Psychiatric sequelae of low birth weight at 11 years of age. *Biological Psychiatry, 47*, 1005-1011.

Breslau, N., Chilcoat, H. D., Johnson, E. O., Andreski, P., & Lucia, V. C. (2000). Neurologic soft signs and low birthweight: Their association and neuropsychiatric implications. *Biological Psychiatry, 47*, 71-79.

Buck, G. M., Msall, M. E., Schisterman, E. F., Lyon, N. R., & Rogers, B. T. (2000). Extreme prematurity and school outcomes. *Paediatric and Perinatal Epidemiology, 14*, 324-331.

Burns, B. M., Chang, F., Snyder, E., Robinson, J., Davis, D. W., Weatherholt, T., et al. (in press). Self-regulation in children of poverty. In *Child Psychology: New Research.* New York: Nova Science Publishers, Inc.

Chang, F., & Burns, B. (2005). Attention in preschoolers: Associations with effortful control and motivation. *Child Development, 76*, 247-263.

D'Agostino, J. A., & Clifford, P. (1998). Neurodevelopmental consequences associated with the premature neonate. *Advanced Practice in Acute Critical Care, 9*(1), 11-24.

Davis, D. W. (2003). Cognitive outcomes in school-age children born prematurely. *Neonatal Network: The Journal of Neonatal Nursing, 22*, 27-38.

Davis, D. W., Burns, B., Snyder, E., Dossett, D., & Wilkerson, S. A. (2004). Parent-child interaction and attention regulation in children born prematurely. *Journal for Specialists in Pediatric Nursing, 9*(3), 85-94.

Davis, D. W., Burns, B., Snyder, E., & Robinson, J. B. (in press). Attention problems in very low birth weight preschoolers: Are new screening measures needed for this special population? *Journal of Child & Adolescent Psychiatric Nursing.*

Elgen, I., Lundervold, A. J., & Sommerfelt, K. (2004). Aspects of inattention in low birth weight children. *Pediatric Neurology, 30*, 92-98.

Emsley, H. C. A., Wardle, S. P., Sims, D. G., Chiswick, M. L., & D'Souza, S. W. (1998). Increased survival and deteriorating developmental outcome in 23 to 25 week old gestation infants, 1990-4 compared with 1984-9. *Archives of Diseases in Childhood: Fetal and Neonatal Edition, 78*, F99-F104.

Hack, M., Flannery, D. J., Schluchter, M., Cartar, L., Borowski, E., & Klein, N. (2002). Outcomes in young adulthood for very-low-birth-weight infants. *New England Journal of Medicine, 346*(3), 149-157.

Hack, M., Friedman, H., & Fanaroff, A. A. (1996). Outcomes of extremely low birth weight infants. *Pediatrics, 98*(5), 931-937.

Halsey, C. L., Collin, M. F., & Anderson, C. L. (1996). Extremely low-birth-weight children and their peers: A comparison of school-age outcomes. *Archives of Pediatric and Adolescent Medicine, 150*, 790-794.

Hille, E., Ouden, A., Saroj, S., Wolke, D., Lambert, M., Whitaker, A., et al. (2001). Behavioral problems in children who weigh 1000 grams or less at birth in four countries. *The Lancet, 357*, 1641-1643.

Horwood, L. J., Mogridge, N., & Darlow, B. A. (1998). Cognitive, educational, and behavioural outcomes at 7 to 8 years in a national very low birth weight cohort. *Archives of Diseases of Childhood: Fetal & Neonatal Edition, 79*, F12-F20.

Hoy, E. A., Bill, J. M., & Sykes, D. H. (1988). Very low birthweight: A long-term developmental impairment? *International Journal of Behavioral Development, 11*(1), 37-67.

Indredavik, M. S., Vik, T., Heyerdahl, S., Kulseng, S., Fayer, P., & Brubakk, A. M. (2004). Psychiatric symptoms and disorders in adolescents with low birth weight. *Archives of Disease in Childhood Fetal and Neonatal Edition, 89*, F445-F450.

Kaufman, A. S., & Kaufman, N. L. (1990). *Kaufman Brief Intelligence Test manual*. Circle Pines, MN: American Guidance Service, Inc.

Marlow, N. (2004). Neurocognitive outcome after very preterm birth. *Archives of Disease In Childhood, 89*, 224-228.

Marlow, N., Wolke, D., Bracewell, M. A., & Samara, M. (2005). Neurologic and developmental disability at six years of age after extremely preterm birth. *New England Journal of Medicine, 352*, 9-19.

McGrath, M., & Sullivan, M. (2002). Birth weight, neonatal morbidities, and school age outcomes in full-term and preterm infants. *Issues in Comprehensive Pediatric Nursing, 25*, 231-254.

Mezzacappa, E. (2004). Alerting, orienting, and executive attention: Developmental properties and sociodemographic correlates in an epidemiological sample of young, urban children. *Child Development, 75*, 1373-1386.

O'Callaghan, M. J., Burns, Y. R., Gray, P. H., Harvey, J. M., Mohay, H., Rogers, Y. M., et al. (1996). School performance of ELBW children: A controlled study. *Developmental Medicine and Child Neurology, 38*, 917-926.

Posner, M. I., & Petersen, S. E. (1990). The attention system of the human brain. *Annual Review of Neuroscience, 13*, 25-42.

Posner, M. I., & Rogers, M. G. (1978). Chronometric analysis of abstraction and recognition. In W. K. Estes (Ed.), *Handbook of learning and cognitive processes: V. Human information* (pp. 143-188). Oxford, England: Erlbaum.

Rothbart, M. K., Posner, M. I., & Hershey, K. L. (1995). Temperament, attention, and developmental psychopathology. In D. Cicchetti & D. J. Cohen (Eds.), *Developmental psychopathology, Vol 1: Theory and methods* (pp. 315-340). Oxford, England: John Wiley & Sons.

Rueda, M. R., Posner, M., & Rothbart, M. K. (2005). The development of executive attention: Contributions to the emergence of self-regulation. *Developmental Neuropsychology, 28*, 573-594.

Saigal, S., Hoult, L. A., Streiner, D. L., Stoskopf, B., & Rosenbaum, P. L. (2000). School difficulties at adolescence in a regional cohort of children who were extremely low birth weight. *Pediatrics, 105*, 325-331.

Saigal, S., Szatmari, P., & Rosenbaum, P. (1992). Can learning disabilities in children who were extremely low birth weight be identified at school entry? *Developmental and Behavioral Pediatrics, 13*(5), 356-362.

Snyder, E., Burns, B., & Davis, D. W. (2006). An investigation of attention networks and visual attention abilities in children with hearing impairments. Manuscript submitted for publication.

Sommerfelt, K., Troland, K., Ellertsen, B., & Markestad, T. (1996). Behavioral problems in low-birthweight preschoolers. *Developmental Medicine and Child Neurology, 38*, 927-940.

Spiker, D., Kraemer, H. C., Constantine, N. A., & Bryant, D. (1992). Reliability and validity of behavior problem checklists as measures of stable traits in low birth weight, premature preschoolers. *Child Development, 63*, 1481-1496.

Sykes, D. H., Hoy, E. A., Bill, J. M., McClure, B. G., Halliday, H. L., & Reid, M. M. (1997). Behavioral adjustment in school of very low birthweight children. *Journal of Child Psychology and Psychiatry, 38*(3), 315-325.

Szatmari, P., Saigal, S., Rosenbaum, P., Campbell, D., & King, S. (1990). Psychiatric disorders at five years among children with birthweights <1000g: A regional perspective. *Developmental Medicine and Child Neurology, 32*, 954-962.

Taylor, H. G., Klein, N., Minich, N. M., & Hack, M. (2000). Middle-school-age outcomes in children with very low birthweight. *Child Development, 71*, 1495-1511.

Teplin, S. W., Burchinal, M., Johnson-Martin, N., Humphry, R. A., & Kraybill, E. N. (1991). Neurodevelopmental, health, and growth status at age 6 years of children with birth weights less than 1001 grams. *Journal of Pediatrics, 118*(5), 768-777.

Vohr, B. R., Wright, L. L., Dusick, A. M., Mele, L., Verter, J., Steichen, J. J., et al. (2000). Neurodevelopmental and functional outcomes of extremely low birth weight infants in NICHD Neonatal Research Network, 1993-1994. *Pediatrics, 105*(6), 1216-1226.

Whitfield, M. F., Grunau, R. V., & Holsti, L. (1997). Extremely premature (< 800 g) school children: Multiple areas of hidden disability. *Archives of Diseases in Childhood, 77*, F85-F90.

Wolke, D., & Meyer, R. (1999). Cognitive status, language attainment, and pre-reading skills of 6-year-old very preterm children and their peers: The Bavarian Longitudinal Study. *Developmental Medicine and Child Neurology, 41*, 94-109.

Author Note

Elizabeth H. Snyder is now at the Center for Child and Family Policy, Duke University, Durham, NC.

Julia B. Robinson is now in the Department of Psychology, Eastern Kentucky University, Richmond, KY.

Support for this study was provided by the University Pediatrics Foundation, Inc., University of Louisville; the Neonatal Follow-up Programs at the University of Louisville and Cincinnati Children's Hospital Medical Center; and a grant to Dr. Davis from the National Institute for Nursing Research, NIH (5 K01 NR 156-2). Their generous support is greatly appreciated. The authors would also like to thank the parents & children who participated in the study.

Structural Validity of the Early Childhood Longitudinal Study Measure of Parental Beliefs about School Readiness

Rebecca J. Morgan & James C. DiPerna
The Pennsylvania State University

The purpose of the current study was to evaluate the reliability and validity of The Early Childhood Longitudinal Study, Kindergarten Class of 1998-1999 (ECLS-K) measure of parental beliefs about school readiness. Parent responses ($n = 13,693$) included in the current study were obtained through schools participating in the ECLS-K, and exploratory factor analyses were used to examine dimensions of parental beliefs about school readiness. Results indicated that a one-factor solution best represented parents' beliefs about school readiness as measured by the ECLS-K parent interview. Implications of findings for the measurement of parents' school readiness beliefs are discussed.

Since the establishment of the National Education Goals in the late 1980s, professionals have been trying to determine not only the meaning of school readiness but also the methods to assess and ensure readiness for all children beginning school (Meisels, 1999). Competing philosophies of school readiness have resulted in failed attempts to obtain a consensus for the term (Kagan, 2003; National Association of Early Childhood Specialists; NAECS, 2000). In addition, changes in the philosophical and social approaches to kindergarten education have influenced parent and educator views of readiness (Welch & White, 1999). Kagan (1992) acknowledged that professionals within the field of education have failed to obtain an operational definition of school readiness, and the term is often associated with a high degree of ambiguity.

Despite the lack of agreement among professionals regarding school readiness, parents have been charged with the responsibility of preparing their children for school and making subsequent school decisions. Parent beliefs about school readiness influence how parents prepare their children for school (Brooker, 2003;

All correspondence should be addressed to Rebecca Morgan, Pennsylvania State University, 111 CEDAR Building, University Park, PA 16802. Electronic mail may be sent to rjm365@psu.edu

Graue, 1992; NAECS, 2000; Pelletier & Brent, 2002; Shepard & Smith; 1985, Stipek, Milburn, Clements, & Daniels, 1992; Wesley & Buysse, 2003). In addition, parent beliefs about school readiness influence their support of school and community programs (Snow, 2006). The purpose of the current study was to examine the reliability and structural validity of the measure of parental beliefs about school readiness used in the Early Childhood Longitudinal Study, Kindergarten Class of 1998-99 (ECLS-K).

Readiness: Complexity, Dimensions, and Consequences

Welch and White (1999) explained that the complexity of school readiness stems from the lack of agreement among stakeholders as to how to operationally define the construct. Snow (2006) identified the lack of a coherent theory that specifies each component of school readiness as one of the main challenges to defining school readiness. Several national panels and school readiness experts, however, have proposed definitions. For example, Shore (1998) reported the objectives and recommendations of the Goal 1 Ready Schools Resource Group, a subcommittee of the National Education Goals Panel. Members of this subcommittee indicated that the construct of "readiness" encompassed five dimensions of early learning and development: (a) physical well-being and motor development, (b) social and emotional development, (c) approaches toward learning, (d) language usage, and (e) cognition and general knowledge (Prince, 1992; Shore, 1998).

Kagan (1992, 2003) outlined two predominant constructs of school readiness: readiness to learn and readiness for school. Readiness to learn is described as the level of development in which an individual of any age can acquire new tasks (Kagan, 1992). Readiness to learn reflects the fluidity of educational contexts and the idea that learning can be fostered. Readiness for school however, "has been regarded as a more finite construct, embracing specific cognitive and linguistic skills" (Kagan, 1992, p. 48). Supporters of this construct of readiness view educational contexts as static and believe that readiness is expected rather than fostered (Kagan, 1992). Kagan (2003) explained that parents and politicians associate this construct with being "ready" to learn to read.

Kagan (1992) also proposed a third readiness concept, maturational readiness, which includes readiness to learn and readiness for school. Kagan defined maturational readiness as the entry level of development that children should attain prior to beginning school (i.e., readiness for school) and as the recognition that children must be given time to develop according to their developmental timetable (i.e., readiness to learn). Advocates for maturational readiness seek to ensure that a child is not placed in an educational environment that exceeds current developmental capabilities, and they support practices such as readiness tests (Kagan; NAECS, 2000). For example, the National Association for the Education of Young Children (1995) stated that it is the school's responsibility to address a child's needs while considering individual variation resulting from developmental and experiential differences.

Finally, social constructivism defines readiness as a construct derived from society. Within a social constructivist context, Graue (1992) defined readiness as a set of standards that emerge from "community values and expectations and are related to individual children in terms of attributes like their age, sex, and preschool experience" (p. 226). Consistent with this idea, Piotrkowski, Botsko, and Matthews (2000) suggested that beliefs about readiness vary between communities. For example, Piotrkowski et al. purported that children in high need communities "may be expected to have more extensive and concrete readiness resources at school entry than children in more affluent families and communities" (p. 541). Beliefs about individual school readiness may be emphasized in an attempt to account for the lack of resources in family and school environments.

In sum, similarities and differences exist between the various definitions of school readiness. The National Educational Goals Panel Report outlined five dimensions of school readiness (Prince, 1992; Shore, 1998). In contrast to this integrated view of readiness, Kagan (1992, 2003) identified three underlying readiness constructs that primarily focus on the individual within the environment. Graue (1992) and Piotrkowski et al. (2000) argued that readiness is primarily the result of community values and expectations.

These divergent views of the school readiness construct have resulted in the development and application of unfair policies and practices. For example, the school readiness construct has been used to justify policies that ignore individual differences in children (e.g., readiness determined by chronological age; Meisels, 1992). The school readiness construct also has been used to support practices that enable existing social inequities (e.g., retention practices occur more often for students belonging to an ethnic minority; Meisels, 1992, 1999; NAECS, 2000). Finally, combinations of school readiness practices, such as increased entry age paired with the practice of redshirting (i.e., practice of delaying a child's entry into kindergarten by a year; Meisels, 1992; Oshima & Domaleski, 2006), have resulted in an advancement of kindergarten curriculum (Kagan, 1992; NAECS, 2000). That is, kindergarten expectations have become more sophisticated to accommodate the needs of older students (Kagan, 1992). An inability to reach a consensus defining the construct of school readiness has resulted in the development of varied perspectives and inconsistent readiness practices.

Implications of Parent Beliefs about School Readiness

Numerous sources have acknowledged parents' responsibility to prepare their children for school (Kagan, 1992; Pelletier & Brent, 2002; Perry, Dockett, & Tracey, 1998). Many readiness practices are conducted solely by parents or through collaboration between parents and teachers. Parents have an essential role in preparing their child for school and implementing readiness practices, and several researchers have identified implications of parental beliefs about readiness. For example, Graue (1992) suggested that parent beliefs about school readiness influence the choice of activities in which they engage their children as well as the experiences they arrange for their children. Stipek et al. (1992) supported this conclusion, reporting that parent beliefs about readiness influence the teaching methods they use with their children (e.g., didactic versus child-centered approaches). Similarly, Brooker (2003) examined cultural beliefs about education and subsequent readiness behaviors of parents identified as Anglo and Bangladeshi. Brooker found that, when preparing children for formal education, Anglo families encouraged child exploration of his or her environment while Bangladeshi families engaged in didactic instruction of English, Arabic, and Bengali alphabets.

Furthermore, parents and professionals agree that kindergarten curricula and expectations have changed in recent years (Wesley & Buysse, 2003). NAECS (2000) stated that advanced expectations in kindergarten curricula, specifically that children learn to read, have been the result of parental pressure. In addition, several researchers have purported that various parent characteristics affect their kindergarten entry decisions (e.g., delaying entry) and willingness to heed educators' advice regarding readiness practices (e.g., retention; NAECS, 2000; Shepard & Smith, 1985). Moreover, Wesley and Buysse (2003) concluded that many parents and professionals are not aware of ongoing opportunities to develop home-school partnerships, are not using similar vocabulary (e.g., parent as "first teacher"), or are not sharing strategies to meet kindergarten expectations.

Parent beliefs impact their readiness practices as well as home-school relationships. Furthermore, two decades of position statements and research suggest ongoing interest in parent beliefs about readiness and the educational decisions parents make for their children. Therefore, it is important that we have technically adequate measures to assess parental beliefs.

Measurement of Parent Beliefs about School Readiness

Two previous studies assessed parent beliefs about kindergarten school readiness. The first, a study conducted by West, Hausken, and Collins (1993), compared the perceived importance of readiness characteristics across two key educational stakeholders – parents of preschoolers and kindergarten teachers. Parent information was collected through the use of the 1993 National Household Education Survey (NHES:93). West et al. clustered the readiness-related items on the NHES:93 into two groups: social-emotional development and cognitive development (Prince, 1992; Shore, 1998). West et al. referred to the two clustered groups as behavior-related and school-related. Respondents were asked to rate how important they thought each item was for a child to be ready for kindergarten using a 5-point scale ranging from 1 (*essential*) to 5 (*not at all important*). West et al. concluded that parent education influenced parent beliefs about readiness characteristics. Specifically, parents who had lower levels of educational attainment were more likely to rate school-related items as very important or essential when compared with the ratings of parents with higher levels of educational attainment.

Diamond, Reagan, and Bandyk (2000) conducted a second study examining parent beliefs about readiness as they relate to parent-child engagement in home activities. Diamond et al. used data collected from parents with children 4- to 6-years-old that had not started kindergarten ($n = 2,509$). Parent responses were collected through their participation in NHES:93. As in the West et al. (1993) study, parents were asked to rate how important they thought each readiness item was for a child to be prepared for kindergarten. Prior to an examination of differences in parent readiness beliefs, Diamond et al. (2000) conducted a principal components analysis of the seven readiness items. This analysis yielded a one-factor solution, representing a unitary construct of school readiness.

West et al. (1993) and Diamond et al. (2000) examined parent beliefs about school readiness using parent responses to seven items included on the NHES:93. Despite using the same items, West et al. (1993) clustered the seven items into two categories (i.e., school-related and behavior-related) while Diamond et al. (2000) concluded the seven items supported a unitary construct of school readiness.

A more recent national study, The Early Childhood Longitudinal Study-Kindergarten Class of 1998-1999 (ECLS-K), used a parental beliefs about school readiness measure that included six of the seven items from the West et al. (1993) and Diamond et al. (2000) studies. Researchers interested in using this ECLS-K measure need to have confidence that the scale adequately assesses parental beliefs about school readiness. Given the lack of consistency in conceptualizing the structure of this readiness measure in previous research (Diamond et al., 2000; West et al., 1993), the purpose of the current study was to evaluate the reliability and structural validity of the ECLS-K measure of parental beliefs about school readiness. Based on the research of Diamond et al. (2000), it was hypothesized that parent beliefs about school readiness, as measured by the ECLS-K, reflected one dimension of school readiness.

Method

Participants

The parent sample included in the current study was obtained through schools participating in The Early Childhood Longitudinal Study-Kindergarten Class of 1998-1999 (ECLS-K). Parents ($n = 13,693$) selected from the ECLS-K database for the current study had children ranging from 4- to 7-years old. Parents with complete interview data and whose child was attending kindergarten for the first time were included in the sample for the current study. Mean age for mothers included in the current sample was 32 years while mean age for fathers was 28 years. Sixty-nine percent of mothers reported being married at the time of their child's birth while 24.3% of mothers reported that they were not married at the time of their child's birth.

Although other members of the household were permitted to answer the interview items, the child's mother usually was the respondent (National Center for Education Statistics; NCES, 2001). As such, percentages of mother's race for the participants selected for the current study, mother's race in the total ECLS-K sample, and race of persons 18 years of age and older collected by the 2000 U.S. Census are shown in Table 1.

Measures

The current study examined parent beliefs about school readiness, which were measured by specific survey items included in the ECLS-K parent interview. Readiness items examined in the current study were developed by Zill et al. (1993) as part of the NHES:93 School Readiness Questionnaire (SRQ). The SRQ focused on several relevant issues (e.g., developmental milestones, home activities, and experience in early childcare) to early childhood development and guided by these issues, provided an approach to school readiness (NCES, 1994, p. 1-2). Six of the seven readiness items from the SRQ were included in the ECLS-K Parent Interview. An explicit rationale for the exclusion of the seventh item, "Is enthusiastic and curious in approaching new activities", was not provided by NCES (2001). The readiness items included on the ECLS-K identified academic (e.g., can count to 20 or more,) and behavioral skills (e.g., takes turns and shares). Parents were asked to rate the importance of each item using a 5-point scale from 1 (*essential*) to 5 (*not important*). Validity and reliability estimates for readiness items found on the ECLS-K were not published previously.

Procedure

Responses collected from the ECLS-K Parent Interview in the kindergarten year (i.e., Fall 1998 and Spring 1999) were examined in the current study. Although the child's mother typically was the respondent, other members of the household were permitted to answer the interview items. The respondent was required to be 18 years of age or older, living in the household with the child, and knowledgeable about the child (NCES, 2001).

A computer-assisted telephone interview was used to collect the information for most families; however, if families did not have a telephone, a computer-assisted personal interview was used (NCES, 2001). The interviewer asked respondents to provide information about a number of different domains including family demographics (e.g., parent education level), educational expectations for their child, and home activities. The parent interview required approximately 50 minutes to complete and was administered primarily by telephone from

Table 1

Percentages of Race for Mothers in Selected Sample, Total ECLS-K Sample, and Individuals 18 Years and Older Reported in 2000 U.S. Census

Race	[a]Selected	[b]ECLS-K	U.S. Census
American Indian /Alaskan Native	1.7	1.5	0.6
Asian	5.7	5.3	3.7
Black or African American	13.2	12.4	11.2
[c]Hispanic or Latino	14.9	14.1	11.0
Native Hawaiian/ Pacific Islander	1.3	1.1	0.1
[d]White	61.0	56.5	72.0
Other Race Alone	0.0	0.0	0.1
[e]More Than One Race	0.6	0.6	1.3
Not Applicable	1.7	1.6	0.0
Not Ascertained	0.0	6.6	0.0

Note. Selected Sample (N = 13,693), ECLS-K (N = 17,212), and U.S. Census from 2000 (N = 209,128,094). Due to rounding procedures total may exceed 100%.
[a] Respondents could select more than one race plus Hispanic so total will exceed 100%.
[b] Respondents could select more than one race plus Hispanic, so total will exceed 100%.
[c] Sum of individuals identifying as race specified and no race specified.
[d] Categorical labels are those used by NCES.
[e] More than one race category means respondent indicated "multi-racial" or "bi-racial".

September 1998 through January 1999. Three percent of interviews were conducted in person. Although most of the interviews were conducted in English, accommodations (i.e., translators or a hard copy of the interview written in the native language) were provided for parents who spoke other languages. One percent of the planned interviews were not conducted due to an inability to accommodate language differences. Interviewer demographic information was not available (NCES).

Statistical Procedures

Data were analyzed using SPSS version 11.0 for Windows. Exploratory Factor Analysis (EFA) was used to test the hypothesized relationships among items on the readiness scale for the presence of separate constructs (e.g., academic and behavioral). To ensure the appropriateness of the data for EFA, several preliminary analyses were conducted.

EFA preliminary analyses. Missing data were identified in the ECLS-K total parent sample ($N = 17,212$), and cases with missing data were subsequently deleted for two reasons. First, approximately 17% of cases ($n = 2,891$) were missing the entire parent interview data (reasons for low parent response are outlined in NCES [2001]). Second, the current sample did not include responses from parents with a child attending kindergarten for a second time (4%; $n = 628$). The resulting sample ($n = 13,693$) was more than sufficient for factor analysis (Comrey & Lee, 1992; Tabachnick & Fidell, 2001). Due to the availability of a large sample, cases were randomly divided into two demographically equivalent samples. A factor analysis then was conducted on the first sample ($n = 6,807$) and replicated on a second sample ($n = 6,886$).

Data in the current samples were examined for multivariate normality using several methods. Skewness and kurtosis of the current samples were assessed by a visual inspection of graphed data (i.e., a histogram). West, Finch, and Curran (1995) described standardized skew value $= \pm 2$ and kurtosis value $= \pm 7$ as substantial departure from normality. However, Tabachnick and Fidell (2001) explained that with large samples the significance level of skewness or kurtosis is not as important as the visual appearance reflecting its actual size or deviation from zero. Linearity in the current sample was assessed through visual inspection of scatterplots. Finally, the data were inspected for multicollinearity and singularity through an inspection of the squared multiple correlations (SMC; Tabachnick & Fidell).

Factorability of the correlation matrix was determined through an inspection of the correlation matrix of the readiness items and several statistical tests. Correlations exceeding .30 supported factorability of the matrix (Tabachnick & Fidell, 2001). Bartlett's (1954) test of sphericity was used to test the hypothesis that the correlations in the correlation matrix were zero. Bartlett's test is sensitive to large sample size so it often is significant even if the correlations are very low.

Therefore, Bartlett's Test of Sphericity was used in conjunction with inspection of the anti-image matrix and the Kaiser-Meyer-Olkin test of Sampling Adequacy (KMO; 1970, 1974) to determine the significance of correlations in the correlation matrix (Tabachnick & Fidell).

Exploratory factor analysis. Principal factors extraction (i.e., principal axis factoring via SPSS) using a varimax rotation method was chosen for the current EFA for two reasons. First, principal factors extraction utilizes common variance to produce the factor model while removing the unique and error variance (Tabachnick & Fidell, 2001). Second, principal factors extraction is less likely than other methods to produce improper solutions, and it is not as sensitive to the violation of normal distribution assumptions (Fabrigar, Wegener, MacCallum, & Strahan, 1999; Floyd & Widaman, 1995). Varimax rotation method was chosen because it maximizes the variance of the structure coefficients and is regarded as one of the best rotation methods (Fabrigar et al.; Tabachnick & Fidell). Scree test was conducted through a visual inspection of the plotted eigenvalues to locate the differentiation in slope (Tabachnick & Fidell). Previous research findings also guided decisions about factor retention.

Finally, interpretation of factors was guided by values of the structure coefficients and meaningfulness. Comrey and Lee (1992) recommended guidelines for interpretation of loadings: .71 is considered excellent, .63 is considered very good, .55 is considered good, .45 is considered fair, and .32 is considered poor. Meaningfulness was determined by factors with three or more variables with unique structure coefficients and alignment with theory (Gorsuch, 1983; Tabachnick & Fidell, 2001). Cronbach's alpha coefficients were calculated for the total readiness score obtained from the readiness measure.

Results

Preliminary Analyses

Sample 1. Normality was assessed through an examination of skewness and kurtosis on each of the six readiness items. Visual inspection of histograms of the score distribution revealed positive skewness. In large samples, deviations from normal levels of skewness and kurtosis (i.e., zero) do not have a substantive impact on results of analyses (Tabachnick & Fidell, 2001). However, this violation of normality supported the subsequent use of principal axis factoring because it is not as sensitive to violations of normality (Fabrigar et al., 1999). Linearity was assessed through visual inspections of the scatterplots for pairs of variables. The scatterplots did not reveal nonlinear relationships between the variable pairs nor did they support the existence of strong linear relationships. Inspection of squared multiple correlations using the initial communalities indicated values below 1 and thus did not reveal multicollinearity and singularity. Several correlations exceeded .30 indicating factorability of the correlation matrix (Tabachnick & Fidell; see Table 2). Bartlett's Test of Sphericity was significant at $p < .0001$

and the Kaiser-Meyer-Olkin Test of Sampling Adequacy was .79, which exceeded the suggested minimum criterion of .6 (Tabachnick & Fidell). Finally, inspection of anti-image correlation matrices contained mostly small values (.45 to .10). Results of these criteria indicated suitability of factor analysis for Sample 1.

Table 2
Intercorrelations, Means, and Standard Deviations for Item Scores on Readiness Measure in Sample 1 and Sample 2

Items	M	SD	1	2	3	4	5	6
1. How important child counts	2.34	89	-	.30	.41	.30	.57	.20
	(2.32)	(.90)		(.29)	(.41)	(.32)	(.59)	(.21)
2. How important child shares	1.74	.58		-	.39	.36	.28	.42
	(1.73)	(.57)			(.38)	(.38)	(.28)	(.39)
3. How important child draws	2.09	.76			-	.37	.42	.30
	(2.07)	(.76)				(.37)	(.44)	(.32)
4. How important child is calm	1.96	.68				-	.37	.33
	(1.94)	(.68)					(.37)	(.33)
5. How important child knows letters	2.20	.83					-	.26
	(2.19)	(.82)						(.28)
6. How important child communicates well	1.72	.59						-
	(1.72)	(.59)						

Note. Sample 1 ($N = 6,807$) and Sample 2 ($N = 6,886$). All correlations are significant at $p < .0001$. Sample 2 values provided in parentheses.

Sample 2. Normality was assessed through an examination of skewness and kurtosis on each of the six readiness items. Visual inspection of histograms of the sample distribution revealed positive skewness. Linearity was assessed through visual inspections of the scatterplots for pairs of variables. The scatterplots neither revealed nonlinear relationships between the variable pairs nor did they support the existence of strong linear relationships. Inspection of squared multiple correlations using the initial communalities indicated that values were less than 1 and thus, did not reveal multicollinearity and singularity. Several correlations exceeded .30 indicating factorability of the correlation matrix (Tabachnick &

Fidell, 2001; see Table 2). Bartlett's Test of Sphericity was significant at $p <$ .0001 and the Kaiser-Meyer-Olkin Test of Sampling Adequacy was .79. Finally, inspection of anti-image correlation matrices contained mostly small values (.47 to .09). Results of these criteria indicated suitability of factor analysis for Sample 2.

Exploratory Factor Analyses

   Sample 1. Principal axis factoring using a varimax rotation was used to examine dimensions of school readiness as measured by the ECLS-K Parent Interview. Inspection of the scree plot revealed a break preceding the first factor, resulting in a visual indication of the existence of one factor. All structure coefficients exceeded the minimum criteria (Tabachnick & Fidell, 2001; see Table 3). These criteria supported one readiness factor that accounted for 46% of the total variance.

Table 3
Structure Coefficients and Communalities from the Single Factor Solution for Sample 1 and Sample 2

Item	Structure Coefficient	Communality
1. How important child counts	.615 (.629)	.366 (.385)
2. How important child shares	.569 (.553)	.285 (.270)
3. How important child draws	.655 (.650)	.313 (.312)
4. How important child is calm	.572 (.585)	.252 (.264)
5. How important child knows letters	.661 (.686)	.392 (.420)
6. How important child communicates well	.484 (.484)	.227 (.219)

Note. Sample 1 (N = 6,807) and Sample 2 (N = 6,886). Sample 2 values provided in parentheses.

   Previous research (West et al., 1993) had suggested at least two dimensions of readiness. Therefore, a two-factor solution was tested as well. When two factors were extracted, two items exhibited cross-loadings (see Table 4). Although four of the items demonstrated large structure coefficient values only on factors consistent with predictions (i.e., academic and behavioral items), two items exhibited large structure coefficient values on both factors. Thus, the two-factor solution failed to meet the criteria for three unique items loading on a factor. Each factor accounted for 23% and 21% of the total variance, respectively. Cumulative variance for a two-factor solution was 44%. In sum, the two-factor solution did not provide evidence of strong structure coefficients and theoretical fit. A three factor solution was not investigated due to failure to meet the criteria for three items with unique structure coefficients on a factor (Gorsuch, 1983; Tabachnick & Fidell, 2001). The one-factor solution of readiness provided the best statistical and theoretical fit and demonstrated adequate internal consistency ($\alpha = .76$) for Sample 1.

Table 4

Structure Coefficients and Communalities From the Two-Factor Solution for Sample 1 and Sample 2

Item	Structure Coefficients		Communality
	1	2	
5. How important child knows letters	**.722 (.741)**	.242 (.262)	.437 (.470)
1. How important child counts	**.714 (.721)**	.192 (.205)	.379 (.395)
3. How important child draws	**.452 (.435)**	**.444 (.457)**	.429 (.422)
2. How important child shares	.205 (.188)	**.645 (.638)**	.323 (.306)
6. How important child communicates well	.135 (.149)	**.591 (.566)**	.234 (.234)
4. How important child is calm	**.322 (.315)**	**.476 (.505)**	.328 (.342)

Note. Sample 1 ($N = 6,807$) and Sample 2 ($N = 6,886$). Bold indicates a salient ($\geq .32$) structure coefficient and include rounded estimates. Sample 2 values provided in parentheses.

Sample 2. The factor analysis methodology used with the first sample was replicated with Sample 2. Inspection of scree revealed a break preceding the first factor, suggesting a single-factor solution. All structure coefficients exceeded the minimum criteria (Tabachnick & Fidell, 2001; see Table 3), and the resulting factor accounted for 47% of the total variance.

A two-factor solution also was investigated. When two factors were extracted, the two items that exhibited salient structure coefficient values with both factors in Sample 1 demonstrated the same pattern in Sample 2 (see Table 4). Consistent with Sample 1, four items had unique structure coefficient values predicted in previous research (i.e., academic and behavioral items). The factors failed to meet the criteria for three unique items loading on a factor (Gorsuch, 1983; Tabachnick & Fidell, 2001). Each factor accounted for 24% and 21% of the total variance, respectively. Cumulative variance for a two-factor solution was

45%. A two-factor solution did not yield statistical results indicative of strong structure coefficients. Thus, factor analysis with Sample 2 also indicated that a one-factor solution of readiness provided the best statistical and theoretical fit and demonstrated adequate internal consistency ($\alpha = .77$).

Discussion

The current study investigated the reliability and validity of the ECLS-K measure of parental beliefs about school readiness. Factor analyses were conducted to determine the number of dimensions represented by the measure of parent beliefs about readiness included in the ECLS-K Fall Parent Interview. Results indicated one school readiness factor was represented by the readiness measure included in the parent interview.

Researchers have offered several definitions of school readiness (Graue, 1992; Kagan, 1992, 2003; Piotrkowski et al., 2000; Shore, 1998). Furthermore, West et al. (1993) and Diamond et al. (2000) examined parent beliefs about the importance of readiness skills using seven items included on the NHES:93. With the exception of one item ("Is enthusiastic and curious in approaching new activities"), readiness items found on the NHES:93 were included on the ECLS-K readiness measure. West et al. conducted the first study using these seven readiness items and created two readiness domains: behavioral and school-related. Diamond et al. utilized principal components analysis to determine relationships between the seven items included on the readiness measure, and results of this analysis supported one readiness factor.

Based upon previous research by Diamond et al. (2000), it was predicted that parent beliefs about school readiness as measured by the six readiness items included on the ECLS-K Parent Interview would reflect one dimension of school readiness. Consistent with this prediction, results of the current study revealed that one dimension of school readiness accounted for the most total variance and provided the best theoretical fit for the 6-item ECLS-K measure. Therefore, current results did not provide support for the existence of two dimensions of school readiness as suggested by West et al. (1993).

Results revealed weak construct validity for the ECLS-K readiness measure. Communalities, that is the variance in each item accounted for by the factor or factors, ranged from 21% to 43%. This suggests that the six items included on the readiness measure are not representing a large portion of parent beliefs about school readiness. Furthermore, in the two-factor solution, item 3 ("How important a child draws") and item 4 ("How important child is calm") loaded on both factors, and they had low communality values. These findings indicate that these items may be capturing another school readiness dimension that is not academic or behavioral. Conversely, these findings could suggest that these items may not be capturing readiness at all. Overall, these results reveal that the readiness measure included on the ECLS-K demonstrates weak construct validity relative to a two-factor (academic and behavioral) model of school readiness as used in prior literature (e.g., West et al., 1993).

Limitations and Directions for Future Research

The primary limitation of the current study was that the ECLS-K readiness measure contained a limited number of items addressing various dimensions of school readiness (purportedly, three items for behavioral and three items for academic). Although these items had been used in a previous study to represent two dimensions of school readiness (West et al., 1993), results of the current study revealed that the readiness items represented one readiness factor. Researchers and practitioners have suggested more than one dimension of school readiness (Graue, 1992; Kagan, 1992; NAECS, 2000; Piotrkowski et al., 2000; Shore, 1998; West et al., 1993). Given the multiple conceptualizations of readiness, the measure included in the current study may have lacked adequate representation of the school readiness domain. Furthermore, the limited scope of the readiness measure did not allow for an examination of parent readiness beliefs relative to separate dimensions (e.g., behavioral or academic). Results of factor analyses not only failed to support the existence of more than one dimension of school readiness but also failed to rule out the possibility that each item was measuring only one dimension.

Future research examining parent beliefs about readiness should lead to the development of a comprehensive measure of the construct. Creation of such a measure will provide a more complete assessment of parents' readiness beliefs. Construct validity of the readiness measure in the current study may be increased after revision of certain items. For example, items that appear to be measuring more than one dimension while explaining little variance could be replaced or could be considered to be a more accurate measure of a different school dimension (e.g., social rather than behavioral). In order to obtain greater insight about importance ratings of readiness provided by parents, future studies should include questions about parents' prior knowledge of early child development and individual differences to examine the impact of prior knowledge on parent beliefs (West et al., 1993).

In conclusion, results from the current study indicate that the parental beliefs about school readiness included in the ECLS-K Parent Interview represent a single school readiness factor. As a result, researchers who intend to use this variable from the ECLS-K dataset (or the ECLS-K parental beliefs about readiness measure) in future studies should use a one-factor model of interpretation because results indicate that the six items represent a unitary school readiness construct. Moreover, researchers and practitioners should be cautious when drawing inferences about parent school readiness beliefs and making decisions about a child's school readiness based on this measure. These professionals also should work to develop a measure of parental beliefs about readiness that encompasses the multiple dimensions of school readiness identified by national panels and practitioners.

References

Bartlett, M. S. (1954). A note on the multiplying of factors for various chi-square approximations. *Journal of the Royal Statistical Society, 16 (Series B),* 296-298.

Brooker, L. (2003). Learning how to learn: Parental ethnotheories and young children's preparation for school. *International Journal of Early Years Education, 11,* 117-128.

Comrey, A. L., & Lee, H. B. (1992). *A first course in factor analysis* (2nd ed.). Hillsdale, NJ: Erlbaum.

Diamond, K. E., Reagan, A. J., & Bandyk, J. E. (2000). Parents' conceptions of kindergarten readiness: Relationships with race, ethnicity, and development. *The Journal of Educational Research, 94,* 93-100.

Fabrigar, L. R., Wegener, D. T., MacCallum, R. C., & Strahan, E. J. (1999). Evaluating the use of exploratory factor analysis in psychological research. *Psychological Methods, 4,* 272-299.

Floyd, F. J., & Widaman, K. F. (1995). Factor analysis in the development and refinement of clinical assessment instruments. *Psychological Assessment, 7,* 286-299.

Gorsuch, R. L. (1983). *Factor analysis* (2nd ed.). Hillsdale, NJ: Erlbaum.

Graue, E. M. (1992). Social interpretations of readiness for kindergarten. *Early Childhood Research Quarterly, 7,* 225-243.

Kagan, S. L. (1992). Readiness past, present, and future: Shaping the agenda. *Young Children, 48,* 48-53.

Kagan, S. L. (2003). Children's readiness for school: Issues in assessment. *International Journal of Early Childhood, 35,* 114-120.

Kaiser, H. F. (1970). A second generation Little Jiffy. *Psychometrika, 35,* 401-415.

Kaiser, H. F. (1974). An index of factorial simplicity. *Psychometrika, 39,* 31-36.

Meisels, S. J. (1992). Doing harm by doing good: Iatrogenic effects of early childhood enrollment and promotion policies. *Early Childhood Research Quarterly, 7,* 155-174.

Meisels, S. J. (1999). Assessing readiness. In R. C. Pianta & M. J. Cox (Eds.), *The Transition to kindergarten* (pp. 39-66). Baltimore, MD: Paul H. Brookes Publishing Co.

National Association of Early Childhood Specialists (2000). *STILL unacceptable trends in kindergarten entry and placement.* Retrieved August 24, 2006 from http://www.naeyc.org/about/positions/pdf/Psunacc.pdf#xml=http:// naeychq.naeyc.org/texis/search/pdf

National Association for the Education of Young Children (1995). *School readiness: A position statement of the national association for the education of young children.* Retrieved August 23, 2006, from http://www. naeyc.org/about/positions/pdf/readiness.pdf

National Center for Education Statistics (1994). *National Household Education Survey of 1993: School readiness data file user's manual.* Washington, DC: Office of Educational Research and Improvement.

National Center for Education Statistics. (2001). *User's manual for the ECLS-K base year public-use data files and electronic codebook.* Washington, D.C.: Author.

Oshima, C., & Domaleski, C. S. (2006). Academic performance gap between summer-birthday and fall-birthday children in grades K-8 [Electronic version]. *Journal of Educational Research, 99,* 212-217.

Pelletier, J., & Brent, J. M. (2002). Parent participation in children school readiness: The effects of parental self-efficacy, cultural diversity and teacher strategies [Electronic version]. *International Journal of Early Childhood, 34,* 45-60.

Perry, B., Dockett, S., & Tracey, D. (1998). *Ready to learn: Exploring the concept of school readiness and its implications.* (ERIC Document Reproduction Service No. ED421249)

Piotrkowski, C. S., Botsko, M., & Matthews, E. (2000). Parents' and teachers' beliefs about children's school readiness in a high-need community. *Early Childhood Research Quarterly, 15,* 537-558.

Prince, C. (1992). *Reactions to the Goal 1 Technical Planning Subgroup report on school readiness.* Washington, DC: National Education Goals Panel.

Shepard, L. A., & Smith, M. L. (1985). Synthesis of research on school readiness and kindergarten retention. *Educational Leadership, 44,* 78-88.

Shore, R. (1998). *Ready schools: A report of the Goal 1 Ready Schools Resource Group.* Retrieved August 24, 2006 from http://govinfo.library.unt.edu /negp/Reports/readysch.pdf#search=%22Ready%20Schools%20Rima %20Shore%22

Snow, K. L. (2006). Measuring school readiness: Conceptual and practical considerations [Electronic version]. *Early Education and Development, 17,* 7-41.

Stipek, D. J., Milburn, S., Clements, D., & Daniels, D. H. (1992). Parents' beliefs about appropriate education for young children. *Journal of Applied Developmental Psychology, 13,* 293-310.

Tabachnick, B. G., & Fidell, L. S. (2001). *Using multivariate statistics* (4th ed.). Needham Heights, MA: Allyn & Bacon.

U. S. Census Bureau. (2000). Summary File 1 (SF 1). Retrieved April 4, 2005, from http://factfinder.census.gov

Welch, M. D., & White, B. (1999). *Teacher and parent expectations for kindergarten readiness.* (ERIC Document Reproduction Service No. ED437225).

Wesley, P. W., & Buysse, V. (2003). Making meaning of school readiness in schools and communities [Electronic version]. *Early Childhood Research Quarterly, 18,* 351-375.

West, S. G., Finch, J. F., & Curran, P. J. (1995). Structural equation models with nonnormal variables: Problems and remedies. In R. H. Hoyle (Ed.), *Structural equation modeling: Concepts, issues, and applications* (pp. 56-75). Newbury Park, CA: Sage.

West, J., Hausken, E. G., & Collins, M. (1993). *Readiness for kindergarten: Parent and teacher beliefs.* Washington, D.C.: U.S. Department of Education, National Center for Education Statistics.

Zill, N., Collins, M., Brick, M., Hofferth, S., Chandler, K., & West, J. (1993). School Readiness Questionnaire. In National Center for Education Statistics (Ed.), *National Household Education Survey of 1993: School readiness data file user's manual* (pp. A-9-A-28). Washington, DC: Office of Educational Research and Improvement.

Bayley III: A Preliminary Overview

Madeline Fernández
Pace University, New York City

Michele Zaccario
Pace University and NYU Medical Center, New York City

The latest revision of the Bayley scales, the Bayley Scales of Infant and Toddler Development—Third Edition (Bayley-III; Bayley, 2006), was conducted to improve the overall clinical utility of the instrument and to address specific criticisms raised by infant/toddler researchers and practitioners. In this review, a brief description of the revisions implemented and a preliminary critique of these revisions are provided. Suggestions for further research and development are also offered.

The Bayley Scales of Infant and Toddler Development—Third Edition (Bayley-III; Bayley, 2006) is the latest revision of the Bayley scales (Bayley, 1969, 1993), a widely utilized standardized instrument designed to individually assess the developmental functioning of infants and young children between the ages of 1 month and 42 months. This Bayley revision was conducted to improve the overall quality and utility of the instrument (Bayley, 2006). Specifically, the Bayley-III revision attempts to significantly address previous criticisms of the instrument, including: complicated administration procedures, administration and scoring concerns, inadequate floor and ceiling, limited information for intervention, and limited clinical utility (Alfonso, Russo, Fortugno & Rader, 2005; Gauthier, Bauer, Messinger, & Closius, 1999; Lichtenberger, 2005; Mayes, 1997; Ross & Lawson, 1997).

In response to the established literature regarding the poor predictability of cognitive ability assessed in infancy and early childhood on later IQ and academic functioning (Black & Matula, 2000; Lichtenberger, 2005), this revision seems to emphasize more clearly than in previous manuals that the Bayley-III is

All correspondence should be addressed to Dr. Madeline Fernandez or Dr. Michele Zaccario, Pace University, Psychology Department, 41 Park Row, New York, NY 10038. Electronic mail may be sent to: MFernandez@pace.edu or MZaccario@pace.edu.

not an intelligence test, nor should it be used to predict later academic achievement. It is also emphasized that the Bayley-III is not meant to be used as a measure of deficits in a specific skill area, and that referrals for further evaluation with
other more narrow-band assessment measures be made for that purpose. Instead,
the developers describe the Bayley-III's primary purpose as one of identifying
children with developmental delays and providing information for intervention
planning (Bayley, 2006).

In the development of the Bayley-III, several specific revision goals were
identified:

> 1) to update the normative data; 2) to develop five distinct
> scales; 3) to strengthen the psychometric quality of the instru-
> ment; 4) to improve the clinical utility of the instrument; 5) to
> simplify administration procedures; 6) to update item adminis-
> tration; 7) to update the stimulus materials; and 8) to maintain
> the basic qualities of the Bayley Scales (Bayley, 2006, p. 11).

The purpose of this review is to offer a brief description and preliminary critique
of the aforementioned revisions, specifically discussing areas of obvious
improvement, delineating areas of potential continued difficulty, and articulating
possibilities for future consideration and research.

Development of Five Distinct Scales

One major change that evaluators will note immediately upon perusal of the
instrument is the development of five distinct scales. Whereas the Bayley Scales
of Infant Development-II (BSID-II) yield three scores (a Mental Development
Index (MDI), a Psychomotor Development Index (PDI), and a Behavior Rating
Scale (BRS) Total Score), the Bayley-III yeilds scores for five developmental
domains: Cognitive, Language, Physical, Social/Emotional and Adaptive. The
five scales included were chosen to correspond to the Individuals with
Disabilities Education Improvement Act (IDEA) guidelines (1990, 1997, 2004)
for assessment of early childhood. Of the five scales, three (i.e., Cognitive,
Language and Motor) are administered individually by the examiner to the child.
The language-dependent MDI had been a major source of difficulty and criticism
of the BSID-II when used to assess children whose language development is
delayed (Lichtenberger, 2005). Often the MDIs of these children were underesti-
mated due to the high language demands of the scale. An attempt has been made
to differentiate between the assessment of cognitive and language skills, with a
reduction in the language load in the Cognitive Scale, allowing for naturalistic
directional cues such as gestures, permitting examiners to "accept responses that
'show evidence' of the target response... and provid[ing] graded levels of support
during the administration of an item" (Bayley, 2006, Administration Manual, p.
220). The end result decreases the effects of expressive and receptive language

skills for the assessment of cognitive abilities. However, anecdotal feedback from practitioners who have administered the Bayley-III suggests that language issues may persist in the Cognitive Scales: the occasional stilted language utilized in the administration of some items may not always be readily understood by an infant or toddler.

The Bayley-III Cognitive Scale is reported to assess sensorimotor development, exploration and manipulation, object relatedness, concept formation, and memory. Both the Language and Motor Scales are comprised of two subtests. The Language scale includes the Receptive Communication and Expressive Communication subtests. Items from the BSID-II that were identified as measuring primarily language skills and additional items adapted from the Preschool Language Scale-4th Edition (PLS-4; Zimmerman, Steiner, & Pond, 2002) were included in the Language Scale. The Motor Scale subtests, Fine Motor and Gross Motor, include items from the BSID-II Motor and Mental Scales that were identified as clearly measuring fine or gross motor skills. In addition, new items that emphasize quality of movement were added.

The remaining two scales, the Social-Emotional Scale and the Adaptive Behavior scale, are caregiver report questionnaires that are written at a sixth grade language level. Both scales are measures that had been previously developed by other authors. The Social-Emotional scale was adapted from Greenspan's *Social-Emotional Growth Chart: A screening questionnaire for infants and young children* (Greenspan, 2004). This scale is purported to assess a child's ability to demonstrate self-regulation, communication of needs, level of relatedness, and purposeful use of emotions. Six stages that reflect the mastery of a functional emotional milestone are assessed and a child's overall level is identified. A Sensory Processing score can also be obtained from the first eight items of the Social-Emotional Scale. The Adaptive Behavior Scale consists of a subset of items from the Adaptive Behavioral Assessment System- Second Edition (ABAS-II; Harrison & Oakland, 2003) and it requires the caregiver to rate the child (ages birth-5) on a range of activities of daily living, including: communication skills, home living skills, leisure skills, self-care abilities, and social skills. There is also an additional optional questionnaire, the Behavior Observation Inventory, that replaces the BRS of the BSID-II. This is to be completed by the examiner and the caregiver for qualitative assessment of the child's behavior during the administration of the Bayley-III.

The development of the five scales would appear to pose difficulties for investigators involved in longitudinal studies with the BSID-II due to compatibility issues between the scales. In addition, while the five- scale format of the Bayley-III certainly represents a conceptual improvement over the BSID-II by making the interpretation of data more clinically facile and relevant, the addition of the Adaptive Behavior scales and the Social-Emotional Scale also poses some potential challenges. For example, there are no response bias indices embedded within these report measures; thus, it is difficult to quantitatively gauge caregiver over- and under-reporting tendencies. The results gleaned from the latter two scales can also differ from the other portions of the Bayley-III, and the meaning and nature of these differences is left to the evaluator to interpret. In the end, an evaluator needs to have a substantial working knowledge of cognitive development, as well as social-emotional development, in order to reconcile and properly interpret differences between the scales.

Normative Data/Clinical Utility

The Bayley-III normative data for the three scales that are administered individually (Cognitive, Language and Motor) was collected in the United States from January to October 2004. The sample was derived from 1,700 children ranging in age from 16 days to 43 months 15 days. These children were divided into age groups in one-month intervals, from ages 1 month to 42 months, with each group composed of 100 children. Males and females were equally represented, and for each age group the proportions of Whites, African Americans, Hispanics, Asians, and Other racial/ethnic groups represented the proportions of those children within the United States based on 2000 U.S. census data. The sample was also stratified according to five parent education levels (less than or equal to 8 years, 9-11 years, 12 years, 13-15 years, and greater than or equal to 16 years) as well as four US geographic locations (Midwest, Northeast, South, and West)(Bayley, 2006).

A considerable improvement over the BSID-II is the Bayley-III's expanded norms tables. Specifically, while the BSID-II provided norms in one-month intervals only, the Bayley-III now offers 10-day increment tables for children ages 16 days to 5 months 15 days. These additional increments were provided in order to better account for the rapid developmental growth that takes place in the first six months of infancy.

Norms for the Social-Emotional Scale were derived from 456 children ages 16 days to 42 months in the *Social-Emotional Growth Chart: A screening questionnaire for infants and young children* sample (Greenspan, 2004). Norms for the Adaptive Behavior Scale were derived from 1,350 children (birth to 5 years 11 months) from the ABAS-II standardization sample (Harrison & Oakland, 2003).

Scaled scores ranging from 1 to 19 with a mean of 10 and a standard deviation of 3 are available for all subtests. Composite scores, derived from the sums of the subtest scaled scores, range from 40 to160 with a mean of 100 and standard deviation of 15 for the Language, Motor and Adaptive Behavior Scales. Composite score equivalents are available for the Cognitive and Social-Emotional Scales. Percentile ranks, growth scores, and developmental age equivalents are also available. Although comparisons between scaled scores are the most psychometrically sound, the charting of growth scores is recommended to track responses to treatment interventions since the scaled scores are not sensitive enough.

The improved clinical utility of the Bayley-III through the collection of data on children with clinical diagnoses is also a promising feature. It is anticipated that the nine special group studies of children (Pervasive Developmental Disorders [PDD], Down syndrome, Specific Language Impairment [SLI], fetal alcohol exposure [FAS/FAE], Cerebral Palsy [CP], intrapartum asphyxia, infants who were small for gestational age [SGA], and infants born prematurely or with low birth weight) will facilitate practitioners' comparisons and discrepancy analysis between subtests for these specific groups. However, caution should be utilized given the limited diagnostic range included, the lack of adequate differentiation within each of the clinical groups (e.g., PDD versus Autism, Asperger's disorder, Childhood Disintegrative Disorder, Rett's syndrome, PDD Not Otherwise Specified, Autistic Spectrum Disorder) and the relatively small sample size (Down syndrome, $n = 90$; PDD, $n = 70$; CP, $n = 73$; SLI, $n = 94$; Asphyxiation at birth, $n = 43$; FAS/FAE, $n = 48$; SGA, $n = 44$; premature or low birth weight, $n = 85$).

A significant criticism of the Bayley-III standardization sample is that no apparent attempts were made to identify or include children who are English-language learners (ELL). There are also no references about the use of the Bayley-III with ELLs in the Technical and Administration Manuals. Thus, it would appear that addressing the developmental assessment needs of ELLs was not an objective in the development of the Bayley-III. However, young ELLs in the United States, particularly in parts of the West, South and Northeast regions, constitute a substantial percentage of the children in early intervention programs (Lollock, 2001; NAEYC, 2005). Given the growing concerns of over-identification of these children in special education programs, often based on assessments that at best incorporate non-standardized administrations or qualitative descriptions of the child's abilities and at worst include the administration of inadequate instruments and reporting of invalid scores, it would seem that the Bayley-III's neglect to address this population in their standardization reflects a significant omission. The complicated issues involved in translating assessment instruments are well known. However, similar to the efforts made to include special group studies during the collection of standardization data for the Bayley-III, the provision of standardization data for a sample of children who are not English-proficient due to second language acquisition factors would have been a significant first step in increasing the instrument's utility for practitioners who work extensively with young ELLs. The Bayley-III falls short in addressing recommendations towards developing instruments that are culturally and linguistically responsive and appropriate for young ELL (NAEYC, 2005).

Psychometric Properties

While a thorough review of the psychometric properties of the Bayley-III is beyond the scope and intention of this article, a brief description of reliability and validity is discussed. The reader should consult the Technical Manual of the Bayley-III (Bayley, 2006) for a more thorough analysis of its psychometric features.

As compared to the BSID-II, the scales of the Bayley-III boast a lower floor and a higher ceiling in an attempt to expand content coverage. These expansions were accomplished via data collected on children diagnosed with developmental delays during the tryout phase of development and from special studies on children with Down syndrome and PDD during standardization. Pilot studies on especially bright preschool children provided additional data in order to extend the instrument's ceiling (Bayley, 2006).

Additionally, the Technical Manual (Bayley, 2006) reports that extensive reliability and validity studies were conducted on all five of the Bayley Scales which yielded results equal to or surpassing those established by earlier versions of the instrument. Specifically, internal consistency reliability coefficients on the normative sample ranged from .86 to .91 for the Fine Motor, Receptive Communication, Cognitive, Expressive Communication, and Gross Motor subtests. These coefficients were reportedly even higher for special clinical populations, ranging from .84 to .99. Internal consistency for the Social-Emotional Scale, as reported by the Greenspan Social-Emotional Growth Chart, ranged from .83 to .94 for the Social-Emotional items and from .76 to .91 for the Sensory Processing items. Internal consistency for the Adaptive Behavior Scale, as established by the ABAS-II Parent/Primary Caregiver Form, ranged from .79 to .98 and inter-rater reliability for two respondents was found to range from .59 to .86. Test-retest reliability coefficients for the Bayley-III also demonstrated a high degree of stability over time across all subtests, and as expected, show a slight increase in stability across age groups.

Construct validity was established for the scales of the Bayley-III by a series of studies that indicated that individual items were found to have higher correlations with the scale in which they were ultimately placed, as compared to other scales of the Bayley. Thus, cognitive items correlated higher with the Cognitive Scale than the Language Scale and vice versa. Additionally, correlations between the scales across ages tended to be in the low-to-moderate range (Bayley, 2006).

Furthermore, the Bayley-III was found to correlate with other instruments in the manner and degree expected. The Technical Manual (Bayley, 2006) provides evidence that this revision is sensitive to performance differences between children in the normative sample and samples of children with various developmental difficulties. It is expected that future studies utilizing the Bayley-III will provide additional evidence of the instrument's utility for clinical assessment and research.

Update of Test Materials

Despite attempts to make the testing kit more portable and user-friendly, the Bayley-III continues to be quite expansive and bulky. It contains many new play-based items with which examiners must become familiar. In addition, there continues to be additional required materials that the examiner is expected to provide, namely, coins, food pellets, unlined index cards, scissors, a set of stairs, a stopwatch, copies of the designs sheet, unlined paper and tissues. However, the Bayley-III materials were also designed to increase children's interest and engage them more easily in the examination process. Examiners are afforded more flexibility through the broadening of the specification of materials that may be used to administer some of the items (e.g., Cheerios as a finger food, toy substitutions). Attempts also appear to have been made to address some of the feedback from the BSID-II with regard to the quality of the materials (Black & Matula, 2000). It is perhaps too early to determine whether the improvements made will hold up to the test of time and use. However, there is an initial appeal for children and examiners alike, as the toys in the kit are more likely to be part of real-life play repertoires, and pictorial items are larger, more crisply drawn, and often brightly colored. Many of the materials in the Bayley-III will be recognizable to examiners who are familiar with the BSID-II. However, maintaining the organization of the materials in their respective locations during administration remains difficult, and accessing the items in a timely manner may also present a challenge.

The Bayley-III kit also includes the Administration Manual, Technical Manual, Stimulus Book, Record Form, Social-Emotional Questionnaire, Adaptive Behavior Questionnaire, and the Caregiver Report (a form to provide feedback for caregivers). It appears that an attempt to address suggestions for improved ease of testing (Alfonso et al., 2005; Nellis & Gridley, 1994) was made through the separation of the Technical and Administration Manuals and the inclusion of scoring criteria on the Record Form. Despite having separate manuals, however, the Administration Manual continues to be large in size and somewhat challenging for examiners to manage during the administration of items, while simultaneously referring to the Stimulus Book or items and recording responses on the Record Form. The Bayley-III handheld Personal Digital Assistant (PDA) Administration Software, an optional administration option that is available from the publisher, promises to offer more ease with administration and scoring. It is to be used in place of the Administration Manual and Record Form. However, given the added cost, institutions' willingness to purchase the PDA software application for examiners is questionable. If purchased together with a Bayley-III Complete Kit ($895 list price), the current cost is an additional $100 for the Scoring Assistant and PDA Administration Software that includes 10 Electronic Record Forms. Each additional purchase of 25 Electronic Record Forms is listed at $78 (PsychCorp, 2007).

There are welcomed changes to the Stimulus Book, as the layout is more examiner-friendly with an easel included for positioning during administration of the items. Administration instructions are printed on the examiner's side similar to other assessment instruments such as the Stanford-Binet, 5th Edition (Roid, 2003) and Wechsler Preschool and Primary Scale of Intelligence-Third Edition (WPPSI-III; Wechsler, 2002). New and updated items/pictures are also noted. The Record Form includes the scoring criteria for the items, in addition to easily identifying the start points. However, the child's starting position (e.g., elevated supine, cradled, supported sitting) when administering items would have also been helpful to include on the Record Form.

Simplification of the Administrative Process and Update of Item Administration

Administration time for children under one year of age is suggested at 50 minutes and 90 minutes is suggested for older children, although examiners should expect slightly higher time frames for the first few assessments and when testing special populations. The use of item sets has been eliminated and examiners are no longer given the flexibility of choosing the item set at which to begin. This seems to be a direct effort to address the scoring difficulties and limitations reported with the age-specific items in the BSID-II that yielded significantly different scores depending on the item set chosen by the examiner (Alfonso et al., 2005; Nellis & Gridley, 1994; Ross & Lawson, 1997). The start points for the scales continue to be based on the child's chronological age. A standard approach based on the child's responses, rather than clinical judgment, is utilized by the examiner to determine any start point changes. The basal (i.e., score of 1 on the first three consecutive items administered at a start point) and ceiling (i.e., score of 0 for five consecutive items) rules are consistent across the three administered scales for all ages. If a child is unable to respond successfully on the first three consecutive items of the start point for his or her chronological age, the examiner must then administer the first item of the previous start point until a basal level is obtained. The developers of the Bayley-III note that by using this approach it is possible to establish two basal levels, and recommend using the higher one when this occurs. The only exception recommended for not using the start point commensurate with the child's chronological age is for children who were born prematurely. Age adjustments for prematurity are indicated through 24 months of chronological age.

Trials and series items remain in the Bayley-III, and there are some items that require separate administrations on the left and right side. Incidental scoring is allowed, which requires that the examiner be very familiar with these items beforehand. While caregiver reports are noted, they are not scored. However, caregiver involvement is encouraged as an important component of the administration of the Bayley-III, as well as a vehicle for providing parents with a better understanding of their child's functioning level. Standardized caregiver involvement was included in the standardization sample with a reported 25% of the assessments administered in the home. Other than the required administration of the Receptive Communication subtest prior to the Expressive Communication subtest, the examiner has flexibility in determining the order of subtest administration to facilitate engagement with the child (Bayley, 2006).

With the Social-Emotional Scale, age determines the discontinue criterion for the items that the caregiver must complete. The entire Adaptive Behavior Scale is completed by the caregiver, with the exception of three areas that are not relevant for children ages birth to 11 months.

Conclusions

The Bayley-III revision has incorporated significant improvements and this preliminary review of the objectives identified by the developers highlights the efforts made to address some of the BSID-II shortcomings. Overall, practitioners have been provided with a better assessment instrument that allows for a comprehensive evaluation to assist in the development of appropriate interventions and in planning for infants and young children. Some limitations persist, particularly with regard to the assessment of ELL. The true benefits of this revision, however, remain to be determined with practitioner use of the scale and further field research.

References

Alfonso, V. C., Russo, P. M., Fortugno, D. A., & Rader, D. E. (2005). Critical review of the Bayley Scales of Infant Development – Second Edition: Implications for assessing young children with developmental delays. *The School Psychologist, 59(2)*, 67-73.

Bayley, N. (1969). *Bayley Scales of Infant Development*. San Antonio, TX: The Psychological Corporation.

Bayley, N. (1993). *Bayley Scales of Infant Development (2nd ed.)*. San Antonio, TX: The Psychological Corporation.

Bayley, N. (2006). *Bayley Scales of Infant and Toddler Development (3rd ed.)*. San Antonio, TX: Harcourt Assesment, Inc.

Bell, S., & Allen, B. (2000). Bayley Scales of Infant Development, Second Edition: Manual [Book Review]. *Journal of Psychoeducational Assessment, 18* (2), 185-195.

Black, M. M., & Matula, K. (2000). *Essentials of Bayley Scales of Infant Development – II Assessment*. New Jersey: John Wiley & Sons Inc.

Gauthier, S. M., Bauer, C. R., Messinger, D. S., & Closius, J. M. (1999). The Bayley Scales of Infant Development-II: Where to start? *Journal of Developmental & Behavioral Pediatrics, 20(2),* 75-79.

Greenspan, S. I. (2004). *Greenspan Social-Emotional Growth Chart: A screening questionnaire for infants and young children*. San Antonio, TX: Harcourt Assessment, Inc.

Harrison, P. L., & Oakland, T. (2003). *Adaptive Behavior Assessment System* (2nd ed.). San Antonio, TX: The Psychological Corporation.

Individuals with Disabilities Education Act of 1997. Pub. L. No. 105-17. (IDEA Reauthorized), U.S. Statutes at Large (1997).

Individuals with Disabilities Education Act of 1990. Pub. L. No. 101-476, §307,20 U.S.C., § 1400 et seq. (1990).

Individuals with Disabilities Education Improvement Act of 2004, Pub. L. No. 108-446.(IDEA Reauthorized), U.S. Statutes at Large 118 (2004):2647.

Lichtenberger, E. O. (2005). General measures of cognition for the preschool child. *Mental Retardation and Developmental Disabilities Research Reviews, 11,* 197-208.

Lollock, L. (2001). The foreign population born in the United States: March 2000. *Current Population Reports,* Washington, DC: US Census Bureau. 20-534.

Mayes, S. D. (1997). Potential scoring problems using the Bayley Scales of Infant Development-II Mental Scale. *Journal of Early Intervention, 21,* 36-44.

National Association for the Education of Young Children (NAEYC). (2005). *Screening and assessment of young English-language learners: Supplement to the NAEYC position statement on early childhood curriculum, assessment, and program evaluation.* Washington, DC: Author.

Nellis, L., & Gridley, B. E. (1994). Review of the Bayley Scales of Infant Development – Second Edition. *Journal of School Psychology, 32(2),* 201-209.

PsychCorp (2007). *Psychological assessment products: Annual catalog 2007*. San Antonio, TX: Harcourt Assessment.

Roid, G. H. (2003). *Stanford-Binet Intelligence Scales, Fifth edition*. Ithaca, IL: Riverside.

Ross, G., & Lawson, K. (1997). Using the Bayley-II: Unresolved issues in assessing the development of prematurely born children. *Journal of Developmental & Behavioral Pediatrics, 18(2),* 109-111.

Wechsler, D. (2002). *Wechsler Preschool and Primary Scale of Intelligence for Children-Third edition.* San Antonio, TX: The Psychological Corporation.

Zimmerman, I. L., Steiner, V. G., & Pond, R. E. (2002). *Preschool Language Scale- Fourth edition.* San Antonio, TX: The Psychological Corporation.

VanFleet, Rise. (Second Edition 2005). *Filial Therapy: Strengthening Parent-Child Relationships Through Play.* Sarasota, FL: Professional Resource Press

Nicole Pernod
Pace University, New York City

Rise VanFleet's second edition of *Filial Therapy: Strengthening Parent-Child Relationships Through Play* concisely describes the benefits of implementing play therapy in a way that includes parents in order to promote growth and understanding in children. Since the first edition eleven years ago, filial therapy has increased in use, with a greater variety of professionals. In the current edition, VanFleet seeks to present the latest information on implementing the model and to present empirical data that supports its therapeutic efficacy.

Filial therapy was developed during the 1960s by Dr. Louise Guerney and Dr. Bernard Guerney as a treatment for children with social, emotional, and behavioral problems (e.g., Guerney, 1964, 1976; Guerney, 2000). VanFleet reports that the technique has received increasing recognition by the clinical and research communities as an effective approach to strengthening parent, child, and family relationships.

VanFleet describes filial therapy as a process that allows parents to become the primary change agents as they learn to conduct child-centered play sessions with their children. Filial therapists, using a competence-oriented psychoeducational framework, teach parents to conduct specialized play sessions, supervise parents during these play sessions, and help them eventually integrate the play sessions and parenting skills at home. The technique is most frequently used with children aged 3 to 12 years. However, VanFleet also discusses several techniques that allow the intervention to be implemented with adolescents.

Filial therapy is a form of play therapy that differs from other available methods in that it directly involves parents. Recent research indicates that VanFleet's report of the efficacy of filial therapy tends to hold true. In 2005, Bratton, Ray, Rhine and Jones conducted a meta-analysis of 93-controlled outcome studies published from 1953 to 2000. The purpose of the meta-analysis was to assess the overall efficacy of play therapy and to determine factors that might impact its effectiveness. Results indicated that the overall treatment effect for play therapy interventions was .80. Further analysis revealed that out of all possible forms of

All correspondence should be addressed to Ms. Nicole Pernod, Pace University, Psychology Department, 41 Park Row, New York, NY 10038. Electronic mail may be sent to: ncpernod@yahoo.com.

play therapy conducted using parents in play therapy produced the largest thera-peutic gains. While play therapy has lacked empirical validation in the past, VanFleet hopes that researchers will continue to assess the validity of the numer-ous forms of play therapy currently utilized by practitioners.

Most therapists are aware of the importance of children's play. Skilled ther-apists usually are confident that they can positively effect a child's intrapsychic state by offering thoughtful reflections, modeling socially appropriate behavior and validating different feeling states, all within clear and consistent boundaries. VanFleet briefly discusses filial therapy's implications for behavioral changes, however, she does not fully elaborate on the information that children's play offers. Children's play contains a plethora of information regarding language and motoric capacities, interpersonal relationships, coping, and level of abstract rea-soning. Therefore, parents being trained in filial therapy must be skilled enough to notice the content of children's play and reflect it back to them in a meaning-ful manner. VanFleet does not fully address parental difficulties that may result from lack of familiarity with important psychological concepts. In addition, par-ents may find progress hard to assess; therapists may need to educate parents regarding what behaviors signal growth and how to assist children to generalize their new abilities to different settings (e.g., school).

Research indicates that play therapy is a communicative tool that enables therapists to enter a child's inner world when words are not readily available (LeBlanc & Ritchie, 2001). Filial therapy seems to successfully blend the bene-fits of play therapy with the importance of including caregivers in treatment plans. More specifically, filial therapy utilizes the parent-child bond as a tool to enable children to expand their skills and emotional understanding. Likewise, filial therapy enables parents to become a catalyst for adaptive psychological growth in their children. The combination may increase the generalization of treatment effectiveness.

Van Fleet states that teaching parents the core values of filial therapy facili-tates a greater understanding of their children's emotional states and aids children in developing healthier emotional expression and problem solving strategies. There are a number of core values of filial therapy including: honesty, openness, respect, empathy, empowerment, collaboration and emotional expression. Parents are educated on the importance of numerous core values and, with proper train-ing from a skilled therapist, develop their abilities to model these core values for their children. Through play, parents teach children emotional modulation and adaptive coping skills. Children are taught through the content of play, while spending time with caregivers.

VanFleet describes filial therapy as a technique that offers results in a some-what short duration of time. Filial therapy follows the principles of child-centered play therapy and children are in charge of the play, with few rules imposed. The goal is to create an open atmosphere in which children feel comfortable expressing thoughts and feelings. Boundaries such as length of time and rules regarding maladaptive behavior are communicated to children and reinforced when necessary.

Parents are educated by the therapist on the importance of children's play. Upon assessment of the parent-child dyad, a filial therapist takes a psychoeducational approach and offers parents numerous ways to analyze their children's behavior, play themes and emotional expressions. Initially, parents are invited to watch their child's play with the therapist behind a two-way mirror and, after several mock sessions with the therapist, play with their child while the therapist supervises and provides feedback. The goal of these initial sessions is to enable parents to interact with their child in a different type of way by validating children's feelings, exploring themes and applying firm boundaries consistently. The therapist then meets alone with the parents, provides feedback on their performance and offers commentary regarding the session and further appropriate interventions. Van Fleet states that both parents are involved and each has weekly sessions with their child. However, she maintains that any caregiver can implement filial therapy, as long as the therapy occurs in a consistent fashion.

After 3 or 4 supervised sessions, parents transition filial therapy to the home setting while encouraged to maintain the boundaries associated with therapy. The parents are invited to call the filial therapist with any questions and also meet several weeks post-transition in order to discuss the progress of the intervention.

VanFleet offers mock sessions in order to describe initial meetings between parents and a filial therapist. She also outlines play sessions and appropriate interventions that would be used in hypothetical situations. Upon transitioning filial therapy to the home setting, success is greatly dependent on the environment used by the family. VanFleet discusses the possible limitations of filial therapy and ways to circumvent problems caused by a lack of resources. She also provides a list of potential toys to illicit imaginary play and themes important for a child's developmental level.

VanFleet describes filial therapy in a manner that supports the validity of the technique. For example, she offers a review of filial therapy's empirical history as well as ongoing research. VanFleet then clearly depicts the course of therapy from: (a) assessment, (b) training, (c) initial play sessions, (d) therapist-supervised play sessions, (e) transfer of play sessions to the home setting, (f) generalization of skills, and (g) closing.

The overall appeal of filial therapy lies in the inclusion of parents in play therapy. The therapeutic intervention offers parents the tools necessary to increase their perceptions regarding the antecedents and consequences surrounding behavior, while recognizing and providing validation of children's feelings. *Filial Therapy: Strengthening Parent-Child Relationships Through Play* also serves as an important reminder for therapists concerning the importance of family dynamics and parental involvement. Regardless of theoretical orientation, any practitioner working with this population would benefit from reflecting upon their own interactions with parents and the value of educating parents on ways of communicating with their children in a therapeutic manner.

Upon reading this book, one may ask, "What about the parents who do not have the resources to undergo training in filial therapy and/or implement it in their home?" VanFleet responds to several of these limitations by offering ideas regarding conducting filial therapy in an apartment setting using toys that already exist in the home for therapeutic means. However, for parents who lack sufficient monetary resources, filial therapy may still be out of reach. A single parent may not be able to devote a scheduled amount of time to the child if he or she is the primary caregiver and has other children that need to be supervised. Also, meeting several times with a filial therapist during the assessment and training stages may pose difficulties related to taking time off from work and arranging child care. However, it is important to note that these limitations also exist within other forms of child therapy, even those that do not involve the parent to such an extent.

The success of filial therapy is dependent upon the competency of the caregivers that implement it. While VanFleet discusses the training involved with parents, she does not discuss objective measures of competency that therapists can use to assess parental progress. Rather, therapists are encouraged to gauge a parent's therapeutic level of ability via direct observation. Filial therapists would benefit from quantifying perceived competency in parents and only then encouraging filial therapy to transition to the home setting. As practitioners, it is our job to assess the progress and psychological status of our clients. Therapists should be confident about the transition of filial therapy and the parent's ability to truly empathize with his or her child while setting clear boundaries and encouraging all types of emotional expression and thematic material. Therapists are ethically bound to provide a service to children, and one must feel confident in transitioning therapy to a person who has not received formal training in the areas of child therapy.

VanFleet's depiction of filial therapy allows the reader to grasp the key concepts of the technique and to formulate ideas ranging from complete implementation to the incorporation of these ideas into already established modes of child therapy. While the book targets practicing child therapists, parents could benefit from VanFleet's summarization of filial therapy and its core values. One could argue that all therapists should seek to incorporate parents in the treatment of children by educating them on the importance of validating emotional expression and setting clear boundaries. Only then can the work that occurs in play generalize to the time outside of sessions.

References

Bratton, S. C., Ray, D., Rhine, T. & Jones, L. (2005). The efficacy of play ther-
    apy with children: A meta-analytic review of treatment outcomes.
    Professional Psychology: Research and Practice, 36, 376-390.
Guerney, B. G. (1964). Filial therapy: Description and rationale. *Journal of
    Consulting Psychology, 28,* 450-460.
Guerney, B. G. (1976). Filial therapy used as a treatment method for disturbed
    children. *Evaluation, 3,* 34-35.
Guerney, L. (2000). Filial therapy into the 21st century. *International Journal of
    Play Thearpy, 9,* 1-17.
LeBlanc, M., & Ritchie, M. (2001). A meta-analysis of play therapy outcomes.
    Counseling Psychology Quarterly, 14, 149-163.

www.ingramcontent.com/pod-product-compliance
Lightning Source LLC
Chambersburg PA
CBHW061008280326
41935CB00009B/887